INVENTING EQUALITY

INVENTING
EQUALITY

*President of the United States shall be President of the Senate
e shall chuse their other Officers, and also a President pro ter.*

Reconstructing the
CONSTITUTION
in the Aftermath of the
CIVIL WAR

Michael A. Bellesiles

St. Martin's Press
New York

First published in the United States by St. Martin's Press,
an imprint of St. Martin's Publishing Group

INVENTING EQUALITY. Copyright © 2020 by Michael A. Bellesiles.
All rights reserved. Printed in the United States of America.
For information, address St. Martin's Publishing Group,
120 Broadway, New York, NY 10271.

www.stmartins.com

Designed by Karen Minster

Library of Congress Cataloging-in-Publication Data

Names: Bellesiles, Michael A., author.
Title: Inventing equality : reconstructing the Constitution in the aftermath of
 the Civil War / Michael A. Bellesiles.
Description: First edition. | New York : St. Martin's Press, [2020] |
 Includes bibliographical references and index.
Identifiers: LCCN 2020021904 | ISBN 9781250091918 (hardcover) |
 ISBN 9781250096180 (ebook)
Subjects: LCSH: Equality before the law—United States—History. | Constitutional
 history—United States. | Slavery—Law and legislation—United States—History. |
 Race discrimination—Law and legislation—United States—History. |
 United States. Supreme Court—Decision making—History.
Classification: LCC KF4764 .B45 2020 | DDC 342.7308/5—dc23
LC record available at https://lccn.loc.gov/2020021904

Our books may be purchased in bulk for promotional, educational,
or business use. Please contact your local bookseller
or the Macmillan Corporate and Premium Sales Department
at 1-800-221-7945, extension 5442, or by email
at MacmillanSpecialMarkets@macmillan.com.

First Edition: 2020

10 9 8 7 6 5 4 3 2 1

For Dan Green

with appreciation for a lifetime

defending free speech

CONTENTS

INVENTING EQUALITY

Introduction

"What to the slave is the Fourth of July?"

On July 4, 1852, Frederick Douglass put this question to an Independence Day celebration in Rochester, New York. No ordinary critic of America's slave system, Douglass existed because a white man had raped an enslaved black woman. Douglass had almost no memories of his mother, from whom he was separated as an infant at the whim of their owner. As a young boy he witnessed slavery's full range of depravity, on one occasion watching in horror as his new owner stripped his aunt, hung her from a ceiling, and whipped her.

Douglass determined at a young age to violate the rigid and brutal constraints of the slave system. Denied the right to exercise what he saw as the natural curiosity of the young, Douglass educated himself in violation of the law and risked a death sentence teaching other slaves to read. His owner quickly identified the young slave as a troublemaker and handed him over to a specialist in "breaking" unruly slaves. The subject of repeated vicious beatings, Douglass stole himself in 1838, fleeing the South and servitude. That flight failed to bring freedom, as he spent the ensuing eight years as a fugitive from American justice, aware that at any moment he could be seized by slave-catchers and returned to slavery.

In spite of this constant peril in the supposedly free North, Douglass frequently spoke out in public settings against American tyranny. Grievously beaten by a mob in Indiana and closely pursued by slave-hunters, Douglass fled to England in 1845 and then to Ireland, where he spoke to large crowds and became an instant celebrity. The publication of his memoirs that year cemented that fame on both sides of the

Atlantic. After British supporters raised the funds to officially purchase his freedom, Douglass returned to the United States in 1846 a free man.

Strikingly handsome and imposing, with a dramatic crown of thick black hair, Douglass possessed a powerful speaking voice, the equal of any contemporary orator's. Douglass knew how to move an audience, as he did that Independence Day in Rochester's Corinthian Hall. As he began his talk, the six hundred primarily white men and women leaned forward. At first he set them at ease, praising the nation's founders for their commitment to human liberty.

Then came a sudden shift in tone. Slowly raising his voice, Douglass directly addressed his audience. They, he pointed out, could safely proclaim the freedoms they possessed as citizens of the United States, but what did "the great principles of political freedom and of natural justice, embodied in that Declaration of Independence," have to do with Americans like him? Black Americans could not be part of this national celebration, which mocked their aspirations as well as the principles white Americans claimed as their own. The Constitution, while granting liberty to some people, validated the subjugation of millions. Making his audience ever more uncomfortable, Douglass emphasized each use of the pronoun "your"—"*your* rights," "*your* liberty." He then hit them in the gut by begging their pardon for asking, but "what have I to do with *your* national independence?" The celebration of American independence only served to underscore the distance between them, demonstrating "the sacrilegious irony" of a country proclaiming its love of freedom while upholding and protecting the institution of slavery.

Douglass spoke a truth few people wanted to hear: that when it came to its own supposed ideals, "America is false to the past, false to the present, and solemnly binds herself to be false to the future." It was well past time to expose the nation's hypocrisy.[1]

The Constitution, in Douglass's words, "is not an abstraction" but the very bond of the Union, exerting great legal, political, and cultural influence. Its power came down firmly in favor of slavery. The Constitutional Convention betrayed the principles of the Revolution in producing a document that was "radically and essentially pro-slavery," making every supposedly free American part of "the body guards of slavery."[2] Little wonder that Douglass's ally William Lloyd Garrison declared the Constitution "a covenant with death, and an agreement with hell."[3] For these reasons, the celebration of American freedom "is a sham . . . your shouts of liberty and equality, hollow mockery." Any slave could speak truth to the slave owners' power, if allowed to speak, and make clear that claims of divine favor and Christian sentiment served as "a thin veil to cover up crimes which would disgrace a nation of savages."[4]

The shocked audience had invited Douglass to speak on a day celebrating freedom, and had likely expected him to offer a hopeful message about America's trend in that direction. Instead, he'd rubbed their noses in their own complicity, revealing the violence and hypocrisy beneath the celebrations of independence and equality. Slaves were also Americans, so the crimes of slavery were visited upon Americans by Americans. How could this perfect document, this Constitution that everyone claimed to venerate, be so flawed, so damaged at birth? No doubt some people dismissed his comments as the bitter rantings of a former slave unable to properly appreciate his good fortune in living in a free state. Yet Douglass raised disturbing points: How could the Constitution defend both freedom and slavery? What happened to the promised ideals of the Declaration of Independence so beautifully expressed in the glorious phrase "all men are created equal"? Why did so few white Americans embrace their own venerated doctrine?

Frederick Douglass saw what so many white Americans could not see or would not admit—that their country promoted and even celebrated inequality. His questions and his doubts about our shared commitment to the ideals we proclaim remain central to the history and development of the United States. We find his words echoing down the years, in documents public and private during the Civil War of 1861–65, and during the conflict for America's future that we know as the Reconstruction era, 1865 to 1877. The questions arise repeatedly during the dark age of segregation and can be heard in Franklin Roosevelt's State of the Union address of 1944 charging that those forced into dire poverty can never know true freedom. Douglass's language lives on in the ringing oratory of the civil rights and women's rights movements, in the great progressive Supreme Court decisions of the 1960s and 1970s, and in the bitter dissents of the twenty-first century. Through the seventeen decades since Douglass asked about the true meaning of the Fourth of July, the fundamental question persists: do we mean what we say about human equality?

American history can be seen as a battle to reconcile the large gap between our stated ideals and the reality of our republic. It is a struggle that cannot honestly be cast as one of steady progress toward ever greater freedom and equality. Every step forward appears to be matched by a step back. But neither can we just dismiss this history as a series of sad footnotes in a losing battle against intolerance. In so many ways the sweep of our history is the story of people fighting to expand the working definition of what it means to be an American citizen, and to determine who is worthy of that designation. It is a story of resistance to the anti-democratic forces fearful of change, and of courageous individuals who will not abandon the fight for human equality.

This book traces the evolution of that battle for true equality from the Revolution through the late nineteenth century. We begin by examining the bright promise of the Revolutionary period, with the high ideals propounded by the Declaration of Independence and the Constitution, showing how both documents ultimately contained the seeds of their own negation. Moving beyond the obvious contradiction of a slave owner declaring that "all men are created equal," Chapter 1 identifies systemic legal flaws that ensured the inability of the nation to attain its stated ideal of legal equality. In a bitter irony, the Supreme Court itself made the case for the inherent weakness of the Constitution in its notorious *Dred Scott* decision, which jettisoned any pretense of respect for legal equality—or historical accuracy—in denying citizenship to millions of native-born Americans. That corruption of American ideals is the subject of Chapter 2, which ends with the fulfillment of Abraham Lincoln's prophecy that "a house divided against itself cannot stand."

The *Dred Scott* decision led inexorably to the bloodiest conflict in this nation's history, the Civil War. Chapter 3 argues that this war quickly transformed the United States by teaching tens of thousands of Americans the reality and value of equality. For the first time, white Americans took seriously the notion that black men could truly be the equal of whites. Within the global context, an even more dramatic shift came with the spreading perception that maybe women also should enjoy the benefits of legal equality.

By the war's end, millions of Americans believed that their Constitution needed to be fixed in order to secure the rights of all. Chapters 4 and 5 examine this development, which occurred over the period of a few brief years when Congress acted with vigor to repair the Constitution's fundamental rent with three amendments ending slavery, defining citizenship while protecting the rights of all those born or naturalized in the United States, and guaranteeing the right to vote to all men. But that last qualifier marked a great betrayal of the principles and promises of the Civil War and Reconstruction, and is the subject of Chapter 6. By excluding women from constitutional protections, Congress validated a second-class citizenship for half the population and ultimately undermined the positive results of the long, bloody war.

A commitment to various forms of inequality did not fade with the passage of the Fourteenth Amendment, with far too many white males finding no reason to share their "democracy." That counterattack on equality is the theme of Chapter 7, which demonstrates the Supreme Court's hostility to a humane interpretation of the Reconstruction amendments in favor of restrictive policies establishing distinctive levels of citizenship. This reactionary stance by the nation's highest court found academic support from the proponents of the pseudo-science of social Darwinism, as well as from southern white politicians intent on restoring slavery under a different guise. Their combined efforts destroyed most of the progressive advances resulting from the Civil

War, thrusting the nation back into a primitive white tribalism buttressed by a patina of alleged scientific rationalism.

If we end the story there, we are left with nothing but another historical tragedy. However, the seeming triumph of inequality in the late
nineteenth century did not go unchallenged. As the Epilogue suggests,
the advocates of equality did not meekly accept either the Supreme
Court's efforts to turn back the clock or congressional quiescence.
Often overlooked by historians, large numbers of women and men
persisted in their battle for true legal equality. Though they usually
lost in their efforts to gain respect and rights, these brave warriors
laid the groundwork for later challenges to discriminatory legislation
and unjust systems. Over the years these advocates of equality highlighted the remarkable power of the opening paragraph of the Fourteenth Amendment, which promised full legal rights for all citizens.
A later war against the forces of tyranny inspired another generation
of heroic figures to return to the fight, resuscitating the Fourteenth
Amendment and with it the dormant concept of equality.

As we near the 250th anniversary of the Declaration of Independence, Americans continue to debate equality. It is hoped that this book
will inform that conversation while reminding the citizens of the United
States, a nation whose foundational document promises in its opening
sentence to "secure the blessings of liberty" for all people without exception, that our work is not done.

CHAPTER 1

Corrupted from the Start

*Or, how Americans abandoned their
stated ideals and embraced inequality*

Frederick Douglass asked how the Constitution could protect both freedom and slavery. Anyone who looked closely at the Constitution knew the answer, though they generally avoided acknowledging it: the Constitution failed to define citizenship and quietly allowed some people to be categorized as property. How had the geniuses of Philadelphia in 1787 allowed such an oversight?

Many of those present at the creation thought they had no choice. The majority of the Framers despised slavery. Though twenty-five of the fifty-five members of the Constitutional Convention owned slaves, many of the slave owners joined most of the northern representatives in speaking out against perpetuating that institution. But the wealthiest people in the southern states, who perceived no evil in coerced labor, would not allow any interference with their power over slaves. At the Constitutional Convention, the representatives of Georgia and the Carolinas made clear that they would sooner see the new nation fail than allow slavery to be subject to limitations. Fellow slave owners, such as James Madison of Virginia, appealed to the logic of liberty. They would damage the effort to form a united nation if they inserted "in the Constitution the idea that there could be property in men," for slaves were "not like merchandize," they were people. Madison's logic had no effect on the entrenched self-interest of his rich neighbors, who did not care that slavery contradicted republican principles and who threatened on several occasions to walk out in the face of criticism.[1]

The slave owners knew they had little to fear, since there was no major organized effort to outlaw slavery in 1787. Only Vermont and Massachusetts had outlawed slavery, the small New York Manumission Society was just two years old, and the British Committee for the Abolition of the Slave Trade had been founded just three days before the convention began its deliberations. In the absence of any sustained opposition to slavery, convention delegates hoping for a unified country saw no alternative to repeatedly giving in to slavery's proponents, though Madison and Gouverneur Morris did succeed in keeping the word "slavery" out of the finished document. The opponents of slavery clung to such small victories, hoping they might someday lead to the end of this intentional denial of everything in which they professed to believe.

The timidity of the opponents of slavery before the take-it-or-leave-it stance of the pro-slavery faction is evident in the development of Article I, Section 9, concerning the international slave trade. Anyone looking into James Madison's *Notes of Debates in the Federal Convention of 1787*, first published in 1840, can see the competing currents at the convention. In the face of calls for federal regulation of the slave trade, the Committee of Detail, chaired by South Carolina's John Rutledge, produced a pro-slavery draft that forbade Congress from taxing the "Importation of such Persons as the several States shall think proper to admit." While upholding the slave trade, the draft included language acknowledging the humanity of the slaves as "persons."[2]

The ensuing debate revealed severe disagreements among the Framers in their vision for the country. Connecticut's Oliver Ellsworth thought the matter not worthy of discussion since slavery would surely die out on its own. In contrast, the delegates from the Carolinas and Georgia found no fault with a system they claimed had been in existence since the dawn of time and warned that they would jettison the Union rather than abandon the slave trade. Delaware's John Dickinson could not contain his disgust with slavery and its defenders. In his view, slavery posed a threat to the new nation's honor and safety as it clearly violated America's proclaimed values while also posing the danger of slave uprisings. Dickinson might be dismissed as a representative from a state with few slaves, but Maryland's Luther Martin, a slave owner, agreed with Dickinson, finding slavery "inconsistent with the principles of the revolution and dishonorable to the American character," while George Mason, one of the largest slave owners in Virginia, firmly stated that "every master of slaves is born a petty tyrant" who would bring down "the judgment of heaven" on America. With Virginia's delegation firmly opposed to the slave trade, which they considered a form of piracy, the South Carolina representatives proposed a twenty-year period of unrestrained trade in slaves, at which point Congress might review the issue.

Madison feared that twenty years offered more than enough time for the expansion of slavery, as the profit motive would lead to the importation of thousands of slaves—an accurate prediction. The growth of slavery posed a clear threat to American liberty, Madison charged, and he called for an immediate end to the slave trade. But in the face of repeated movements toward the door by the three southernmost states, the convention accepted the new wording by a vote of seven to four, with delegates from New Jersey, Pennsylvania, Delaware, and Virginia rejecting even this language as immoral and an unwarranted appeasement.[3]

This single debate offers ample evidence that slavery endangered national unity from the start, with at least three states willing to form a separate union rather than allow any limitations on human bondage. Even more revealing was the controversy over how to count slaves as part of the population. It quickly became clear that the presence of slavery in a country dedicated to liberty embarrassed the majority of delegates at the Constitutional Convention. Madison declared, "We have seen the mere distinction of colour made in the most enlightened period of time, a ground of the most oppressive dominion ever exercised by man over man." But once more the delegates from South Carolina would not give way, demanding that their slaves—who, after all, constituted half of their state's population—should be counted as people for the purposes of representation. Others observed that if they are people worthy of being counted for representation, then they are subject to the same liberties promised to all Americans and could not be held in bondage. Slavery just could not be made to make sense.[4]

However, slavery made perfect sense to Pierce Butler, John Rutledge, Charles Pinckney, and Charles Cotesworth Pinckney, the delegates from South Carolina. These white men set the groundwork for the defense of slavery over the next several decades, their arguments persistently slipping into the passive voice. Slaves were property; it was that simple. As property, they did not enjoy human rights, though they should still be counted as people when it served their owners' purposes.

The argument kept going in circles, the debate returning repeatedly to disrupt the convention: are slaves people or property? Pennsylvania's Gouverneur Morris cut to the heart of the matter: if slaves are property, yet are counted for purposes of representation, then why not count other forms of property? No principles bolstered slavery, just self-interest. Slavery, Morris maintained, "was the curse of heaven on the States where it prevailed," consigning them to tyranny and poverty, while the free states prospered peacefully without the routine use of violence against other people. If the southern states insisted on remaining retrograde, that was their responsibility, but that did not give them the right to play with language and human rights.[5]

Morris did not end his critique with the obvious contradiction between humanity and property in persons. He went further, casting the Constitution in language that reverberated seventy years later in Frederick Douglass's fiery oratory. The delegates from the Carolinas and Georgia, Morris warned, reframed the new Constitution as a bulwark of slavery. The southern delegates demanded that everyone jettison the American Revolution and its principles, forcing the country to revert to an aristocratic system even worse than the one they had just thrown off by means of war. Slavery promoted an aristocratic government, Morris charged, reducing many Americans to "vassalage." What, he asked his fellow northern representatives, would they get in return "for a sacrifice of every principle of right, of every impulse of humanity"? The answer was shattering, as they would be responsible for defending this cruel bondage. They would bind their states' militia to defend the slave owners in the event of a slave uprising—a rebellion Morris found entirely justified. Meanwhile, the slave owners would expand their system, increasing the danger of future slave rebellions, which the people of the North would have to help crush. Morris concluded that the proposed Constitution actually encouraged slave owners to acquire "fresh supplies of wretched Africans," which would increase their numbers for representational purposes and thus their political influence in the new nation. Pinckney could only respond weakly that the New England fisheries and western frontier were "more burdensome to the U.S. than the slaves."[6]

For several days it appeared that the quarrel over whether to count slaves as people or property would sink the effort to craft a new Constitution. As the representatives of the Carolinas and Georgia prepared to bolt, James Wilson of Pennsylvania and Roger Sherman of Connecticut averted crisis by proposing that a slave be counted as three-fifths of a person. While the number was seemingly selected at random, the choice of three-fifths rather than the equally baseless one-half or five-eighths made a huge difference to the southernmost states. If slaves were not counted toward representation, then South Carolina would fall from a population of 250,000 to 140,000 and Georgia from 82,000 to 50,000. With these numbers, South Carolina would rank behind New Jersey, and Georgia would become the smallest state in the Union in terms of official population and would have just one delegate in the House of Representatives.[7]

The "Three-Fifths Compromise" is one of the most unfortunate misnomers in American history, implying as it does a reasonable middle ground. It was but one of a series of deals made by the majority to keep the powerful slave owners of the Carolinas and Georgia within the Union. Despite the power granted Congress to regulate trade, it could not interfere with the foreign slave trade until 1808. Congress could tax imports, which fueled the northern economy, but not exports, the source of southern economic development. Northern states were required to return runaway slaves and, as Morris had warned, must help crush slave rebellions. In return for all of that, the slave owners agreed to not strangle the Union at its inception.

Through the nineteenth and twentieth centuries, most commentators viewed the Three-Fifths Compromise as dealing solely with the issue of representation and the resulting balance of power between the states. In the traditional telling, outraged northerners thought the South gained an unfair advantage by getting to count slaves as three-fifths of a person. This version of the story is correct but not complete. As the convention debates and later controversies indicate, the three-fifths clause crafted a diminished legal and cultural identity for blacks as not fully people. For most representatives at the Constitutional Convention, including the entire Virginia delegation, seeing slaves as less than a whole person was exactly the issue. Slavery, each said in turn, is wrong; slaves are people and need to be seen as such. If they are people, then they should enjoy the same rights as other citizens of the United States. Did three-fifths of a person get three-fifths of the rights of an American? The Framers of the Constitution asked these questions but offered no useful answer, allowing the confusion of the three-fifths clause to become part of the Constitution. As Morris warned, the decisions made in the summer of 1787 had long-lasting consequences.[8]

The only way the Convention found to respond to these deeply troubling questions about the personhood of black Americans was to ignore them—setting the pattern for the next seven decades. The Federalist Papers, written by Alexander Hamilton, John Jay, and James Madison in support of the Constitution during the debates over ratification in 1787 and 1788, contain only a single discussion of the three-fifths clause. Federalist No. 54, generally attributed to Madison, recognized the illogic of the three-fifths clause while embracing it as a necessity. He denied that the Constitution labeled slaves "merely as property, and in no respect whatever as persons," but this did not mean that they are solely one or the other; rather, they are both and neither. Sounding like a layperson attempting to explain the Trinity, Madison had the Constitution coming down "with great propriety" on the side of splitting the difference between person and property. That might suggest that the slave should be half of a person, but the math seems fair since slaves are "debased by their servitude below the level of free inhabitants" by two-fifths. With that sleight of hand and admission of avoidance, Madison breathed a sigh of relief and moved on to more sensible topics.[9]

Since that is the only reference to the three-fifths clause in the Federalist Papers, it is safe to assume that the authors preferred that no one talk about it. Some anti-federalists—opponents of the Constitution who feared it would establish a strong central government—briefly raised the issue, only to also abandon it as too dangerous to both their logic and society. Melancton Smith of New York felt that slaves should not be counted at all, since they had no free will, but admitted that it confused him and he might be mistaken. The anonymous Brutus (probably Robert Yates) condemned slavery as defying "every idea of benevolence, justice, and religion, and contrary to all the principles of liberty, which had been publickly avowed in the late glorious revolution." He then unknowingly echoed Gouverneur Morris in arguing that if the three-fifths clause "be a just ground for representation, the horses in some states, and the oxen in others, ought to be represented." Brutus undermined the moral power of his objection by framing it entirely within the context of an unfair representation for the southern states. Similarly, at the Massachusetts ratifying convention, opponents of the Constitution asked what justified slave owners evading paying taxes on two-fifths of their professed property, while New Englanders paid tax on 100 percent of their livestock? Confused by the formulation, these anti-federalists quickly dropped it for more comprehensible flaws.[10]

Northern opponents of the Constitution thought the three-fifths clause conceded too much to the southern states, while those living in the South warned that it did not grant the slave owners sufficient security in their property. Both foundered on the core problem: the northerner who thought slaves should count for nothing was then saying that slaves were not people, while the southerner who thought the slave should be counted as a whole person implied that slaves enjoyed equal personhood. It is little wonder that most anti-federalists avoided the three-fifths clause as much as did the federalists.

The Framers of the Constitution struggled with the concept of human equality. The Constitution may have begun with the statement "We the People," but it failed to define who those people might be. Under the three-fifths clause, the law accepted less-than-human people, a minimization of personhood that could easily be extended to other groups, including, of course, women. Further problems arose as a consequence of the passive voice used in the Constitution's fugitive slave clause. "No person held to service or labour" in one state could avoid that labor by escaping into another state. Not only did the Constitution thus avoid the word "slave," it also held that such a runaway worker would be "delivered up" to the person to whom the labor was due. But delivered by whom? There was the rub, and most northern states eventually determined that every runaway slave posed a moral rebuke to the Constitution and the country, and that capturing and returning these fugitives was not their job.

The Constitutional Convention compounded the embedded defect of slavery by failing to address the nature of citizenship. During the Revolution, the United States had moved away from the traditional European concept of subjectship—the notion that a person owed undying allegiance to the monarch of the state into which he was born. In its place, the new republic created a concept of citizenship based upon a chosen allegiance—a person became a citizen of a free society as an exercise of free will.

While a radical reimagining of society, citizenship remained ambiguous and received surprisingly little attention at the Constitutional Convention. Since Article IV, Section 2 seemingly established legal equality—"The citizens of each State shall be entitled to all privileges and immunities of citizens in the several States"—the definition of citizenship is obviously vital. Bluntly stated: it matters who deserves the rights and privileges of citizenship. Yet the Constitution did not define citizenship, deliberately leaving vague which people would enjoy the basic and essential legal equality promised by Article IV, Section 2. How then, did the Framers intend for citizenship to be understood and legal equality protected?

Madison's notes indicate that the convention returned often to the issue of citizenship, but almost entirely within the context of eligibility for serving in Congress. Several delegates observed that the states had distinctive qualifications for citizenship, voting, and office-holding, leading to different levels of rights. No one objected to the absence of a unified process of naturalization, nor did anyone attempt to define citizenship, though James Wilson did remind the convention that the citizen of one state was a citizen of all the states. Without debate, the convention granted Congress the power "to establish an uniform rule of naturalization," something Congress did not get around to until the 1920s.[11]

There was a telling moment, however, in the debate over the slave trade. Gouverneur Morris proposed that Article I, Section 9 specify that "the importation of slaves into North Carolina, South Carolina, and Georgia, shall not be prohibited." He favored the specification of the states involved not only to make a political point that the convention was bowing to their interests but also to remove any ambiguity about the states' right to grant citizenship as they saw fit. Permitting the slave trade on the national level, Morris warned, not only confused the process by which states made citizens but also implied that some people—such as slaves—could never become citizens. However, delegates objected both to the naming of the states that demanded the slave trade and to the use of the word "slaves."[12]

In 1789, Madison, a member of the first House of Representatives, admitted that the Constitution should have defined citizenship in order to secure legal equality. Even in this first year of constitutional government, the confusions piled up. Could a person be a citizen and a slave, a woman and a citizen, an immigrant and an American? In the absence of constitutional guidance, Madison proposed that citizenship follow the place of birth, though he avoided complicated particulars and "peculiar" circumstances, such as slavery, gender, and immigration. Madison hoped to clarify that a person born in the United States was definitively a citizen, while kicking the larger issues down the road to some later Congress to sort out. But Congress found the specifics troubling, recognizing that if a person born in the United States was a citizen, then very soon slaves and women would step forth to demand their equal rights. Congress therefore refused to even debate Madison's proposal, leaving the essential problem of an unclear standard for citizenship embedded in American law.[13]

This lack of clarity on citizenship plagued every branch of government. In 1821, Attorney General William Wirt attempted to determine who enjoyed citizenship rights under the Constitution. Strict legal logic led Wirt irrevocably to insist that free blacks must be citizens entitled to all the privileges of citizenship. Yet Wirt, the longest-serving attorney general in the nation's history, could not bring himself to accept his own logic, and he lamely concluded that the matter rested with the states. The states would not prove to be the firmest defenders of legal rights.[14]

The failure of the Constitution to identify citizens continually imperiled free blacks. For instance, in 1832, Prudence Crandall's school for girls in Canterbury, Connecticut, accepted white and black students. When local parents objected to Crandall's integration policy, she transformed the school to exclusively serve blacks. The parents appealed to the legislature, which passed the "Black Law" prohibiting schools for black students without the approval of local authorities. Crandall defended herself in court by appealing to Article IV, Section 2 of the Constitution and its grant of citizenship rights across state borders. The court responded that free blacks were not citizens, so constitutional protections did not apply to black students. When Crandall still refused to change her policies, a mob attacked the school and closed it down. Similarly, the Constitution's inability to provide guidance on the issue of citizenship permitted Pennsylvania's chief judge, John Bannister Gibson, to disenfranchise every black in the state in 1837. Gibson cited no evidence to support his assertion that blacks could not be citizens beyond observing that since slaves were black, free blacks existed only at the state's sufferance.[15]

Chief Justice Lemuel Shaw of the Massachusetts Supreme Court, considered one of the preeminent jurists of his time, read the law in opposite directions on the tangled issue of legal equality. In 1836, Shaw relied on the principle of legal equality to free Med, a six-year-old slave residing in Boston. Since the Massachusetts constitution declared all people equal, Shaw reasoned, then Med ceased to be a slave the moment she breathed the state's free air. Shaw accepted that other states could have slavery through the implementation of positive law—legislative acts—but Massachusetts had chosen freedom for all.[16]

However, racism mangled Shaw's elegant logic. In the 1840s black parents challenged Boston's segregated schools, relying on the principle of legal equality Shaw had defended in the Med decision. Appearing before Justice Shaw in the case *Roberts v. City of Boston*, the parents' attorney, Charles Sumner, argued that "any institution founded on inequality" violated the Massachusetts constitution, which guaranteed equality and prohibited "exclusive privileges." Shaw agreed with Sumner that everyone is equal before the law, and yet some people are more equal than others because of "the actual and various conditions of persons in society." Shaw thus offered a perfect legal tautology: inequality is legally permissible because inequality exists in society. Since natural differences exist between men and women, blacks and whites, old and young, the legislature can grant or deny rights to groups as it sees fit. Shaw's decision became the cornerstone of segregation, the legal justification to which state and federal courts turned until 1954.[17]

The Supreme Court did no better in parsing constitutional standards of citizenship. Its only interstate slave trade decision came in 1841, with the complicated case of *Groves v. Slaughter* responding to Mississippi's efforts to prevent the importation of slaves from other states. The seven justices split into five positions that mixed interstate commerce, which the Constitution clearly placed under congressional oversight, and personhood, returning to the thorny issue of whether slaves are people or property. Justice John McLean demanded that the Court confront the core issue, insisting that even slaves enjoyed the status of people under the Constitution. Justice Henry Baldwin angrily responded that the Constitution treated slaves as property and that states could not therefore prohibit the slave trade, as the owners' rights were protected under the Fifth Amendment's due process clause. The Court's majority sidestepped the matter entirely by calling for further legislation.[18]

The white public appeared widely indifferent to the courts' confusion, preferring to accept the contradictions and get on with their affairs. The famed French traveler Alexis de Tocqueville praised this willful ignorance: "I have never been more struck by the good sense and the practical judgment of the Americans than in the manner in which they elude the numberless difficulties resulting from their Federal Constitution." Tocqueville echoed Jefferson's 1814 advice to Edward Coles in recommending that Americans leave the resolution of fundamental problems to some later generation.[19]

By the time Tocqueville visited in the 1830s, Americans had successfully constructed a self-image that had no relation to their actual world. Within a few years of Tocqueville's famous warning that equality posed the greatest threat to liberty, the anomalies would become too burdensome and the American people would pay a high price for failing to confront the large crack in the nation's foundation. Avoidance and procrastination would cost hundreds of thousands of lives.

=

How had the American people turned away so quickly from Thomas Jefferson's ringing avowal of human equality to make the United States the land of inequality? Of greatest significance is the simple fact that legal equality threatened every preexisting social arrangement. More than a brutal system of coerced labor was at stake. Equality would overturn hierarchies of gender, ethnicity, religion, and class. Intellectual consistency can be terrifying.

In March 1776, Abigail Adams famously wrote her husband, John, a member of the Continental Congress on the verge of declaring independence: "I desire you would remember the ladies and be more generous and favorable to them than your ancestors." She reminded her husband of the hard truth that "all men would be tyrants if they could," and that women pay the price for that tyranny. Less well known is John's response: "I cannot but laugh." He declared her "saucy," and insisted that he would rather lose the war than submit "to the despotism of the petticoat." The emerging nation's leaders intended to keep their revolution within strict limits.[20]

The Declaration of Independence included soaring rhetoric about the right of revolution and human equality that made many Americans, including John Adams, uncomfortable. He had no problem with propertied white men demanding control over their local political structure, but he could not tolerate his wife using their language of legal equality.

Over the nation's first seventy years, some Americans rejected the Declaration's language promoting equality as a silly error on Jefferson's part, while others promoted its words but not its meaning. Speaker of the House Robert Hunter took the former position in 1845, dismissing equality as an abstraction lacking relevance to political and social realities. Another doubter of the American Revolution, Fisher Ames, a member of the first Congress under the Constitution, saw equality undermining culture, appealing only to irrational emotions, and productive of "agitation and alarm." The illusion of equality made men dissatisfied with their lot in life. Ames succinctly expressed the fears of many educated Americans that the rhetoric of the Revolution might inspire their social inferiors to seek equality. This wholesale dismissal of the core ideas of the young nation led to reframing the Revolution as a conservative movement. Ames was joined in this task by most of the country's leading intellectuals.[21]

The word "equality" chafed on the intellects and interests of many prominent Americans, carrying with it a whiff of Revolutionary gunpowder. Rufus Choate, a congressman and leader of the legal profession who gave many July Fourth orations in his long career, dismissed the "glittering and sounding generalities of natural right which make up the Declaration of Independence." Jurist William Harper utterly rejected Jefferson's call for equality as sentimental and "palpably false." After all, women are rational humans and often "better qualified to exercise political privileges, and to attain the distinctions of society, than many men," yet no one suggested granting them full legal equality. That great champion of dissent John Quincy Adams scoffed, like his father, at the idea of women citizens. He based his logic not on the Constitution or any legal principle but rather on the biblical story of the Garden of Eden. God denied women any say in government because of Eve's disobedience to the divine command, a penalty that all women must pay until "the final redemption of the race." Men alone could participate in politics until the end of time.[22]

James Fenimore Cooper, the leading American novelist of the first half of the nineteenth century, expressed well the elite's disdain for equality. He mocked the concept as nothing more than empty electioneering promises, "a maxim that is true in neither nature, revealed morals, nor political theory." Cooper spoke directly to the great and obvious contradiction of all American protestations of justice and equality: slavery. Its continuation gave the lie to patriotic boasts and proved that no one really believed in equality. The language of equality served a purpose, manipulated by the wealthy and politically ambitious to flatter and control the common man. Americans might like the language of the Declaration, but inequality is everyone's daily experience, with everyone finding someone over whom they might claim superiority. The rhetoric of equality could not alter the fact that nature made men unequal, a position reinforced by the Bible. The United States distributed rights based on birth, inheritance, and property. Cooper saw an unequal society and thought it good.[23]

Belief in inequality tainted scholarship as well. The leading historian of the antebellum period, George Bancroft, a prominent spokesman for the Democratic Party, saw himself as a defender of the "common man." He praised the Declaration for giving the nation ideals that overturned false distinctions between men. But he distrusted immigrants, had no time for women, complained that Catholics just followed orders from the Pope, and justified slavery by pointing to its ancient roots, as in imperial Rome, where "everybody was served by slaves"—a logical absurdity unless the slaves had slaves. Similarly, John L. O'Sullivan's opening editorial in the first issue of his prominent *Democratic Review* found the United States guided by a "pervading spirit of democratic equality" in its mission of universal emancipation. Yet in the very next paragraph he reminded his readers that this call to arms did not extend to slavery, which must remain untouched. Like so many proclaimed adherents of Jeffersonian democracy, O'Sullivan spoke in favor of both equality and slavery, refusing to admit any contradiction.[24]

It is notable that all the above critics of equality were northerners. Southern intellectuals unsurprisingly shared this celebration of inequality. In 1838, the *Southern Literary Messenger* maintained that Jefferson did not intend his call for equality to extend beyond white men, since slaves could not enter into contracts and thus had no legal standing, and women were, well, women. The infamous and comically inept Dr. Samuel Cartwright, who crafted a pseudo-science demonstrating white superiority, shared the consensus view that the Declaration's promise of equality applied only to white men, since blacks were not really human but an inferior order of being. Another prominent equality denier was the chancellor of South Carolina College, William Harper, whose influential 1838 *Memoir on Slavery* considered slavery a rational means of maintaining social order and race a reasonable way of determining who should be enslaved. As he framed the question: "If there are sordid, servile, and laborious offices to be performed, is it not better that there should be sordid, servile, and laborious beings to perform them?" Conveniently, those servile people were not white but black, marked by God for slavery. Similarly, the pedophile senator James Hammond held that all societies required "a class to do the menial duties," one that needs neither intellect nor skill, but only physical strength and docility, and "constitutes the very mud-sill of society" upon which all else is built. There was no need to ask the slaves how they felt about such an arrangement, as "the *status* in which we have placed them is an elevation."[25]

Outside of the South, America's political leaders preferred to pretend that everything was as Jefferson said, and that the beneficent glow of equality and democracy spread across the land. A sentimental and myopic vision of equality developed that described an imagined golden city on a hill. In his popular "Junius Tracts," published in 1844, Calvin Colton captured the prevailing ideology of Jacksonian America as a country where men of humble origin can rise to wealth and prestige through hard work and virtuous conduct. No privileges based on birth, and "no civil or political disqualifications" barred anyone's path to prosperity. Coining a phrase used to this day, Colton proclaimed, "This is a country of *self-made men*." Colton crafted a vision of a land of economic equality where a laborer "is never compelled to work for wages fixed by employers," because he can always quit and find work elsewhere. It is unlikely that any contemporary American worker would have recognized this portrait of economic equality, but the court system consistently operated on the ideological certainty that labor relations were fixed by two free wills entering into an open and fair contract.[26]

Freed from the need for evidence, an abstract notion of equality filled the popular vision. The first issue of the influential *American Review* included an editorial by Henry Bellows, a leading Unitarian minister, proclaiming the United States a land of total freedom. "There are here no established limits within which the hopes of any class of society must be confined." As with so many of these early propagandists of the pure and good America, Reverend Bellows compared his country to the class-based oppressions of Europe: "It is a glorious thing that we have no serfs, with the large and unfortunate exception of our slaves—no artificial distinctions— . . . no station which merit may not fill." That clause contained it all: the great "unfortunate exception" of slavery and the certainty that no other distinctions existed. A pity about slavery, but what could one do? One should certainly not let this single exception interfere with the general celebration of America's exceptionalism.[27]

The Revolutionary generation had made good use of the language of equality in their struggle against Britain. But the moment they won the war, they turned their collective backs on the ideal and began implementing the laws necessary to institute inequality. It is of course easy—and accurate—to call these leaders hypocrites, but their ideas and actions fell well within the traditions of the Enlightenment world they inhabited. Jefferson and his peers were familiar with Aristotle, who warned against the dangers of unchecked equality. If people believe they are equal, he argued, they will claim the right to rule, leading to revolution and the end of stable government. The law exists to maintain appropriate levels of inequality, keeping everyone, including the rulers, in their place. America's founders also knew the writings of Thomas Hobbes, who celebrated inequality as necessary to social stability. Without government, Hobbes held, all men are equally able to kill one another. The law institutes inequality and keeps people from routinely committing homicide to promote their self-interest.[28]

While they admired Aristotle and Hobbes, the Revolutionary generation venerated John Locke, who maintained that all men are born equal and that distinctions are the result of social and legal actions. What set Locke apart from previous philosophers was his realization that just as society creates artificial inequalities, so it can also promote equality. Through education and a spirit of progressive reform, society can re-create itself to protect and enhance humanity's "natural

freedom," and government can ensure that no one falls under the will
of another man. Locke saw legislation as capable of fostering either
inequality or equality; the law and human society are both elastic.
This philosophical perception of the law as able to promote equality
remained a quiet undercurrent in American life until the very fabric of
the nation began to unravel in 1860, when a wide range of the public
perceived legal equality as the only way to save their country.[29]

The Constitution had declared itself formulated in the name of
"We the People of the United States." For the first seventy years of
the nation's existence, those who held social, economic, political, and
cultural power limited that collective noun to white males. Those who
attempted to broaden the definition of "the people" were routinely
defeated, as in the Dorr Rebellion of 1841–42, which sought to bring
democracy to Rhode Island, and at the Virginia Constitutional Convention of 1829–30. At the latter, conservative delegates fearfully argued
that any expansion of white manhood suffrage, then limited to those
with landed property, threatened to undermine the right of property
in people. So the convention left suffrage linked to property. White
male suffrage expanded in 1851, but cautiously and without any ringing
endorsement of the concept of equality.

White opponents of slavery remained timid until the debut of William
Lloyd Garrison's newspaper *The Liberator* in 1831. Garrison differed from
previous white opponents of slavery in demanding its complete and immediate abolition. While few white abolitionists shared Garrison's conviction
regarding human equality, they did broadcast a deep-seated moral revul-
sion to slavery. Though its circulation remained insignificant, *The Liberator* exerted enormous influence and unhinged southern slave owners. The
defenders of slavery saw the abolitionists as a profound social threat who
could not be allowed to speak their dangerous words of freedom.

The slave owners' campaign to silence dissent gained significant aid
in the mid-1830s when the Democratic Party made the fateful decision

to tie itself to the slave South. In 1836, the Democratic majority in Congress forced through a gag rule forbidding the presentation of anti-slavery petitions, in clear violation of the First Amendment's protection of the people's right to petition their government, and condemned books questioning the wisdom of slavery, such as Hinton Helper's *The Impending Crisis of the South*, as "insurrectionary and hostile to the domestic peace and tranquility of the country." Southern states offered rewards for the assassination of leading abolitionists, including Garrison and Douglass, and even members of Congress, such as New York's Seth Gates.[30]

Americans liked the rhetoric, if not the reality, of equality. Kentucky's 1792 constitution began, "That all power is inherent in the people, and all free governments are founded on their authority and instituted for their peace, safety, and happiness." Almost the exact same wording can be found in the constitutions of Alabama in 1819, Delaware in 1831, Arkansas in 1836, and Florida in 1838. These states all protected slavery while limiting rights for poor whites and women despite the constitutional promises of liberty. As late as the 1840s, Rhode Island put such stringent property qualifications on suffrage that only one in ten adult white males in Providence could vote, while South Carolina's class-based franchise persisted until the end of the Civil War. Numerous states limited voting to taxpayers, and most states did not allow immigrants to vote; some states denied the franchise to Catholics, as Maryland did to Jews, while others required long residency as a prerequisite. And voting was public, subject to community pressure.[31]

There were missed opportunities to clarify legal equality. As early as 1806, Virginia's chancellor, George Wythe, Jefferson's mentor, ruled that the state's Declaration of Rights granted "freedom as the birthright of every human being." However, the state's Supreme Court of Appeals quickly overturned Wythe's ruling, noting that equality certainly did not extend to black people.[32] There were also rare moments of honesty, as when New Jersey's high court dismissed equality as "abstract," a nice word that appealed to feelings rather than "to the legal intelligence of the court." The state constitution's proclamation that "all men are by nature free and independent" was never intended to have any real consequence in the law. The state had the right to ignore its own constitution's wording when the principles were inconvenient.[33]

The Constitution's contradictions produced many legal anomalies. Missouri's constitution of 1820 excluded free blacks but not slaves from the state. Several members of Congress pointed out that this clause violated the U.S. Constitution's grant of equal privileges and immunities. During these debates, Representative Joseph Hemphill of Pennsylvania attempted to get Congress to agree on a definition of citizenship. If being born in the United States did not make one a citizen, he asked, what did? Southern representatives responded correctly that the Constitution did not define citizenship, which left the issue to the states. Reversing the logic, they proclaimed that those who did not enjoy full civil rights could not be citizens. Congress allowed the Missouri constitution to stand with a vague caveat that it did not affect national citizenship.[34]

The Democratic Party platform of 1840, the first adopted by a political party, demonstrates the depth of delusion common among white males in Jacksonian America. On the one hand, the party promised to defend the democratic principles put forth in the Declaration of Independence and the Constitution, "which makes ours the land of liberty, and the asylum of the oppressed of every nation." On the other hand, these same people refused to allow any interference with slavery.[35]

Americans had trouble understanding the meaning of the words they most cherished. Charles Jared Ingersoll, a leading Democrat, wrote in an influential 1823 essay of the "almost universal" practice of direct democracy in a country where only one-fifth of the adult population could participate politically. Ingersoll insisted that "justice is openly, fairly, and purely administered" to all Americans, even though three-fourths of the population had almost no legal rights. Among the liberal Whigs, who believed in government support for social and economic improvement, Senator Edward Everett insisted that in America "nothing is bestowed on the chance of birth," with the benefits of equality of opportunity extending to everyone—except those not included.[36]

Historians, too, often have trouble untangling this constitutional knot. Events taken as signs of progress toward equality generally do not hold up to scrutiny. For instance, most textbooks treat the Northwest Ordinance of 1787 as a great progressive step in its prohibition of slavery in the territory north of the Ohio River. But the ordinance did not have an enforcement clause, allowing slave owners to bring their slaves into the region. The 1820 census found 749 slaves in Illinois; it was not until the constitution of 1848 that the state finally outlawed slavery. The Wilmot Proviso of 1847, which would have prevented the spread of slavery to the territories taken from Mexico, is similarly portrayed as a liberal measure. Yet David Wilmot of Pennsylvania left no doubt that his aim was not to combat slavery but to limit western expansion to whites. He wanted to stop the spread of slavery, but only in order to stop the spread of black people: "The negro race already occupy enough of this fair continent; let us keep what remains for ourselves, and our children— . . . for the free white laborer."[37]

Once upon a time, scholars could refer to "the egalitarian urges of American life" as a given, much as Tocqueville wrote of "the equality of their condition" and their "love of that equality" without any fear of refutation. During the triumphal age of American liberalism, one historian even insisted that the years before the Civil War marked "the age of Egalitarianism." But the reality of antebellum America fails to match this liberal vision.[38]

Textbooks often give the impression that the northern states rushed to end slavery after the American Revolution. In fact, only Vermont in 1777 and Massachusetts in 1783 terminated the institution in the Revolutionary period. In the dozen years after the end of the Revolution, just seventeen wills in New York City record the freeing of slaves. That the number of slaves in New York in the 1790s increased by nearly one-quarter indicates continued acceptance of human bondage. When

New York ended slavery in 1799, it did so in the most hesitant fashion imaginable. The Gradual Manumission Act affected only children born to enslaved mothers after July 4, 1799, and even they remained in the service of their "masters" until the women were twenty-five and the males twenty-eight. Those born before that date remained condemned to slavery, a great many of them shipped south just in case the state legislature changed its mind and decided to extend freedom—which New York finally did in 1827.

Meanwhile, southern states built ever higher protective walls around their prized institution. Through the colonial period, inequality had been based largely on informal practice rather than legal codes. With the passage of the Constitution, ambiguities and contradictions increased, most particularly around the questions of blackness and the status of free blacks. With so many slaves the product of rape by white masters, it often became difficult to identify an individual as black, leading the southern courts to struggle over racial definitions. At the same time, many slave owners, either through a sense of guilt or responsibility, granted favored slaves their freedom. This increased sensitivity to the immorality of slavery convinced state legislatures to outlaw manumission—the granting of freedom.

Starting in 1822, southern states constrained the rights of free blacks because of their blackness. The slave uprising led by the Charleston free black Denmark Vesey served as the impetus for these laws. White panic over a supposed plan to kill slave owners and sail to Haiti led the South Carolina legislature to pass the Negro Seaman's Act, which forbade black seamen—even those serving in the U.S. Navy or on foreign vessels—from stepping ashore. Those who violated the law would be sold into slavery. Though the Supreme Court declared the law unconstitutional in *Elkison v. Deliesseline* (1823), the act, copied by other southern states, persisted—and was enforced. When Massachusetts sent two distinguished jurists south to argue for repeal of the legislation, one was nearly lynched and the other imprisoned as a lunatic. When the issue threatened international relations in the 1830s, Attorney General

Roger Taney advised President Jackson to not concern himself since blacks could not be citizens of the United States anyway—a position Taney returned to with devastating effects in 1857.[39]

In short, Thomas Jefferson clearly did not mean what he said in the Declaration of Independence, and most American political and intellectual figures had the good manners to not question him on the issue. July Fourth rhetoric aside, equality found few defenders in the early republic beyond a handful of eccentric, bold, and generally derided thinkers such as Thomas Paine, Ethan Allen, and Frances Wright. The anti-slavery pamphlets and letters of Stanhope Smith, Benjamin Rush, Benjamin Banneker, and James McHenry received little attention. Elijah Lovejoy suffered more than indifference, being murdered by a pro-slavery mob in Alton, Illinois, in 1837. By that date it appeared obvious that there were many Americans who would rather commit murder than confront the reality of inequality.

The rejection of equality accelerated through the 1840s, as the United States expanded the sphere of slavery in its war with Mexico, and reached a fever pitch with the removal of every check on slavery in the 1850s, setting the stage for the ideological and political division of the United States. Many historians have seen "Jacksonian democracy" establishing white male equality by 1840. But given the attitude of many southern Jacksonians to their fellow whites, it is difficult to accept even that limited definition of equality. Class distinctions in the South and the consistent call of southern legislatures to silence and even kill whites who questioned their social order do not speak to any recognizable respect for equality at any level.

The leading political opponent of equality was South Carolina's John C. Calhoun. A senator and vice president of the United States, Calhoun did all he could to silence those "dangerously diseased" individuals who opposed inequality. In Calhoun's twisted vision, advocates of equality sought nothing less than the destruction of the Union, as any move toward the limitation of slavery would produce a civil war "drenching the country in blood, and extirpating one or the other of the races." Calhoun saw himself seizing the moral high ground since slavery was "a positive good"—subjugation being good for inferior people. Anti-slavery agitators sought to reverse the natural order, as legal equality would somehow lead to blacks dominating whites. Calhoun disdained the Declaration of Independence, rejecting completely the notion "that all men are born free and equal" as "the most dangerous of all political errors," which "has done more to retard the cause of civilization . . . than all other causes combined." Southern white supremacists projected their own sexual misconduct with their slaves onto those who opposed slavery; thus ending slavery would lead not only to sexual relations between the races but also, Calhoun warned, to forced interracial marriage. The logic may be difficult to grasp, yet it obviously worked with southern white voters, becoming a zombie ideology that continued to eat the brains of racists for generations.[40]

A demented philosopher of injustice, Calhoun composed a theory of progress through inequality and the thorough exploitation of workers. George Fitzhugh, Calhoun's successor as the South's leading ideologue, took that perspective to its logical conclusion of enslaving white workers as well, proposing that society and the poor themselves would benefit from enslavement. "Human Equality," Fitzhugh wrote, "is practically impossible, and directly conflicts with all government, all separate property, and all social existence." Southern apologists for slavery did not ignore the question of rights. Rather, they just perceived a single right: their right to property in humans. When George Washington's nephew and heir, Supreme Court justice Bushrod Washington, received criticism for selling fifty-four slaves from Mount Vernon to a Georgia slave trader, Washington responded with outrage that anyone would question what he chose to do with his property.[41]

Such contempt for even the most limited concept of equality was not confined to the South. During the 1840s and 1850s a new political movement calling itself the American Party, known to history as the

Know-Nothings, captured political offices throughout the North and appeared primed to become the chief political competitor to Jackson's Democratic Party. The Know-Nothings sought to deny rights to immigrants they deemed dangerous, specifically Catholics. The chief propagandist and financial backer of the party, Samuel F. B. Morse, saw no contradiction between exclusion and democracy. Morse, inventor of the telegraph, warned that Catholics could not think for themselves, posed a critical danger to the nation, and must be excluded from the rights of citizenship in order to secure those rights for true independent Americans. Morse evoked Jefferson in warning of "the great danger to the country of this introduction of foreigners."[42]

Some observers did see a contradiction between the many forms of inequality in America and its self-image as the land of the free. Unlike Tocqueville, the French engineer Michel Chevalier, who also traveled through the United States in the 1830s, examined slavery as the basis for an unequal society, with the slave owners as aristocrats. The economist William Gouge saw a class system in which the wealthy seized political power and perpetuated economic inequality like perverse Robin Hoods—taking from the working poor to give to the unproductive rich. Gouge stands out among his male contemporaries for noticing gender inequality and its economic consequences, as women are paid less or not at all for the same work. Frances Trollope, an entrepreneur and caustic critic of American culture, thought the rhetoric of equality a giant fraud and Jefferson little better than a rapist for the way he treated his slave women.[43]

However, those who questioned the mythology of American equality often undermined their critiques and proposed reforms with other forms of bigotry. For example, early labor unions claimed to believe in equality, but until the creation of the Knights of Labor in 1878 they did not practice equality within their own membership. Antebellum unions saw economic inequality destroying the promise of American life and wanted to know what happened to the promise of universal education. Yet these same workers did not hesitate to exclude blacks, the

foreign-born, and women. Similarly, Transcendentalism, that supposedly authentic American philosophy, superficially embraced a language
of spiritual equality but remained hazy on the details. Ralph Waldo
Emerson anticipated Nietzsche: "Some will always be above others.—
Destroy the inequality to-day, and it will appear again to-morrow."
He believed in the superiority of intellect, which placed a few men
above others—and most specifically above women: "Man is the will,
and Woman the sentiment." Ultimately, he recommended that women
take "a vow of silence" and pay close attention to men of genius such
as himself.[44]

Among those who ignored Emerson's counsel were the Grimké sisters of Charleston, South Carolina. Sarah and Angelina witnessed the
horrors of slavery at a young age and struggled to avoid complicity, publishing *American Slavery As It Is: Testimony of a Thousand Witnesses*
in 1839. Relying on a variety of sources, including advertisements for
runaway slaves, *American Slavery As It Is*, which is still in print, confronted the American public with one of the most powerful condemna-
tions of slavery in the antebellum period. Outraged white southerners
censured, banned, and burned the book, and forced the sisters to flee
the South for Philadelphia. While abolitionists celebrated Sarah Grimké
for her courage in confronting the horrors of slavery, most denounced
her groundbreaking 1838 call for gender equality, *Letters on the Equality of the Sexes*. A majority of male opponents of slavery could not
acknowledge the equal humanity of women.[45]

The Grimké sisters' writings and public speeches sparked one of
the most significant and unexpected cultural movements in the antebellum period. In the decade after the appearance of the Grimké sisters on the national stage, an ever increasing number of women came
to feel that their opposition to slavery formed a necessary part of an
even larger struggle for human equality. In 1848 a group of the nation's
first feminists met at Seneca Falls, New York. Adopting the Declaration's language, they proclaimed "that all men and women are created
equal." Lucretia Mott and Elizabeth Cady Stanton played key roles in

organizing the Seneca Falls Convention, which launched this first women's movement. A number of male allies, including Frederick Douglass, aided their campaign. Only one of their resolutions failed to gain unanimous support: a call for women's right to vote. Opponents feared that demanding the franchise would "make the whole movement ridiculous." Stanton and Douglass persuaded a bare majority to support the resolution, but within a few years the movement channeled its energies into abolitionism as the more pressing cause.[46]

Most white American males ignored the vast inequality in their country until activists made it impossible to avoid. In the 1850s slavery moved to the center of American political life, and those attempting to make self-congratulatory and inaccurate generalizations about freedom no longer went unchallenged.

Rather than the traditional progressive vision of history in which democracy steadily advances, the first half of the nineteenth century in the United States witnessed the tightening of social controls and the promotion of inequality. The nation's political and intellectual elite gradually reduced equality to a rhetorical flourish applicable only to a specific subset of white males. Leading ministers and scientists moved aggressively to the side of virulent racism, while prominent politicians sought to silence those who rejected the repressive consensus. In 1835, South Carolina's governor, George McDuffie, told the legislature that no institution "is more manifestly consistent with the will of God than domestic slavery," its "increasing inequality" producing social stability. He therefore called on the legislature to pass laws to imprison those who called for any alteration in slavery. McDuffie repeated the formulations of his mentor, John Calhoun, who insisted that states, not people, are equal.[47]

Slavery may have begun in North America as an economic system for extracting labor from people, but by the 1850s it had become a means for the southern elite to control the entire population of their region, whites included. The African American poet Frances Ellen Watkins, considered one of the most eloquent speakers on the abolitionist circuit, saw through the pretenses of slavery's defenders. Underneath all their rhetoric was the simple proposition that money came before human life. The slave owners had crafted "a fearful alchemy" to transform human blood into gold. "Instead of listening to the cry of agony, they listen to the ring of dollars."[48]

To support slavery, white supremacists had to warp their political ideals, legal institutions, social relations, and Christianity. Believers in the inerrant words of the Bible held that humanity began with Adam and Eve, with everyone descended from that first pair. Many racist Christians struggled with a convoluted logic and careful misreading of the Bible to explain blacks as the descendants of Noah's son Ham. Racists with a more scientific bent created the notion of a separate creation, with the races literally different species. The movement away from a strict reading of the Bible came quickly for the defenders of slavery in the 1840s. For instance, in 1842 the *Democratic Review* adhered to the traditional notion that "the various races of man constitute a single species." Just eight years later the same magazine wrote that modern science showed "that there are several distinct races of men on the face of the earth, with entirely different capacities, physical and mental." Scientific research made clear that blacks must be kept as slaves not only because they were fit for nothing better but also for their own good, as otherwise they would die out. The magazine admitted the paucity of scientific research, much of it based on the study of skulls, but confidently predicted that future scholarship would validate the "ultimate predominance of the white race on the face of the globe."[49]

While science offered little further clarification, the certainty of white separateness and superiority grew. As John Van Evrie insisted in an 1861 book whose title stated its entire argument (*White Supremacy and Negro Subordination; or, Negroes a Subordinate Race, and (So-Called) Slavery Its Normal Condition*): "It is a palpable and unavoidable fact that Negroes are a different species." He thought his evidence obvious: blacks are different from whites, therefore they must be a different species. When scientific proof was required, racists made it up. Representative Samuel Cox of Ohio authoritatively told Congress: "The physiologist will tell the gentleman that the mulatto does not live; he does not recreate his kind; he is a monster. Such hybrid races, by a law of Providence, scarcely survive beyond one generation." By kicking blacks out of the human race, these scientific racists could easily justify kicking them out of citizenship, preparing the way for the Supreme Court to resolve the legal crisis. The Constitution might not say it, but only whites could be citizens, since only they were truly human.[50]

A perverted reasoning took hold of America's intellectuals, with words holding contrary meanings and logic turned on its head. Writing in *DeBow's Review* in 1847, the Missouri attorney John McKrum insisted that the law must be *"equal and impartial to all."* This "equality of rights," in law, society, and politics, must apply to everyone. What initially sounds like a straightforward affirmation of equality suddenly descends into a justification for the grossest forms of inequality. The law must treat all equally, except when doing so violates the natural order. Written constitutions did not deserve respect unless they adhered to these higher standards, which express themselves in "the *inequalities* arising from the disparity of men's physical and moral constitutions." The law "should leave men as it found them—strong if they were strong before—and weak if they were weak." The law cannot confer rights on those who did not have them at birth.

Thirty years before social Darwinism emerged in the United States, McKrum was laying its groundwork. Nature created the weak and the strong, and any effort to interfere with that natural ordering not only would fail but also would prove counterproductive. "In short, government has nothing to bestow upon any one; it can only serve to protect men in what they have." Like so many nineteenth-century intellectuals, McKrum contemptuously dismissed the sweeping assertion of equality found in the Declaration of Independence, pretending to revere the document while rejecting its substance.[51]

This emerging theory of inequality served the slave owners, misogynists, and bigots of all kinds well. It fed the sadism of southern whites who conducted a system based on torture and humiliation. Robert E. Lee has often been presented as a kindly master, yet when three of his slaves attempted to escape, he punished them fiercely. Ordering the man and two women stripped to the waist, Lee had a constable whip them between twenty and fifty times each, shouting for the constable to "lay it on well." When Frederick Law Olmsted was sickened by watching a grotesque sexualized beating, his host mocked him as weak. No rules or standards guided the forms and extent of punishment; "the overseers and drivers punished the negroes whenever they deemed it necessary, and in such manner, and with such severity as they thought fit." Olmsted asked one overseer if he did not find punishing the slaves "disagreeable," to which the overseer replied: "Why, sir, I wouldn't mind killing a nigger more than I would a dog."[52]

The slave owners' dehumanization of those beneath them extended to other whites, most particularly those who had to work for a living. The southern elite deployed a number of derogatory phrases to describe less fortunate whites, such as "clay-eaters" and "white trash," and looked upon white northerners with contempt. Northern whites, according to George Fitzhugh, belonged to "a slave race, the descendants of the Saxon serfs." The hated Yankee was "little more than a cold-blooded, amphibious biped." Little wonder that Fitzhugh felt poor whites should enjoy the benefits of enslavement.[53]

The United States in the 1850s became a nation divided culturally as well as politically and economically. As northern society became ever more urban, industrial, and bourgeois, the South embraced its violent, feudal ways with greater fervor. Every slave owner knew theirs was a tyrannical system, though many hated to call it that. Mary Chesnut described her father-in-law, the prominent planter James Chesnut, "as absolute a tyrant as the Czar of Russia, the Khan of Tartary, or the Sultan of Turkey." Slave owners, she wrote in her diary, "would brook no interference with their own sweet will by man, woman, or devil."

The notion that slave owners' will must dominate—which is so anathema to democracy and equality—would prove of key significance in the crisis of the Union.[54]

Only a small and ill-organized collection of free blacks and white reformers opposed the slave owners and their political allies at the start of the 1850s. The slave owners appeared to possess not just the power but also the intellectual authority to support their position. The Declaration of Independence seemed forgotten, and they wielded the Constitution like a broadsword against anyone who would dare to limit slavery's expansion.

Frederick Douglass understood the Constitution as neither pro-slavery nor anti-slavery, which was precisely the problem, as the Constitution allowed slavery to flourish without explicitly endorsing it. He also understood that the majority of white Americans rejected human equality. Independence Day rhetoric made white men feel better about themselves while refusing to act on its language. Douglass challenged American whites to make use of the openings to freedom offered by the Declaration and Constitution; taken together, they aimed to promote not slavery but liberty. Their unfulfilled promise was both the flaw and the opportunity. The slave owners used the Constitution to promote slavery; the time had surely come for the proponents of freedom to use it as well.[55]

Frederick Douglass offered one of the most powerful and sophisticated critiques of the United States Constitution in the antebellum period. With great lucidity and precision, he saw the text as both deeply damaged and repairable. Ignoring the obvious contradictions, Douglass pointed out, required a willful abdication of the powers of reason. Chief Justice Roger Taney was willing to make that sacrifice.

CHAPTER 2

The Supreme Court Chooses Inequality

*Or, Chief Justice Roger Taney rewrites
history and the Constitution*

I n declaring its independence in 1776, the United States seemingly
dedicated itself to the enhancement of human equality. The Constitutional Convention of 1787 appeared to follow that commitment to
equality with its preamble, in which "We the People" created their Constitution to "establish Justice . . . and secure the Blessings of Liberty to
ourselves and our Posterity."

Yet that same Constitution offered legal support to the institution of
human bondage, though without using the dread word "slavery." Further complicating the contradiction, the Constitution failed to define
citizenship, to clarify who "We the People" are and who is entitled to
the law's protection.

In the ensuing seven decades, those who held power in the United
States gave every indication that they were comfortable with inequality on several levels. With every seemingly progressive step forward,
such as the extension of voting rights to include most white males,
came retrograde motions, none more obvious than the Fugitive Slave
Act of 1850, which nationalized the protection of slavery, followed by
the Kansas-Nebraska Act of 1854, which threatened to further expand
slavery.

By 1857 it was evident that America's political leaders would not
resolve the fundamental division between the competing impulses
toward tyranny and freedom inherent in American life. In that year,

the United States Supreme Court issued a decision that further deep-
ened the national divide.

Roger Taney, who came from a wealthy slave-owning Maryland family,
made his mark as a ruthlessly effective lawyer and politician who rose
to power over the corpse of the Bank of the United States. After two
secretaries of the treasury refused to withdraw federal funds from the
Bank for fear it would plunge the country into a depression, President
Andrew Jackson turned to Taney, who withdrew the funds, killed the
Bank, and sent the nation into a severe economic crisis. When Chief
Justice John Marshall died in 1835, Jackson rewarded Taney's loyalty
by appointing him to the Supreme Court, the first Catholic to sit on the
Court. In 1857 the Court heard a case that provided Taney the oppor-
tunity to clarify the essential role of slavery in the life of the republic
and resolve the problem for good.

The basic facts of what happened to Dred Scott are clear and uncontested. Slaveholder John Emerson took Scott and his family into territories that did not permit slavery. Scott, who first tried to purchase his
family's freedom, brought suit in the Missouri courts, arguing that he
and his family had become free people under the Missouri Compromise
of 1820, which had excluded slavery from new northern territories. A
federal district court agreed with Scott, declaring that those who were
once free, as Scott and his family became when they entered free territory, were forever free.

In his decision for the majority, Chief Justice Taney overturned the
lower court's decision in favor of freedom and moved quickly to resolve
the essential question: could people be property? Taney answered yes,
absolutely, so long as the people in question were "negroes of the African race." Taney's dismissal of Scott's claim to freedom was direct and
thorough. He began by finding the Missouri Compromise of 1820,
which prohibited the expansion of slavery into new territories north of
the 36°30′ parallel (Missouri's southern border), unconstitutional since

Congress could not legislate for the territories but held them in trust for all the people in the Union, those who owned slaves and those who did not. Uniting the rights of property with the right to hold people as property, Taney ruled that Congress could not deprive a citizen "of his liberty of property." Such an act "could hardly be dignified with the name of due process of law."

Taney further declared that Scott had no right to bring suit in a federal court in the first place, since he was not a citizen. No black person could sue in a federal court, because no black person could be a citizen of the United States. The original intent of the Framers was clear on this point, since they never included blacks "under the word 'citizen' in the Constitution"—though, in fact, the Constitution never included anyone under the word "citizen." There were no black citizens in any states in 1787, he held, since the Framers regarded blacks as "an article of property." He was wrong about this; several Framers expressly stated the opposite.

One could object that the Constitution does not define citizenship. For Taney, that failure was precisely the point. Since the Framers did not define citizenship, we must assume that they meant citizenship for white men only, since they were all white—and all male, which excluded women. Taney constructed a perfect circle in which the Constitution protects personal rights, but only of those persons included in the political community as he defined it.

Taney's logic ran away from him when he declared that whites formed the United States "for them and their posterity, but for no one else." Rejecting birthright citizenship and the concept of a unitary American citizenship—both of which had long been standards upheld by state and federal courts—Taney apparently excluded immigrants and their children from citizenship, since citizenship is inherited. The chief justice wriggled out of this awkward position by quickly tying citizenship to race and denying the right of states to determine other paths to citizenship, in the process contradicting an earlier dissent in the *Passenger Cases* of 1849 in which he had written that "every citizen of a State is also a citizen of the United States" with an unhindered right of free passage. But Taney shrugged off all inconsistencies in crafting a principle of dual citizenship: a citizen of a state was not the same thing as a citizen of the United States.

Taney's decision in the *Dred Scott* case limited full legal rights to the white male descendants of the founding generation. He found evidence for his position not in the language of the Constitution but in its silences—and in the carefully selected behavior of the Framers. If the Framers meant for blacks to be citizens, then they would have granted rights to their slaves, which conflicts with the owners' self-interest and therefore makes no sense. Blacks "were never thought of or spoken of except as property" and should therefore be viewed that way by the law. The Constitution defends these property rights with the fugitive slave clause. Even Jefferson's noble words from the Declaration of Independence that "all men are created equal" serve as further proof that blacks reside outside the American community. For "it is too clear for dispute," Taney insisted, that Jefferson never intended blacks to be included in his famous formulation. If the Declaration included black Americans, then "the conduct of the distinguished men who framed the Declaration of Independence would have been utterly and flagrantly inconsistent with the principles they asserted."

Taney effectively twisted the logic of human and constitutional rights into a pretzel. The history of a crime became justification for its continuance. "No one of that race had ever migrated to the United States voluntarily; all of them had been brought here as articles of merchandise." As a consequence, Taney reasoned, the law must continue to treat them and their progeny as just so much merchandise, and the legally recognized owner can take that property anywhere he wants, just as he would his horse. The Constitution protects property rights, making no distinction between types of property, and no legislature has the right to create such a distinction. Following John C. Calhoun, Taney maintained that since the Constitution defended slavery, the federal government must do so as well. The only power the Constitution conferred on Congress was "of guarding and protecting the [slave] owner in his rights."

Taney spoke for the majority in this 7-to-2 decision, but the biting dissents by Justices John McLean and Benjamin R. Curtis offered a completely different interpretation of the Constitution, human rights, and history. The Constitution, they argued, gave Congress the right to make "all needful rules and regulations" for the territories in Article IV, Section 3. Additionally, blacks had been citizens in five states, including in the South, at the time of the Constitution's ratification, and these black citizens had voted for representatives to the several ratifying conventions. Having the power to act politically made them part of the nation from its creation, the dissenters argued, and Chief Justice Taney had no right to deny their existence or take away the citizenship of their descendants. Under the Constitution, Curtis wrote, "every free person born on the soil of a State, who is a citizen of that State . . . is also a citizen of the United States." It is unfortunate that the Constitution does not say so outright, but Article IV, Section 2 implies it.

Curtis wanted to know where Taney got the idea that the "Constitution was made exclusively by and for the white race." There is nothing in the Constitution or any of its supporting documents, such as the Federalist Papers, that makes this assertion. The opening words of the Constitution contradict Taney's assumption, clearly stating that the nation was "established by the people of the United States, for themselves and their posterity." Given the presence of black citizens in several states, Curtis continues, they and their posterity enjoyed the rights of citizenship. McLean, in turn, reminded Taney of the actual practice of the law in the United States, where no naturalization is required for a person born within its borders. The country had never "been very fastidious" about granting citizenship; after all, under the recent Treaty of Guadalupe Hidalgo ending the Mexican War, "we have citizens of all grades, combinations, and colors," as was the case when Louisiana and Florida became part of the United States. The Supreme Court's precedents repeatedly perceived slavery as a state construction—meaning slavery did not exist without state law. In the absence of such legislation, "the presumption, without regard to color, is in favor of freedom." Taney proposed that the slave owner can take the laws of his home state with him into territories that do not have slave laws. What, McLean asked, gives the individual slave owner this power, which not even Congress can exercise? McLean strikes the one truly moral note in this exchange, reminding his fellow justices that "a slave is not a mere chattel. He bears the impress of his Maker."

Most significant, McLean accused Taney of reading the Constitution as a dead document written by a single mind. That singularity of authorship was far from true. As Frederick Douglass and many others had observed, the word "slavery" does not appear in the Constitution for a reason: the Framers carefully kept that terrible reality out of the nation's founding document. Yet, McLean observed, the three passages referring to slavery—Article I, Section 2 (the three-fifths clause) and Section 9 (the slave trade), and Article IV, Section 2 (the fugitive slave clause)—all use the word "persons." Slaves are not called property in Madison's convention notes, in the Constitution, or in the Federalist Papers; and these are the places we should look for constitutional meaning, rather than relying on the assertions of Roger Taney.[1]

As his own notes later revealed, Taney knew he was just making it up. But he insisted that he did so to save the country from a slide into fanaticism and chaos. That he was wrong about nearly everything did not matter, since the majority—with President James Buchanan applying considerable pressure to change the vote of at least one justice—sided with Taney.

With the *Dred Scott* decision, black Americans in all states lost their legal rights. It appeared that the United States had definitively chosen inequality as its guiding principle and national identity. The United States was, of course, a slave republic in 1857. But for a large portion of the white population, the commitment to inequality ran deeper than just support for slavery, forming the core of their collective character. Mobs opposed to immigrants, minority religions, and dissident political views rampaged across the country, and women who dared to demand their civil rights faced contempt and hostility. One's identity, no matter how constructed, quickly became one's way of life, immune to rational discourse and resistant to change. For many white Americans, an adherence to inequality formed such a significant part of their self-perception that they proved willing to destroy their country and risk death in order to preserve it. Taney's great, unintended accomplishment with his *Dred Scott* decision rapidly became evident: he forced the American people to finally confront the issue of equality, and choose sides.

Chief Justice Taney thought that he had solved the great national crisis constitutionally. He found widespread support for that perception, with racists across the nation celebrating the *Dred Scott* decision. As the Augusta *Constitutionalist* put it, the southern view of slavery "is now the supreme law of the land . . . and opposition to southern opinion upon this subject is now opposition to the Constitution, and morally treason against the Government." Taney tried to make the Constitution into a pro-slavery document, casting the Framers as defenders of human bondage. As the historian Don Fehrenbacher wrote, the *Dred Scott* decision was "a work of unmitigated partisanship, polemical in spirit though judicial in its language, and more like an ultimatum than a formula for sectional accommodation."[2]

But Taney was wrong if he thought the matter settled. The *Dred Scott* case forced white Americans to confront issues they preferred to avoid, pushing equality and its meaning to the center of the nation's debates. Taney came under withering fire, even from conservative legal scholars and politicians. John Codman Hurd, who wrote a massive book defending slavery, nonetheless criticized Taney's decision for exceeding the law and the facts; the first law review article on the case saw it as a stain on the Court's reputation. In an extraordinary act, the Maine and Ohio supreme courts rejected Taney's history and logic, the former stating that blacks could vote in state and federal elections, the latter finding that any slave who made it to Ohio was automatically free. Predictably, Democratic president James Buchanan sided with Taney and intended to implement his decision. The *Washington Union*, considered the administration's official paper, asserted that statutes outlawing slavery in the northern states were now unconstitutional violations of Fifth Amendment guarantees of property rights.[3]

The implications of the *Dred Scott* decision could not be clearer: the slave states could treat black people as they pleased, but the free states could not. Taney transformed the Supreme Court into the major bulwark against freedom, as his decision constituted the first significant step toward the nationalization of slavery. As Justice McLean warned, under Taney's logic slave owners would be able, at will, "to introduce slavery into a free State." Many contemporaries believed, correctly, that a *Dred Scott* II was in the works, another case that would realize McLean's warnings and grant slave owners the power to take their slaves into free states. Vermont's legislature warned of exactly this next step in the expansion of slavery when it passed a sweeping Freedom Act in 1858. The legislature concluded that the Supreme Court's reading of the Constitution, if "applied, would convert every State into a slaveholding State, precisely as it now makes every Territory a slaveholding Territory."[4]

Dred Scott unified northern opposition to "the Slave Power"—as the southern elite was labeled—and transformed American politics. This Supreme Court decision followed two acts of Congress that appeared to many northerners as outrageous extensions of southern supremacy over the national government: the Fugitive Slave Act of 1850, which made the northern states responsible for the return of runaway slaves, and the Kansas-Nebraska Act of 1854, which employed Stephen Douglas's concept of "popular sovereignty" to allow the settlers of a territory to choose to become a free or slave state. The former nationalized the policing of slavery, while the latter made evident that there would be no limits on the westward expansion of slavery.

Seeking some way to contain the Slave Power, northern voters turned in growing numbers to the Republican Party, founded in 1854. In 1859, newly elected Representative John Bingham of Ohio—who will play an important role in this story—spoke for many Republicans when he charged that Justice Taney corrupted American ideals in seeking to make the United States a slave nation. The Constitution might not identify citizens, but Bingham insisted that it must include not just free whites "but all free persons." Nowhere in the Constitution could he find "that word *white*; it is not there." The following year he warned Congress that the "slaveocracy" had taken over every branch of government, including the Supreme Court, in order to pervert the intent of the Constitution away from freedom and toward slavery.[5]

Bingham found validation of this looming threat to freedom not just in Supreme Court decisions but also in the domination of the Democratic Party by southern slave owners. For Democrats, "states' rights" meant protecting slavery from outside intervention, keeping the government weak so that it could not interfere with the personal power of those who owned slaves. Bingham warned that the Slave Power's war on legal equality would destroy the nation. Their next step in spreading the territory of slavery would be using the federal government to attack the rights of free labor while limiting free speech and the right of petition. The *Dred Scott* decision left no doubt that the Slave Power planned to take advantage of the fractured Constitution to make the United States a slave empire.[6]

One voice warning the nation of "a second *Dred Scott*" belonged to the shrewd Illinois attorney Abraham Lincoln. The year following Taney's decision, the Republicans chose Lincoln as their senatorial candidate against incumbent Stephen Douglas.

The resulting contest in Illinois became the most dramatic senatorial campaign of the nineteenth century. Until passage of the Seventeenth Amendment in 1913, state legislatures elected senators. As a consequence, senatorial elections usually played out within the nation's legislatures and their backrooms. Lincoln sought to involve the public in what he saw as a crucial moment in national life, inviting incumbent senator Stephen Douglas to publicly debate him. Though Douglas felt confident of victory, he hoped to use the debates to promote himself for the 1860 Democratic presidential nomination. The debates, published in newspapers around the country, led to the nomination of both men for the presidency.

The people of Illinois enjoyed an unprecedented presentation of competing visions for the future of the United States. Thousands of people flooded the seven host towns—one in each congressional district. They watched, and participated, as the two candidates stood before them on raised wooden platforms, battling for up to four hours, responding to hecklers and shouted questions as well as to each other. At six foot four, Lincoln towered over his pugnacious opponent, who was a foot shorter. Lincoln's high-pitched voice could not match Douglas's booming baritone—no one ever asked the latter to speak up. The debates foreground the character of the two men, with Lincoln's relaxed humor and goodwill contrasting sharply with Douglas's combative ill temper and roiling bigotries. Intellectually, the two men were evenly matched: Douglas dominated the Senate as a ferocious debater, while Lincoln had honed his skills as a prominent attorney. But the content of their positions aptly indicated the irreconcilable differences between the two political parties.

The *Dred Scott* decision and the future of slavery swirled through the debates. Lincoln tied Douglas and the Democratic Party firmly to the former, which he insisted ensured the expansion and nationalization of the latter. Douglas accepted the challenge and defended the Supreme Court and its pro-slavery decisions while insisting that it did not matter to him what became of slavery or the slaves.

Lincoln seized the offensive from the start, while Douglas fell back on being offensive. At times the senator seemed to suggest that Lincoln just wanted to have sex with black women, which of course had little to do with the issues of citizenship and equal rights. Douglas repeated Taney's logic: "I say that this government was established on the white basis. It was made by white men, for the benefit of white men and their posterity forever, and never should be administered by any except white men." As far as Douglas was concerned, no black person, regardless of education or place of birth, could ever be equal to the lowliest white man and should never be allowed to vote.[7]

Under his concept of popular sovereignty, Douglas held that "the people"—by which he meant white men—would decide the social and political future of the country. God, Douglas held, clearly did not intend blacks to be the equal of whites. "If he did, he has been a long time demonstrating the fact." Because whites treated blacks unequally, blacks were clearly unequal, or God would have arranged matters differently. Douglas charged that Republicans sought "amalgamation between superior and inferior races."[8]

Lincoln responded to Douglas's racism without directly challenging it. He insisted, for example, that just because he recognized the humanity of blacks did not mean that he intended to marry a black person. Nor did Lincoln make a case for perfect equality, since he thought whites superior to blacks. Instead, he warned of the pernicious effects of a dangerously unbalanced constitutional system, and this resonated with his audiences. As he famously said in his speech accepting the Republican nomination in June 1858, "A house divided against itself cannot stand." Lincoln had the ability, which Douglas did not, to look at American history with unblinking accuracy. He respected the founders, but they were not gods, having created a fractured system, one riven by an obvious flaw that they well knew could not be easily healed: the acceptance of slavery. Looking back, Lincoln saw too many compromises with the Slave Power; looking forward, he saw a dangerous "acquiescence" that could lead to the destruction of freedom in the United States. With rare prescience, Lincoln perceived that "this Government cannot endure permanently half slave and half free." The country had to "become all one thing, or all the other"; he saw no alternative.

Lincoln asked his audience to consider the most perilous possibility: "What is necessary for the nationalization of slavery?" The answer was terrifyingly simple: "The next *Dred Scott* decision." Using Taney's false reasoning, Lincoln made the point often that the Supreme Court could easily determine that no state could exclude slavery. With certainty, he warned that such a case was on the horizon, and unless the people overthrew the Slave Power, freedom in America would end. Lincoln tapped into the northern fear that the Supreme Court would soon extend the logic of *Dred Scott* and transform the United States fully into a slave nation. Douglas was trapped, able to do no more than say that the Supreme Court would never do such a thing.[9]

The *Dred Scott* decision closed the debate for many Americans. Supporters of slavery celebrated that the Supreme Court had spoken with finality and that slavery would remain a permanent presence in American life. Lincoln spoke for those who thought that was precisely the problem, and the advocates of slavery kept feeding their anxiety. The flagship Democratic paper, the *Washington Union*, declared the emancipation of northern slaves "a gross outrage on the rights of property" and "an act of coercive legislation."[10]

For opponents of slavery, Kansas's Lecompton Constitution—adopted by pro-slavery forces through massive fraud, intimidation, and violence—pointed the way to a dark future in its declaration that the "right of an owner of a slave to such slave and its increase [progeny] is the same and as inviolable as the right of the owner of any property whatever." Lincoln pummeled Douglas with the Lecompton Constitution, saying that it resulted from Douglas's pet concept of popular sovereignty, "the most arrant humbug that has ever been attempted on an intelligent community." Lincoln argued that the Lecompton Constitution and the *Dred Scott* decision constituted a coherent effort to expand the realm of slavery. The Democrats thrust the core issue before the

American public: could a person be property? Douglas had to answer in the affirmative, leaving the higher moral ground to Lincoln.[11]

In these debates, Douglas laid out the position from which the Democrats would not deviate through the nineteenth century, completely rejecting legal, political, or social equality. He also rewrote the Declaration of Independence to insert the word "white" wherever necessary. The signers of the Declaration did not mean to include blacks, Indians, "nor any other barbarous race"; rather, they intended equality for white men alone, and no others need apply.[12]

When not spewing racist cant, Douglas responded to Lincoln's concerns with calm certainty that all would be well if only the Republican Party disbanded. Yes, the United States was a house divided, but it had "flourished" that way for seventy years, so why should it not last another seventy? The country would continue to live half slave and half free if only the abolitionist "agitators" would keep quiet.[13]

Silencing the dissident is always the go-to position of those holding power. Abraham Lincoln did not remain silent. His greatest political gift to the United States was thrusting the concept of equality before the public. Taney forced Americans to choose between freedom and slavery; Lincoln gave those who favored freedom a moral language based on legal equality. There would be no turning back for the people of the United States.

The debates highlighted both the widespread celebration of discrimination in the United States and the accelerating challenges to the nation's legal inequality in the late 1850s. Douglas looked to the past, found racism, and projected it into the future. Lincoln looked to the past, found an ideal of freedom, and hoped it was America's future.

Lincoln famously reintroduced the American people to the core concept of equality embedded in the Declaration of Independence. In his 1858 Senate campaign, he repeatedly cited the Declaration as the historical root of the American concept of equality, one that slavery violated every day it existed.

Lincoln's constant reference to the Declaration annoyed Douglas, who charged that his opponent sought to turn Illinois into "an African colony." Douglas followed Taney in proclaiming as historical fact that the Framers meant American liberty for whites only. Lincoln dismissed these racist assumptions as lacking evidence. Instead, he maintained that Jefferson had put forth a simple understanding of equality that entitled everyone to "the natural rights" of "life, liberty, and the pursuit of happiness." Lincoln agreed with Douglas that the black man "is not my equal in many respects" and would probably never enjoy "perfect equality" with whites. "But in the right to eat the bread, without the leave of anybody else, which his own hand earns, he is my equal, and the equal of Judge Douglas, and the equal of every living man." Lincoln thought it reasonable and right to let black Americans decide for themselves how to live, for the Declaration had put forth the radical notion that each individual is best able to determine his own happiness.[14]

Lincoln had anticipated most of the main points in his forthcoming campaign in his speech in Springfield, Illinois, on June 16, 1858, accepting the Republican Party's nomination for senator. The speech, which catapulted Lincoln to national attention with its imagery of a house divided, captured the reality of the political situation in the 1850s: two incompatible visions of equality and the Constitution. For slave owners, the only equality was property. Their property in slaves was equal to any other form of property and should be as transportable as cattle and horses. This vision fed a spreading contempt for human life, as evidenced by the routine violence of southern life. Reports out of the South, such as the powerful *American Slavery As It Is*, portrayed the obscene daily horror of slavery in the slave owners' own words. Representative Preston Brooks's attack on Charles Sumner on the Senate floor in May 1856 became a national symbol of southern violence, with southern whites proclaiming Brooks a hero for nearly beating a United States senator to death with a cane. Similarly, the northern press highlighted

Missouri senator David Atchison's boast that he would lead his "Border Ruffians" into Kansas in order to make it a slave state by any means necessary. Atchison swore to "kill every God-damned abolitionist in the district," which by his definition meant anyone who did not support slavery. Lincoln understood that what had been a political dispute had become a brutal struggle for the future of America.[15]

Under Lincoln's leadership, the Republicans came to acknowledge a shared humanity in an assumed freedom. Lincoln built on a handful of legal precedents to argue that "no law is free law." In other words, slavery required positive law, the position staked out by many northern jurists over the previous twenty years. Only legislative action could create slavery, as people were otherwise free. While not quite endorsing full legal equality, Lincoln laid the foundation for a broadening of the concept and proffered a benign vision of American law that could not have been more different from Roger Taney's.[16]

Lincoln called upon the Declaration of Independence in perceiving freedom as the natural condition of humanity. The chief justice turned instead to his understanding of the original intent of the Framers of the Constitution as granting freedom to white males alone. Taney placed slavery as the starting point for all black people; any freedom they enjoyed was a temporary gift from white folks. Where Lincoln sought to use the Fifth Amendment's grant of due process rights as a bulwark against slavery, Taney made it a defense of slavery, as property took precedence over personhood. Though himself guilty of racism, Lincoln acknowledged the humanity of black people, a humanity the chief justice denied. Lincoln's Constitution acted to promote progress and the expansion of freedom; Taney envisioned a static Constitution, an emasculated Congress, and a slave republic.[17]

Lincoln's formulation of equality appears so simple—if not self-evident—that one must ask why it was necessary for him to reintroduce the Declaration of Independence into the national discourse. Where had it gone?

==

As the slavery debate polarized the nation in the 1850s, few public figures spoke openly in favor of legal equality for everyone. Certainly many women argued for their right to participate in America's democracy, but political leaders completely ignored them. Women fighting to gain some legal equality won a few victories with the passage in a few states of bills that permitted women to own property in their own names. But hostile state judges overturned this legislation in the name of "a higher law"—by higher they meant not the Constitution but rather their vision of what God intended.[18]

Similarly, most white abolitionists carefully differentiated their loathing of slavery from support for equal rights. They framed slavery as unconstitutional under the Fifth Amendment's promise of due process and Article IV's guarantee of republican government, rather than the more amorphous standards of legal or human equality. Ohio's Salmon P. Chase set the model in holding that the federal government should not support slavery, which would ultimately lead to slavery's slow demise while negating any need for direct action against slaveholding and inequality.

However, by the end of the 1850s, voices calling for equality once more unsettled the country's collective conscience. A gifted young German immigrant named Carl Schurz, who had fled the repression that followed the 1848 revolutions in Europe, gained national attention for a speech in Boston's revered Faneuil Hall. Schurz aimed to convince Americans that their country thrived because of equality, whether they recognized that fact or not. Democracy worked only with the acceptance of that great moral truth, "equality of rights." Legal equality promoted the expansion of freedom, while inequality stole freedom from everyone. As much the victims of tyranny as their slaves, southern whites denied themselves freedom in fear that liberty would prove contagious. "The system of slavery has enslaved them all," Schurz proclaimed. Returning to Madison's argument in the Federalist Papers that a multiplicity of interests and beliefs secured liberty, Schurz gloried in America's cultural diversity, calling it the bedrock of "True Americanism" and democracy. Northern newspapers quoted extensively Schurz's portrait of the United States as "the colony of free humanity, whose mother-country is the world ... *the Republic of equal rights, where the title of manhood is the title to citizenship.*"[19]

Until the late 1850s, leading white male opponents of slavery rarely delved much beyond that point to explore social and political equality. Yet even this limited and unthreatening proposal that black Americans should be able to enjoy the humblest rights led defenders of slavery to attack the abolitionists—often physically—as a danger to the republic. President Jackson legitimated these attacks in his Farewell Address (mostly written by Chief Justice Taney), stating that "all efforts on the part of people of other States to cast odium upon" slavery "and all measures calculated to disturb their rights of property ... are in direct opposition to the spirit in which the Union was formed, and must endanger its safety."[20]

Initially it appeared that this limited view of freedom would triumph, as in 1858 the Illinois legislature reelected Stephen Douglas. However, his debates with Lincoln elevated the latter to national prominence. Northern whites held many positions on slavery, from acceptance to moral repugnance; what Lincoln accomplished was giving voice to the shared fear that slave owners were not content for slavery to remain limited to their states but wanted to extend their reach ever outward, to subject ever more territory to their power—and to their coercive labor system. At the very least, Lincoln reminded northern audiences, slave labor endangered free labor.

By 1860, the *Dred Scott* decision had persuaded the majority of Americans outside the South that the Constitution was in fact deeply flawed and had to be repaired, though they were not sure how. Lincoln offered a more practical answer, one that would require no change to the Constitution and would take a long time: block the expansion of slavery. Like most Republicans, Lincoln remained ambivalent about the extent of black equality, but he had no doubt that slavery posed an immoral and existential threat to the United States.

At their Chicago convention in 1860, the Republicans made clear their transition to a greater faith in equality by inserting the words of the Declaration of Independence that "all men are created equal" directly into their platform. They threw down the gauntlet before the Democrats, challenging them to repudiate the founder of their party in the name of slavery. The Democrats willingly jettisoned Jefferson.

The Democratic Party stood firmly behind the institution of slavery. However, the leadership of the southern Democratic Party insisted on a purity test for any presidential candidate: not only must he defend the right of southern whites to own slaves, but he must also defend the superiority of their system to the detriment of free labor. The leading candidate for the nomination, Stephen Douglas, would not take that final step, leading to the division of the party along regional lines in the same way that the leading Protestant churches had divided in the 1840s over the issue of slavery. In the 1860 election, separate Democratic conventions put forth competing northern and southern candidates: Senator Stephen Douglas and Vice President John C. Breckinridge.

Little differentiated the two Democratic platforms, except that Douglas understood that the southern elite needed to stop being so aggressive in their desire to extend slavery if they wished to maintain national power. Douglas charged that Lincoln and "the Black Republicans" intended to destroy the Union, while Breckinridge wanted to guarantee that destruction through secession—the right of states to leave the Union whenever they saw fit. Backers of both candidates claimed that a Republican victory would lead to the total equality of black Americans and interracial sex. Douglas supporters warned that the Republicans wanted "African amalgamation with the fair daughters of the Anglo Saxon, Celtic and Teutonic races." These charges echoed in the South, as Breckinridge supporters warned of the "horror . . . of negro equality," when victorious Republicans would force poor white females to marry black men. The Republicans' goal, one Georgia Democrat warned, is to free the slaves "and leave them in our midst, upon a footing of social and political equality with the whites . . . [a] danger more appalling than death." In 1860 the Democrats deployed equality as a terror weapon.[21]

Democrats found many supporters on both sides of the Mason-Dixon Line. The *Illinois State Register* agreed with Douglas that "the election of Mr. Lincoln will be a national calamity" that would destroy the country. The *Brooklyn Daily Eagle*, which had the largest evening circulation in the nation, supported Breckinridge for the presidency in 1860, finding the racist Douglas soft on the issue of slavery because he would not publicly state that it was a moral system. The Peoria *Democratic Union* thought slavery gave the country the sort of diversity that somehow preserved liberty. America "flourished in the diversity of its institutions"—by which the paper meant free labor and slave labor—and would continue to do so as long as there was not too much freedom or too much slavery.[22]

Northern Democrats deployed racism to tarnish the Republicans as dangerous egalitarians. After a decade in political power, Democrats recognized that this new political party tapped into a fundamental moral, intellectual, and economic issue with their warnings on the expansion of slavery beyond the South's borders. Southern Democrats conceded great persuasive power to the Republicans and could not be certain that poor whites would remain loyal to slavery. Even after twenty years of forbidding any public questioning of slavery, the southern elite saw signs of widespread dissatisfaction among the extensive population of poor whites who grew tired of seeing their hard work derided as unworthy of white men. The *Charleston Mercury* had no doubt that a Lincoln victory would lead to the spread of the Republican Party into the South, with the contest over slavery no longer between sections, but "in the South, between the people of the South." The New Orleans *Daily Delta* warned that under a Republican national government, free speech would flourish and the sectional conflict would divide southern whites, as "armies of our enemies shall be recruited from our own forces."[23]

The southern elite felt the fragility of their system and its justifications and feared free speech, leading them to lash out in every direction, cobbling together a contradictory array of defenses. It is an error to look for consistency in the southern position; even while screaming about states' rights, southern politicians demanded the largest and most intrusive extension of federal power in the nation's history, first through the Fugitive Slave Act and then in their demand for a national slave code. Lacking intellectual coherence, they relied on racism and terror of the unknown.

Republican nominee Abraham Lincoln believed that if Congress could find a way around the *Dred Scott* decision and forbid the taking of slaves into the territories, slavery would, with time, slowly wither and die. He counseled patience to his followers and calm to his opponents, but the opposition embraced panic. The Democratic press in the North charged Republicans with supporting equality—what Stephen Douglas called "a species of insanity." The *New York Herald* described racial inequality as a scientific fact and saw those who found any immorality in slavery as seeking to destroy the nation. The *Chicago Times* joined in charging that equality would lead to "amalgamation." Leading northern religious papers, such as the Catholic *Freeman's Journal* and the Protestant *Observer*, continued to defend slavery months after the firing on Fort Sumter. The Philadelphia *Morning Pennsylvanian* declared those opposed to slavery "atheists."[24]

Despite febrile opposition from many northern newspapers, the Republicans continued to gain strength through 1860. Their argument that the Slave Power had dominated the government for decades and perverted the Constitution appeared matched by the reality of southern aggression. As the election approached and newspaper reports indicated that Lincoln might sweep the North, the southern press lost its grip on reality. Conspiracy theories swept the white southern imagination, including one involving secret plots by Lincoln to use the U.S. Army to launch raids on the South aimed at freeing and arming the slaves. Southern newspapers fed the fires by falsely reporting hundreds of cases of arson and poisonings by slaves. As is generally the case in American politics, it hardly mattered that none of these charges was accurate.

Hysteria seized the South's white population, many of whom joined in beating, whipping, and hanging blacks and whites suspected of Republican connections. Northerners living in the South received warnings to leave at once.

From the start of the election year, the southern elite unveiled their trustiest weapon, the threat to leave the Union. As early as February 1860, nine months before the presidential vote, the Alabama legislature voted to hold special elections for a convention to consider secession if a Republican won. Senator Albert Gallatin Brown of Mississippi, an advocate for the expansion of the United States—and slavery—into Central America and the Caribbean, criticized his northern colleagues for failing to admit that they held distinctive and irreconcilable interpretations of the Constitution. "We claim that there is property in slaves, and they deny it"—it was that simple. Any effort to interfere with the property rights of the slave owner was despotism. Senator Louis T. Wigfall of Texas seconded Brown's view, insisting that the failure to protect slave property in the same way as any other property violated the Constitution and broke the bonds of union.[25]

Every step of the way through the 1850s, slave owners sought to protect what Senator Atchison called their "species of property," no matter what the cost. Jefferson Davis called slavery "a moral, a social, and a political blessing . . . its origin was Divine decree." Nearly every southern senator welcomed talk of secession, which they saw as nothing less than a second American Revolution.[26]

Modern readers may be baffled by the defenders of slavery passionately contending that their rights were under attack. What is difficult to perceive is the extent to which white southerners, even those who did not own slaves, feared losing their freedom to oppress blacks. They could not let go of the idea that they had an unhindered right to own people and do as they willed to those identified as inferior. But we must also not forget that the southern elite planned to be dissatisfied with a Republican victory, as even the "moderate" southerners supporting

Douglas or Unionist candidate John Bell threatened secession if Lincoln won. If they could not win every contest, they no longer wanted to play the game.

Abraham Lincoln won what is probably the most consequential presidential election in American history, though he did not appear on the ballot in ten southern states. Lincoln's victory in the campaign, one southern newspaper stated, was "undoubtedly the greatest evil that has ever befallen this country."[27]

Since the founding of the Republic, the southern elite had grown accustomed to dominating the nation's politics. Nine of the first fifteen presidents came from the South, and southerners had filled most of the key political offices in Congress up until 1861. Despite Lincoln's victory, the Republicans did not control the federal government. Justice Taney's Supreme Court could block any legislation that passed through a deeply divided Senate, where 37 Democrats and Unionists outnumbered 29 Republicans, and House, where Republicans held a slim majority of 120 to 108. Nonetheless, the loss of the executive branch unhinged the South's white leadership. With the election of a northerner to the helm of a political party premised on preventing the further expansion of slavery, the southern political leadership decided that their region could no longer participate.

Southern legislatures refused to recognize the results of the election and prepared to withdraw from the Union in order to preserve slavery. Most Republican leaders, Lincoln included, could not believe that the southern states would actually leave. Southern politicians always threatened secession if they did not get their way, as they had done with the Missouri Compromise of 1820, the tariff crisis starting in 1828, and nearly every debate on the issue of slavery in the next quarter century. But no compromise seemed possible short of Lincoln's refusing to accept office. As a pro-Douglas Atlanta paper stated, "We regard every man in our midst an enemy to the institutions of the South, who does not boldly declare that he believes African Slavery to be a social, moral, and political blessing." Decades of having every need and whim fulfilled by human chattel had made these men impervious to compromise.[28]

The southern leadership had a great deal of room for compromise, particularly because racism cut across party lines in the North. On white supremacy, at least, leaders of the Republican and Democratic parties were in complete agreement. In Illinois, Senator Lyman Trumbull unabashedly declared, "We, the Republican party, are the white man's party," while his state's senior senator, Stephen Douglas, repeatedly claimed that mantle for the Democrats. Some prominent Republicans, such as Representative Thaddeus Stevens of Pennsylvania and Senator Charles Sumner of Massachusetts, spoke in favor of equality, but even their party's standard-bearer, Abraham Lincoln, maintained white supremacy. As a consequence, in the aftermath of the 1860 election most leading Republicans, including Lincoln, publicly called for accommodation with the slave owners.[29]

However, southern intransigence could not get around one fundamental difference. Lincoln might agree with his old friend Alexander Stephens of Georgia in thinking blacks inferior to whites, but Lincoln would not follow where Vice President Stephens of the Confederate States of America went next, in declaring that inequality must be the basis of any republic. Shortly after his election, Lincoln wrote Stephens: "You think slavery is right and ought to be extended; while we think it is wrong and ought to be restricted. That I suppose is the rub." With the exception of Sam Houston of Texas, no prominent southerner would give way on the need to expand slavery now.[30]

At this time no southern leader denied that slavery was the cause of secession. Across the South, politicians and journalists referred to their commitment to slavery as the reason to leave the Union, while also insisting that the Republicans caused the crisis. If the latter had not threatened to place limits on the expansion of slavery, there would have been no trouble. In Alabama, leading secessionist William Lowndes Yancey insisted that they would compromise on any issue except slavery.

As the *Charleston Mercury* bluntly stated, the southern states determined to "rally together to save their institutions from Abolition rule" by forming "a Slave Republic." With the formation of the Confederate States, the *Montgomery Advertiser* boasted, they created a nation "on the basis of liberty, equality and independency for white men, and slavery for negroes."[31]

Secessionists sought not to preserve the Constitution from Republican encroachments but to correct a fundamental flaw in the document: its bias toward freedom. The very idea of equality, Vice President Stephens insisted, had been a terrible mistake. The Constitution did not mention slavery because the Framers "rested upon the assumption of the equality of the races. This was an error." Having dismissed the authors of the Constitution as ignorant neophytes, Stephens explained that "our new government is founded upon exactly the opposite idea; its foundations are laid, its corner-stone rests upon the great truth, that the negro is not equal to the white man; that slavery—subordination to the superior race—is his natural and normal condition." In short, the Confederacy categorically rejected the idea of equality in any form.[32]

Those who created the Confederacy led a movement to retain racial inequality. All but one of the fifty delegates who met in Montgomery, Alabama, in February 1861 owned slaves, and twenty-one were major planters. As Jefferson Davis made his way to Montgomery from his Mississippi plantation, he assured audiences that secession secured slavery and white supremacy for all time, a promise reiterated in his inaugural address. Secretary of State Robert Toombs issued instructions to his diplomats on how to explain secession: the southern states had no choice but to leave the Union because the election of Lincoln threatened "to destroy their social system" based on slave labor. It just made more sense to form their own nation to preserve slavery.[33]

The Confederacy's constitution reflected that social system. Article I forbade any "law denying or impairing the right of property in negro slaves." The Confederate Congress that produced their new frame of government formulated their solution to the great constitutional crisis: rejecting the humanity of slaves.[34]

The southern elite raised the ownership of others into an inherent right. The time had come, proclaimed the planter Richard T. Archer of Mississippi, for southerners to unite and form a government and military, "determined to live or die in defence of the God given right to own the African." They were making a revolution, breaking free of a tyrannical government that would not respect their property rights and "way of life."[35]

Many northerners also saw the election of 1860 as revolutionary, though in a different direction. Frederick Douglass exulted that finally the Slave Power had lost, Lincoln's election having broken its hold on the federal government. Charles Francis Adams, son of John Quincy Adams, wrote that with Lincoln's election "the great revolution has actually taken place and . . . the country has once and for all thrown off the domination of the Slaveholders." While Douglass and Adams were correct, the process of defeating the Slave Power would be neither easy nor peaceful. "The Union is rapidly drifting to dissolution," a New York newspaper proclaimed, "like a canoe above the Falls of Niagara." Many Americans had little confidence that their country could be saved from destruction.[36]

When the Framers of the Constitution refused to confront the issue of human equality, they left a deep chasm in the final draft, one that went beyond just the question of slavery. For the law and the nation's political system to work, a fundamental question had to be answered: Who was a citizen and thus enjoyed legal rights? Faced with a deep divide over the answer to that question, the Constitutional Convention dodged the issue; it would be left to the states to determine the limits of freedom.

Even the Bill of Rights avoided confronting the nature of personal rights directly. Congress could make no law limiting speech or establishing religion, but the states certainly could—and did. For instance, Connecticut maintained a state religion, Congregationalism, until 1818, while the southern states routinely violated freedom of speech, even trampling on federal power by maintaining their authority to monitor the mail for abolitionist literature and sentiment. The Supreme Court upheld this separate standard in *Barron v. Baltimore* in 1833, in which Chief Justice John Marshall declared that the Bill of Rights did not apply to the states. The states remained free to curtail legal rights as their legislatures chose.[37]

Roger Taney thought he had resolved the great constitutional crisis with the *Dred Scott* decision. But that decision concerned more than just the status of black Americans. If the Supreme Court could so nonchalantly rewrite history, could it not exclude the reviled Irish Catholics as well? Were women also ineligible for citizenship and legal rights? Who would be safe when facts no longer mattered? Taney had created more questions and contradictions, and brought on an even greater crisis.

Abraham Lincoln, on the other hand, thought that he had just solved the great national crisis politically. The people had spoken, slavery could not be extended into the territories, and with time the white slave owners would accept this reality. He too would be proven wrong, as the leadership of the southern states found no advantage to remaining within the United States.

Frederick Douglass warned in his July 4 speech that only violence, a second American Revolution, would overthrow this corrupt system. He may have been right, but it was neither he, Taney, nor Lincoln who fixed the Constitution and invented the concept of equality. That task fell to thousands of Americans whose experience of the Civil War transformed their understanding of their country and its people.

The Civil War amply demonstrated that inequality had deformed every aspect of American society. The American elite created a system that theoretically operated on the principle of legal equality, and then they devoted enormous energy to undermining that structure to allow for inequality. As written in 1788, the Constitution allowed the loosest construction of legal equality, as blacks, women, immigrants, Catholics, and the poor all found their status reduced to subjectship rather than citizenship. Governments stripped rights, from freedom of speech to the right to stand before a court of law, from the majority of Americans. Traditional practices and freshly minted laws imposed all sorts of controls even on white males, restricting everything from speaking freely to freeing slaves, from free use of the mails to petitioning Congress. But the whole illogical structure came crashing down in 1861, as Lincoln had predicted.

War changes everything. On July 4, 1852, Frederick Douglass challenged those who remained uncertain in a time of crisis to pick a side: "For it is not light that is needed, but fire; it is not the gentle shower, but thunder. We need the storm, the whirlwind, and the earthquake." That whirlwind would descend on the nation in 1861.[38]

In that pivotal year, Chauncey H. Cooke, a farm boy from Wisconsin who faithfully read the newspapers of his region and listened to his elders argue politics, watched in dismay as his nation divided and went to war against itself. As soon as he could, he enlisted to "save the Union," fought in several battles, and came to see slavery up close. He did not like what he saw and became an abolitionist during the war.[39]

That same year, Robert Smalls, a sailor and a slave living in Charleston, South Carolina, could not help but hear all the whites debating the breakup of the Union. Contrary to the law, he had taught himself to read and had even acquired some smuggled abolitionist tracts. As we shall see, when the opportunity presented itself, Smalls acted with boldness and courage, becoming a hero to those who believed the United States worthy of salvation.[40]

Born a slave in Richmond, Mary Elizabeth Bowser had been freed by her owner's widow in 1843. When Virginia left the Union, Bowser offered her services to the cause of freedom, heroically risking her life to spy on the new Confederate government. Even more surprisingly, Elizabeth Van Lew, the white daughter of Bowser's onetime owners, followed the same path and served as a Union spy.[41]

Days before the 1860 election, Anna Dickinson of Philadelphia turned eighteen. As a young woman, she was supposed to stay home and see to the domestic sphere. But as the southern states seceded from the Union, Dickinson found her voice and quickly became one of the most acclaimed orators in the country, speaking before mass rallies, Congress, and President Lincoln. Her message was simple: the Constitution needed to be amended in order to proclaim and protect human equality.[42]

These are among the thousands of people who reinvented the Constitution and transformed the country. The story is not a simple one with a single hero. Rather, it is a complicated tale of ordinary people grabbing Theodore Parker's arc of the moral universe and bending it toward justice. What they accomplished would not instantly change American society, but it would plant the seed—or, as some saw it, the dangerous time bomb—of equality within the Constitution itself. With time, other ordinary people would seize upon the work of that Civil War generation and, though it would take a long struggle, force the United States to live up to its highest ideals.

CHAPTER 3

Learning Equality

*Or, how Americans once more
came to celebrate equality*

On a July night in 1861, as the war entered its third month, the Union cause gained one of its first, unlikely heroes. On that night, the *Jeff Davis*, a notorious privateer named for the Confederacy's president, captured the schooner *S. J. Waring* in waters off South Carolina. Five Confederates came aboard to guide the prize to Charleston, removing the original crew except for two sailors, who were locked below deck, and the ship's steward, William Tillman. Since racist ideology constantly promoted the myth of black docility, the southern sailors assumed they had nothing to fear from Tillman, and even told him that he would be sold into slavery as soon as they reached port. What Tillman did next bordered on the inconceivable to these defenders of slavery.

Waiting until after midnight, he boldly attacked the captain and his two mates with a hatchet, killing all three. He persuaded two of the remaining southern sailors to aid him and locked up the third. Freeing his fellow Yankees, Tillman took command of the ship and sailed it to New York, where he was widely hailed for vindicating the nation's honor and awarded prize money by the government. As one New York newspaper put it, Tillman exposed the lie of "those who question the Negro's capacity for the enjoyment and defense of liberty."[1]

Black Americans, free and enslaved, recognized the Civil War as a tremendous opportunity in their struggle for freedom and equality. As the war swept through the nation, thousands of African Americans fled plantations, aided and served in Union forces, and demanded acceptance as citizens. The Civil War offered other marginalized groups the chance to finally claim a place in the public sphere. Catholics, German and Irish immigrants, and women all seized the moment to make themselves heard and be recognized as Americans—a recognition they and blacks quickly gained in one of the most dramatic cultural shifts in American history.

However, these changes resulted from four years of unparalleled bloodshed and did not go uncontested. Through those war years and a decade of progressive efforts to transform the country, the majority of Americans battled to make the nation's stated ideals into a reality for all. They confronted powerful reactionary forces fighting to maintain the status quo, first openly on the battlefield, then through clandestine violent organizations such as the Ku Klux Klan, and finally back in the halls of Congress and the marketplace of ideas. As Frederick Douglass correctly predicted: "This struggle . . . may be both moral and physical; but it must be a struggle. Power concedes nothing without a demand. It never did, and it never will."[2]

Americans think of the Civil War primarily as a military struggle, but it became a significant political, social, and constitutional revolution. The war did more than end slavery; it transformed the way Americans saw themselves and one another. Perhaps for the first time in the nation's history, tens of thousands of white male Protestants demonstrated respect for previously marginalized groups, including blacks, women, Catholics, and immigrants. At the same time, members of those groups publicly expressed a long-denied self-respect, demanding the full rights of citizenship. During the four violent years of the Civil War, Americans learned the true nature of equality and its benefits.

President James Buchanan attended a wedding on December 20, 1860. In the midst of this private celebration a commotion arose in the entrance hall, where a telegram had just arrived from Charleston. Sara

Agnes Pryor of Virginia, who would go on to serve the Confederacy as a nurse, brought the news to the president: South Carolina had seceded from the Union. A stunned Buchanan quietly left the party to return to the White House, where he would continue to do nothing until the inauguration of his successor, Abraham Lincoln, on March 4, 1861.[3]

Newspapers quickly bore the terrible news to every corner of the country. By Christmas Day 1860, few Americans did not realize that their country had fallen apart. Even in the face of secession, northern white males initially refused to face the reality of their situation and did all they could to preserve the unequal Union. America's political leaders had apparently forgotten the Constitution's opening words—"We the People." Congress established a cascade of special committees in an effort to avert sundering the Union, struggling to protect the equal rights of the states, not those of the nation's citizens. So thoroughly had equality been discredited and rejected by America's white men that it is fairly certain that inertia would have perpetuated the slave system for decades to come had not the slave-owning elite tried to force their ideology and socioeconomic structure on the rest of the country in the late 1850s.

Advocates of slavery consistently maintained that the abolitionists brought on the crisis by insulting their "way of life." While abolitionists certainly criticized slavery and the Constitution's defense of that institution, they presented no anti-slavery amendments in Congress prior to the Civil War. There were, however, several proposed pro-slavery amendments, culminating in the second session of the 36th Congress— from December 1860 through March 1861—which considered two hundred amendments to the Constitution aimed at keeping the southern states in the Union by protecting slavery.[4]

In his final message to Congress, President Buchanan recommended three amendments: one to recognize the right of property in persons, one to protect slavery in federal territories, and a third that recognized the right of slave owners to recover runaways. Buchanan made clear that his sympathies lay with the southern elite, as he insisted that there would be no "discontent" but for "the long-continued and intemperate interference of the Northern people with the question of slavery in the Southern States." The president would do nothing to interfere with the secession movement. New York senator William Seward neatly summarized Buchanan's position as believing it "is the duty of the President to execute the laws—unless somebody opposes him—and no state has the right to go out of the Union—unless it wants to."[5]

As the secession crisis accelerated, some congressmen sought "compromise" by institutionalizing inequality. Thomas R. Nelson of Tennessee offered a constitutional amendment that would forbid anyone from voting in any election "unless he is of the Caucasian race, and of pure, unmixed blood." Of more significance was the so-called Corwin Amendment, named for Representative Thomas Corwin of Ohio but written by Senator Seward. This proposed amendment prohibited any future amendment to the Constitution from meddling with the institution of slavery in the states where it already existed and forever barring Congress from interfering with slavery. Seward would willingly condemn the nation to slavery in perpetuity to appease southern secessionists. The amendment rushed through both houses of Congress in February 1861 by a vote of 133 to 65 in the House and 24 to 12 in the Senate. President Buchanan immediately signed it—a unique and unrequired action—and sent it to the states for ratification. But only Maryland and Kentucky voted to ratify the amendment before events at Fort Sumter made the issue moot.[6]

Lincoln, too, did his best to dissuade the southern legislatures from seceding, offering up every concession possible short of abandoning his party's principles. Repeatedly between his election on November 6, 1860, and his inauguration on March 4, 1861, Lincoln promised that his administration would protect slavery where it already existed and ensure the internal security of the slave states against possible slave uprisings. What he would not do was allow the further expansion of slavery, which would surely end freedom in the United States. To reassure slave owners, Lincoln proposed a new fugitive slave act that would require all citizens to participate in its enforcement, effectively nullifying northern personal liberty laws that had defended runaway slaves. In a letter to Seward a month before his inauguration, Lincoln said that he would do anything, from allowing slavery to persist in the District of Columbia to protecting the domestic slave trade, so long as the southern states accepted the altered political realities. In what he thought would be a compelling gesture to the southern elite, Lincoln endorsed the proposed new constitutional amendment.[7]

In this last regard, Lincoln stood firmly with his fellow Republicans. Throughout the 1860 election and its aftermath, most leading Republicans left little doubt that they would agree to nearly every compromise with the slaveholders except for the expansion of slavery into new territory or into the free states. While most Republicans opposed slavery as immoral and a violation of the most basic precepts of Christianity and humanity, they did not want to damage the Union's peace by touching the institution where it already existed. If only the Slave Power could be halted in its reckless grasp for ever more territory, they thought, slavery would slowly die out over time. Above all else, slavery must be kept from coming into competition with free labor, to the detriment of the latter.

The southern leadership rejected Lincoln's proffered olive branch out of hand. They even turned their backs on the proposed constitutional amendment that would have given them security in their slave ownership. Republicans and northern Democrats could only maintain the Union if they submitted to the slave owners and accepted the transformation of the United States into a slave nation. The planter elite's occasional protestations of "states' rights"—which would have been protected by the proposed amendment—were beside the point, as they insisted that the federal government must operate more energetically to enforce slavery nationwide. Before South Carolina seceded, thirty southern senators issued a manifesto rejecting any and all efforts by northern political leaders to maintain the Union. The honor "of the Southern people" could only be found in a confederation separate "from an unnatural and hostile Union."[8]

The majority of white southerners preferred to live in a slave nation and to perpetuate a warped republican vision of direct contradictions and oxymorons. The planter elite appropriated and altered longstanding cultural icons in support of slavery. One Louisianan echoed Patrick Henry in calling for secession with the stirring words "Give me the right to own and protect my property, or give me death." Newspaper editor Robert B. Rhett Jr. wrote in his *Charleston Mercury* that by securing slavery, "the master race can establish and perpetuate free government."[9]

Confederate leaders made no secret of the fact that they were fighting against the danger of equality and aimed to define their America as a land of inequality. North Carolina representative David Siler wrote in 1862 that his constituents were not interested in slavery but were unified in their opposition to equality with blacks. To prevent being "equalized with an inferior race," they were willing to fight and die. It is little wonder that in his second inaugural address, Lincoln summarized 1861 succinctly: "Both parties deprecated war, but one of them would *make* war rather than let the nation survive, and the other would *accept* war rather than let it perish, and the war came."[10]

The southern elite felt a sense of relief in secession. Finally they had a slave republic free of those nagging idealists with their talk of "all men are created equal." Finally they had a central government that ensured the expansion of slavery anywhere they desired to go and that would back up their economic and social structure based on racism, torture, and the subjugation of another people. As Confederate vice president Alexander Stephens proclaimed in 1861, the Confederacy's "Constitution has put at rest forever all the agitating questions relating to our peculiar institutions—African slavery as it exists among us—the proper status of the negro in our form of civilization." Lest anyone doubt why they had seceded, Stephens stated that slavery "was the immediate cause of the late rupture and present revolution," as well as the foundation of their new nation, which, he promised, "will become the controlling power on this continent."[11]

The attitude of northern Democrats eased the path to southern secession. Over the previous decade Democrats had accepted as dogma that any questioning of slavery was the equivalent of declaring blacks equal, and that equality meant forced interracial sex—generally called "amalgamation." As evangelist Charles Finney reported, the Democrats in Ohio accused Republicans of attempting to force whites and blacks "to intermarry; and that our object was to introduce a universal system of miscegenation."[12]

Even after eleven slave states seceded from the Union, northern Democrats persisted in making this equation of anti-slavery agitation leading to social equality and then amalgamation. Delaware had only one thousand slaves at the start of the Civil War, yet when Lincoln presented the state legislature with a plan for compensated emancipation, the state's Democrats angrily denounced this ploy "to place the negro on a footing of equality with the white man" as the first step in a plot "to degrade the white man by obliterating the distinction between races." Lincoln's own postmaster general, Montgomery Blair, warned that radical Republicans sought to foster "amalgamation, equality, and fraternity"—a clear play on the slogan of the socially disruptive French Revolution—in a conspiracy to form "a hybrid government, ending, as all such unnatural combinations have ever done, in degraded, if not in abortive generations." Given this context, any effort at compromise faced certain failure.[13]

Lincoln persisted in his efforts to win back the Confederate states through political compromise. In his 1862 annual message to Congress, Lincoln proposed three constitutional amendments: federal compensation to slave owners, a declaration that slaves freed during the war would remain free, and the colonization of blacks in some spot outside the United States. The Confederacy was still not interested, and neither were most African Americans, who would never willingly leave *their* country. They found an unexpected advocate in Maryland senator

Henry Winter Davis, a former anti-immigrant Know-Nothing leader. Davis dismissed talk of compensation for slave owners on the basis of the equality of labor. For generations, blacks had worked without the compensation due to all laborers. The slave owners deserved nothing, as everything in the South "that smiles and blossoms is the work of the negro that they tore from Africa." The logic had been reversed; it was past time for the slave owners to pay black workers for their labor, just as they would white workers.[14]

A year of war had transformed Senator Davis, like many white Americans, from a fearful opponent of abolitionists and foreigners to a champion of the right of blacks to some form of legal equality. Also like Davis, many whites recognized that the war would bring drastic social change. In the war's first year, Susan Wallace, the wife of Union general Lew Wallace, observed, "However we may go into this war, we shall come out of it abolitionists." In North Carolina, Basil Thomasson wrote in 1861 that by seceding, the South would be "killing off her darling institution" faster than the abolitionists could hope. The Tennessee slave owner Oliver P. Temple fought against his state joining the Confederacy, warning that "secession was only a short cut to emancipation." While accurate assessments of the potentially transformative power of war, these voices could not compete with the slave owners' ideology propelling them toward self-destruction.[15]

As the renowned author Octavia Butler warned, "Ignorance protects itself." Despite the obvious dangers secession and war posed to their social order, the white elite embraced the threatened chaos on the basis of an all-consuming racism—the power of which cannot be understated. While slaves rushed toward the freedom Americans had long proclaimed, slave owners saw only "ingratitude"—a word that occurs repeatedly in the accounts of southern whites. It is hard to understand the attitude that people should be grateful for their enslavement, unless one appreciates that most slave owners believed their own defense of slavery as a benign institution. After Union forces captured Port Royal,

South Carolina, in November 1861, Louis Manigault watched in frustration as slaves fled his family's plantation. "This war," he wrote in his diary, "has taught us the perfect impossibility of placing the least confidence in any Negro." Clearly "ingratitude" was an essential feature of "the African character." A year later, Virginia planter Colin Clarke experienced the same shock over slaves running to the Union lines. His disillusionment led him to an "utter, thorough, & deep disgust with the whole race."[16]

Southern whites' response to all these black people delighting in their freedom defies rationality. Virginia's leading promoter of secession and the man who fired the first shot at Fort Sumter to begin the Civil War, Edmund Ruffin, recorded in his diary that he saw all around him the "ingratitude & treachery of slaves to the most considerate & kind of masters." The slaves appeared ignorant "of attachment & loyalty." Of course, the ignorance lay entirely with the region's whites.[17]

More importantly, many northern whites went in the opposite direction, developing respect for the bravery and loyalty of former slaves who escaped and volunteered to help the Union army. "That down-trodden race, who had for years suffered every injustice at the hands of their white oppressors," observed Major George Wood of the 7th Ohio, risked their lives by aiding Union troops as scouts and guides. He respected the sophistication with which they watched troop movements and seized the opportunity to escape slavery.[18]

The military battles of the Civil War are well known. Less appreciated is the conflict of ideas that played such a vital role in determining the war's outcome. Confederate military forces held their own in the military struggle with the United States. But the southern leadership barely contested the war for the hearts and minds of the American people, offering nothing more than the repetition of their core position that slavery is good and that blacks are an inferior people undeserving of freedom as they are incapable of courage, reason, or self-reliance. In contrast, the adherents of the Union framed a number of powerful political and social messages based on the enhancement of human liberty and equality. As it turned out, African Americans proved pivotal in both the military and ideological conflicts.

Essential to the battle for the future of the United States was the ability of African Americans to persuade—through word and deed—white northerners that their self-interest demanded equality for all. Frederick Douglass stated the position well in June 1861: "The ties that bind slaveholders together are stronger than all other ties," and any effort at compromise is doomed to fail. The only hope for preserving the Union would be "rendering the slaveholders powerless," and the only path to that goal required ending slavery and establishing true equality. Douglass admitted that Americans might not yet grasp the justice of his words, but "the inexorable logic of events" will force them to recognize that this "is a war for and against slavery." With time, northern whites would see that their interests and freedom itself were intertwined with the fate of blacks.[19]

As Douglass predicted, "the inexorable logic of events" rather than a sense of equity drove the push for emancipation. As the war dragged on, it became obvious that the Union needed to do all it could to reduce the power and resources of the Confederacy while increasing its own. If nothing else, removing the labor of four million slaves from the Confederate column and adding them to the Union cause would make an enormous difference. The possibility of also gaining tens of thousands of soldiers and allies made that step even more crucial and led the Lincoln administration to sell emancipation to the northern public as an act of military necessity.

This inexorable logic appeared manifest as early as 1861, with the transformation of Massachusetts's Benjamin Butler from Democratic stalwart to liberator. Butler, a lawyer who promoted Jefferson Davis for the presidential nomination in 1860, had defended the institution of slavery throughout his antebellum political career. However, he had an epiphany in December 1860 while meeting with Davis in hopes of preserving the Union. Davis's refusal to consider any compromise convinced Butler that the southern leadership intended to leave the Union no matter what the North offered, and he recommended to President Buchanan the immediate arrest of South Carolina's secessionist representatives for treason. Buchanan ignored him. When the war came, Butler assumed command of the Massachusetts 8th Regiment. He played a key role in keeping Maryland in the Union, threatening to arrest any legislators who voted to secede, earning national attention and command of Fort Monroe at the mouth of the James River in Virginia.

In May 1861, Butler welcomed three runaway slaves who offered to work for him on the fort's defenses. When the "owner" demanded the return of his "property," Butler instantly understood that it made no sense to return workers to those attempting to overthrow the government he defended. Accepting the slave owner's logic that these men were property, Butler declared them war contraband, utilizing a traditional legal principle under which the property of wartime opponents could be seized. When the slave owner raised the Fugitive Slave Act, Butler reminded him that Virginia had seceded from the Union and therefore no longer enjoyed the protection of American laws.[20]

Butler's actions electrified the nation, offering the first solid hint that this war could have much larger repercussions. Republican politicians and the press praised Butler's boldness. The administration gave its tacit approval, though Secretary of War Simon Cameron cautioned that the precise legal status of these runaway slaves must be determined at some future date. Other officers quickly followed Butler's lead, and Representative Owen Lovejoy, whose brother Elijah had been killed by a pro-slavery mob, persuaded Congress to pass a resolution stating that "it is no part of the duty of soldiers of the United States to capture and return fugitive slaves." A direct line ran from Butler's spontaneous action to the Confiscation Act of August 1861, which declared that anyone using slaves in support of the Confederate war effort "forfeit all right" to those slaves.[21]

At this point the fleeing slaves took the military practice of confiscating contraband in an entirely new direction. As word spread through the slave community that General Butler had no intention of returning runaway slaves, a slow trickle became a flood, with nine hundred slaves coming to the fort by August, and then several thousand over the next year, totaling ten thousand by May 1863. Butler and Congress had not anticipated this torrent of slaves fleeing the tortures of a barbarous institution. For too long, many northern whites had accepted the mythology of the contented slave. The reality became evident as thousands of slaves poured into Union lines. It was one thing to have a few men willing to work for a local Union commander and another to respond to the needs of hundreds of families. Butler himself agonized over the legality of his situation, eventually concluding that it was in the military's and government's interest not to own this form of property but rather to treat them as what they were, people like any other.[22]

Meanwhile, the government and army lacked any coherent response to this slowly emerging policy of treating slaves as people. In Tennessee, General Don Carlos Buell returned slaves who entered Union lines to their owners. In his diary, Lieutenant Colonel John Beatty, who served under Buell, described his commander as an "amiable idiot" whose policies wasted resources that could serve the army "in the insane effort to protect men [slave owners] who have forfeited all right to protection."[23]

In contrast, John C. Frémont, the Republicans' first candidate for president back in 1856 and commander of the Department of the West, emancipated the slaves of all Confederate supporters in Missouri. David Hunter, an ardent abolitionist and commander of the Department of the South—which at the beginning of 1862 consisted of only the coastal islands along the southern Atlantic coast—favored not just freeing the slaves but also arming them. However, federal legislation still forbade the enlistment of black troops, leading the War Department to refuse recognition of these first black units. Under orders, Hunter disbanded all but one company—he just did not mention that unit to the War Department. In Kansas, General James H. Lane formed two regiments consisting mostly of escaped slaves from Missouri. Lane twice ignored letters from the secretary of war ordering him to desist, deploying these troops in several battles and praising them for "fighting like tigers."[24]

Frémont, Hunter, and Lane had clearly overstepped their authority in attempting to force the government's hand in favor of emancipation. Lincoln felt compelled to rein in his generals, if only to maintain civilian control of the military, but also from fear that these acts of liberation could cost the Union the support of the border states. In 1861 it was still unclear if the slave states of Missouri, Kentucky, Maryland, and Delaware would remain in the Union. Butler proclaiming runaway slaves contraband and exploiting their labor had demonstrable utility, but adopting a sweeping policy of freeing large numbers of slaves might "alarm our Southern Union friends and turn them against us," Lincoln wrote Frémont in September 1861. In order to not lose border-state support, Lincoln countermanded both Frémont's and Hunter's orders.[25]

Despite Lincoln's caution, many Union troops acted independently in following the logic of freedom. Some generals, such as Henry Halleck and John Dix, took the opposite tack, refusing to allow runaway slaves to enter Union lines as a way of avoiding the entire issue. Lincoln let Halleck's and Dix's orders stand, continuing into 1862 his efforts to accommodate the racist southerners and bring them peacefully back into the Union.[26]

But Lincoln's moderation found few takers in the South, not even in the border states. His trial balloon of compensated emancipation deflated immediately. On July 14, 1862, the majority of border-state congressmen sent Lincoln a public letter upholding their "right to hold slaves," which they had no intention of giving up. Lincoln had hoped that mollifying these representatives would convince ever more white southerners to switch their allegiance from the Confederacy to the Union. But by the summer of 1862 the president began losing confidence in his appeasement policy.[27]

==

Lincoln had some basis for his efforts to forestall emancipation. Many white Unionists lived in the Confederate states, though they tended to be primarily poor farmers in the hill country. In contrast, southern blacks were nearly unanimous in their newly discovered patriotism. That widespread willingness to support the Union, even in the absence of promises of freedom, moved many northerners to favor emancipation. The Ohio soldier John Beatty, like so many other Union soldiers, came to respect the blacks he encountered, and moved toward welcoming their emancipation. Marching through Virginia in March 1862, he wrote in his diary of the slaves flocking to cheer the Union troops, "They are the only friends we find." Beatty was convinced that the war would evolve into a campaign for emancipation, "and when it ends African slavery will have ended also." If he had his way, the army would "commence the work of emancipation at once, and leave every foot of soil behind me free."[28]

As the war continued, this support for emancipation spread through all ranks in the army. Colonel Harrison C. Hobart, a Democrat from Wisconsin, initially opposed any effort to make the war about slavery, but after a year of combat he favored not only emancipation but also the arming of black volunteers. General Winfield Scott, who hailed from Virginia, came to much the same conclusion by the end of 1862, as would Generals Ulysses S. Grant and William T. Sherman. On the issue of equality, the military moved well ahead of civilian opinion. Even ardent abolitionists such as Theodore Parker dreamed of an all-white America, free of blacks, Chinese, Indians, and Irish. Frank P. Blair, a leading Missouri Republican and adviser to Lincoln, introduced legislation to pay for the colonization of Central America by black Americans. Nonetheless, Republican perceptions began changing with the war, as indicated by two symbolic acts in April 1862, when Congress authorized diplomatic relations with the black republics of Haiti and Liberia and voted to allow blacks to work for the post office.[29]

Republican civilians may have moved more slowly than the military in their attitude toward equality, but northern Democrats, who still claimed the loyalty of roughly 40 percent of northern voters, dug in their heels with the vitriolic certainty of white supremacy. The Democratic press fought bitterly against any suggestion that the war had anything to do with slavery. The *Chicago Times* angrily insisted that Union soldiers would "never submit to social and political equality" with blacks, and that "no greater privileges should be asked for negroes than for oxen and asses, for lager beer and swine," since they were just another form of property.[30]

The racism of many northern whites grew not from any familiarity with blacks but from feeling threatened by the very *idea* of ex-slaves competing for their jobs. In August 1862, a mob of Irish workers attacked a tobacco factory in Brooklyn that employed twenty-five blacks, mostly women and children. The rioters set the factory on fire in an effort to kill the blacks, but the police rescued the workers. In March 1863, a white mob attacked the black area of Detroit, burning homes and killing several people. Then in July came the New York anti-draft riots, which began as a protest against unfair conscription policies that allowed the children of wealth to buy their way out of service, but which quickly devolved into genocidal rage. New York's Democratic mayoral candidate, Fernando Wood, poured fuel on the fire by charging that the government planned to replace drafted workers with freed slaves. For three days New York descended into chaos as rioters attacked blacks and burned their homes and businesses, even setting fire to the Colored Orphan Asylum. It took troops straight from the battlefield at Gettysburg to suppress the riots. Because so many bodies were destroyed by fire or thrown into the river, it is impossible to determine the total casualties, which ran somewhere between three hundred and one thousand dead.

Other events indicated that much of the white North remained obdurate in their resistance to treating blacks as fellow Americans. When Lincoln called for volunteers in April 1861, blacks in Boston, Providence, New York, Philadelphia, and Washington organized units and rushed to serve. Arguably, the first volunteer to shed blood in the war was Nicholas Biddle, a runaway slave attacked by a pro-Confederate mob in Baltimore on April 18 as his working-class Pennsylvania regiment marched through the city. Yet white leaders responded with hostility to the very idea of black troops, canceling their musters and mocking their efforts, while President Lincoln treated the martial enthusiasm of northern blacks with contempt: "If we were to arm them, I fear that in a few weeks the arms would be in the hands of the rebels."[31]

Secretary of War Cameron attempted to change Lincoln's mind in December 1861, publicly calling for arming slaves. The *Louisville Journal* objected that black troops would "introduce into a war that is now humane and holy a savage ferocity and brutality that every Christian man and woman should shudder to contemplate." In the House, Kentucky's Charles Wickliffe charged, without evidence, that blacks were "afraid, by nature or instinct, of a gun," and if armed would rampage against all whites. Robert Mallory, another supposed expert on blacks from Kentucky, shared the same contradictory vision: "One shot of a cannon would disperse 30,000 of them," yet the blacks' "depraved nature" would lead them to butcher whites. Lincoln responded by ordering the recall of Cameron's report on arming blacks and fired the secretary of war.[32]

Lincoln reflected the attitude of the majority of northern white civilians in trying to avoid using black troops. Far too many preferred that their children die in combat rather than be tainted by association with black troops. Cincinnati police officers called to disperse a group of blacks trying to volunteer at a recruiting station shouted, "We want you damned niggers to keep out of this; this is a white man's war." More presciently, abolitionist Gerrit Smith predicted in May 1861 that the Union would soon have no recourse but to accept black troops and the white North would all become "radical, uncompromising, slave-arming, slave-freeing Abolitionists."[33]

Some blacks attempted to enlist by "passing" as white. In 1861, Joseph T. Wilson, who would later write a groundbreaking history of black troops, joined a New York regiment in the company of two

Spaniards and managed to pass as one himself. But after just a few days in the ranks, he was recognized and honorably discharged. When a private in the 1st Regiment of Kansas Volunteers was discovered to be African American, a group of fellow soldiers wrote their commander that they would endure privation rather than suffer the ignominy of serving with even a single black soldier. Sailors did not have this issue, as the navy had accepted blacks since the Revolution and they accounted for one-fifth of the serving seamen. In the first two years of war, blacks seeking to serve their unwelcoming country either enlisted in the navy or volunteered to serve in menial army jobs. Amazingly, thousands did so.[34]

The pressure on the government to make better use of the vast reserve of potential black troops increased as the war entered its second year. In 1862, with Union forces at Baton Rouge under sustained attack by superior Confederate numbers, General Benjamin Butler called for reinforcements, only to be told by the War Department that none were available. Butler responded, "I shall call on Africa to intervene, and I do not think I shall call in vain." Hundreds of free blacks had already organized themselves into loyal militia companies, and he asked them for aid "to defend the flag of their native country." Some blacks observed that this country had denied them citizenship, but the majority put these thoughts aside and joined the United States Army without official sanction.[35]

In July 1862, Congress listened to necessity and repealed the sections of the Militia Act of 1792 forbidding black men from serving, opening the door to the recruitment of African American troops. They followed up with the Second Confiscation Act, which moved further than any previous legislation in explicitly stating that all slaves entering Union lines "shall be forever free of their servitude, and not again held as slaves." This act also authorized the president "to employ as many persons of African descent as he may deem necessary and proper for the suppression of this rebellion." These congressional actions altered both the tone of the national conversation on race and the nation's war aims. The explicit justification for war remained the restoration of the Union, but now as part of an implicit battle for human freedom.[36]

Also in July, President Lincoln changed his mind. His refusal to use black troops buckled before the realities of modern warfare. The war began with a conviction on both sides that the struggle would be short. As the second year of the war dawned, there could be little doubt that they were in the midst of a protracted struggle and that it would be foolish for the Union to not exploit the potential advantage of black troops. As Lincoln framed it, the choice was "not a question of sentiment or taste" but one of simple mathematics. Meeting with Secretary of the Navy Gideon Welles and Secretary of State William Seward, Lincoln emphasized the importance of blacks to the war effort, telling them that "we must free the slaves or be ourselves subdued." In his diary, Welles noted this "new departure for the President," who had always "been prompt and emphatic in denouncing any interference" with slavery by the federal government.[37]

Later that same day, Lincoln read his cabinet an initial draft of a proclamation emancipating the slaves. Above all else, the president insisted that the course of war forced him to take this dramatic and pragmatic action. The Confederacy fought for the preservation of slavery; the time had come for the Union to fight for its end. The cabinet recommended caution, not wanting the proclamation to appear to be an act of desperation, and they persuaded Lincoln to wait for a victory.[38]

Lincoln got his victory at Antietam in northwest Maryland on September 17, 1862—the single bloodiest day in American military history. Union forces suffered more than twelve thousand casualties driving back the Confederate effort to bring the war north, inflicting ten thousand casualties on Lee's army. Five days later, Lincoln released the Emancipation Proclamation, which not only declared all slaves within rebel territory free but also announced the implementation of the Second Confiscation Act's grant of authority to enlist black troops. To get the message to slaves who might assist the Union cause, Lincoln ordered soldiers to distribute thousands of copies of the proclamation. Though southern law had long forbidden teaching slaves to read, many had taught themselves and shared the good news with their fellow slaves: the dream of freedom was coming, and it wore a blue uniform.[39]

The Emancipation Proclamation did not meet with universal approval in the North. Unsurprisingly, most Democrats greeted it with racist derision. Campaigning for election as governor of New York, Democrat Horatio Seymour attacked the proclamation with violent racist tropes, deeming it "a proposal for the butchery of women and children, for scenes of lust and rapine, of arson and murder, unparalleled in the history of the world." Seymour won. Ohio's governor, David Tod, insisted "this is a *white* man's government . . . [and] white men are able to defend and protect it." August Belmont, a German immigrant and leader of the northern Democratic Party during the Civil War, initially supported the war effort, even donating money to help raise troops. But with the Emancipation Proclamation he turned against the war. At a dinner at Delmonico's, Belmont persuaded other party leaders to establish and fund the Society for the Diffusion of Political Knowledge, which would print a stream of racist and anti-war tracts. To head the society, Belmont selected the former financier of the Know-Nothing Party, Samuel F. B. Morse.[40]

Emancipation became the central issue of the 1862 elections, in which the Democrats did well in the northern states, gaining thirty-five seats in the House of Representatives. General George McClellan warned the president that the specter of equality "will rapidly disintegrate our present Armies." There was even talk, mostly by McClellan, of a coup.[41]

The Democrats' electoral success in 1862 is not fully reflective of northern public opinion. The Republicans maintained their majority in the House and picked up six seats in the Senate even while facing an electoral handicap, as troops serving in the field could not vote—the preference of soldiers for the Republican Party only became clear with the election of 1864. In 1862, many soldiers shared the view of a New York private who celebrated the Emancipation Proclamation for making clear that the war "is now between Slavery & freedom, & every honest man knows what he is fighting for." A Pennsylvania captain similarly saw the war evolving into "a contest between human rights and human liberty on one side and eternal bondage on the other."[42]

One of the most fascinating and underappreciated aspects of the Civil War is the spreading acceptance of equality by the white men serving in the U.S. military. The general evidence for this evolution is found in their votes in the 1864 election and in the years following the war, but specific examples shine through in a great many of the letters and diaries that survived the conflict. For instance, Chauncey H. Cooke wrote movingly to his family that everywhere his regiment, the 25th Wisconsin, went in the South, slaves rushed out to cheer them on and render aid. As their boat traveled up the Mississippi toward the decisive siege of Vicksburg in 1863, Cooke watched slaves run down to the riverbank and celebrate the appearance of Union troops, dancing, bowing, and dropping "upon their knees and [holding] their hands above their head as if they were praying." These gestures of gratitude stirred the troops on the transport, especially as "every white man and woman was ready to shoot or poison us."[43]

Like so many others, Cooke wrote that the Union troops found that "the negroes were our only friends, and they kept us posted on what the whites were doing and saying," bringing them food with the military intelligence. General O. M. Mitchell wrote Secretary of War Edwin Stanton that "the negroes are our only friends, and in two instances I owe my own safety to their faithfulness." They knew the rugged terrain better than any local white and guided his troops without concern for their own safety. Prisoners of war gave powerful testimonials of slaves risking everything to bring them food and water and aiding them in escaping from the Confederates. Lieutenant Hannibal Johnson of the 3rd Maine Infantry kept a record of his escape with three others from a Confederate prison camp outside Columbia, South Carolina. Fed, hidden, and guided by selfless slaves every step of the way, Johnson wrote in his diary, "If such kindness will not make one an abolitionist, then his heart must be made of stone."[44]

As he traveled through the South, Chauncey Cooke became convinced that slavery had damaged the whites almost as much as the blacks, the elite having deliberately kept poor whites ignorant of the outside world. By his count, only one-tenth of the Confederate prisoners could read and write. When one of his friends asked some prisoners why they fought, they received an answer that would become standard in the years ahead: "You Yanks want us to marry our daughters to the niggers."[45]

While the government evidenced no policy of mandatory interracial marriage, the United States did benefit enormously from the presence of some four million slaves in the Confederacy. Not only were the Confederate states unable to call upon the military services of black adult males, but they also had to divert white forces to the control of these slaves. Thousands of slaves eluded that control now that freedom definitely waited for them at the end of their trek, depriving the Confederacy of their labor. The United States profited from that labor, as well as from the intelligence, supplies, aid to lost and escaped soldiers, and service as guides that these slaves and former slaves offered. But of greatest significance was the enlistment of a quarter of a million African Americans in the Union Army.

Throughout their lives, black Americans, enslaved and free, had heard the charges of their inferiority, making it difficult to feel confidence in their status as humans. The abolitionist movement had played a key role in battling that perception, if only because it foregrounded articulate and heroic blacks including Frederick Douglass, Sojourner Truth, Martin Delany, William Wells Brown, Frances Ellen Watkins, and Dr. John Rock. Rock spoke to this issue in 1860, observing that whites consistently attempted to shift the blame for slavery and its ill effects onto the victims: "Our enemies have taken every advantage of our unhappy situation, and attempt to prove that, because we are unfortunate, we are necessarily an inferior race, incapable of enjoying to a full extent the privileges of citizenship." He saw through racism to its utility for an avaricious elite. Charges of inequality served as a "subterfuge" intended to justify "the infamous treatment which greets the colored man everywhere in this slave cursed land."[46]

The following year the *Anglo-African*, the most popular and influential black newspaper of the 1850s and 1860s, fought back against popular perceptions of black inferiority in an article specifically addressed to whites. To the degree that African Americans were ignorant, the paper charged, the fault lay with whites who "have shut the light of knowledge from our souls and brutalized our instincts." Whites should feel guilty for "what you have made us," but even more for "what you have prevented us from being." Frances Ellen Watkins succinctly characterized slave owners as abandoning the values of their civilization when they listened not "to the cry of agony" but "to the ring of dollars" they extracted from other humans.[47]

In 1863, William Wells Brown published his popular and influential *The Black Man*, which promoted the idea that blacks just needed education to join fully in the life of the nation. Brown highlighted the lives of fifty-seven prominent African Americans who overcame every form of privation and oppression to contribute markedly to American society. Brown did not disguise his anger with whites who called blacks inferior: "It does not become the whites to point the finger of scorn at the blacks, when they have so long been degrading them." Brown embraced Locke's tabula rasa, the belief that the human mind begins as a blank slate upon which experience and education etch character. The black mind had been chained too long by slavery; with freedom and education would come a great renaissance as African Americans would finally be able to rise to their full potential.[48]

By 1864 blacks began organizing Equal Rights Leagues in states as diverse as Louisiana and Ohio, and holding "colored conventions" to demand equality. They issued manifestos, collected signatures on petitions, and wrote pamphlets explaining the nature of equal rights,

since whites obviously required some education in that area. Such public statements may have helped prepare the white mind for the radical
concept of equality, but intellectual arguments were insufficient unless
backed by hard evidence. The performance of black soldiers would provide that evidence for both whites and blacks.

With the Emancipation Proclamation, the Union Army began recruiting black troops. The 1st South Carolina Volunteers, commanded by
Colonel Thomas Wentworth Higginson, was the first black regiment
to gain official recognition. Two months later they fought their initial
skirmish on the St. Mary River, acting with courage but little discipline.
Confident that they would do better in the future, Higginson wrote
in his official dispatch, "No officer in this regiment now doubts that
the key to the successful prosecution of this war lies in the unlimited
employment of black troops." After a second black regiment captured
Jacksonville, General Hunter wrote that he thought "the prejudices of
certain of our white soldiers against these indispensable allies are rapidly softening or fading out."[49]

Once Lincoln made the decision to accept black troops, he and
his administration proceeded with energy. Secretary of War Stanton
appointed Adjutant General Lorenzo Thomas to recruit these new soldiers. Thomas had enormous power, including the ability to grant commissions and to throw racists out of the army, exerting federal authority
to change attitudes. In his speeches, Thomas said that it gave him great
pleasure to rid the army of racists as unworthy of the uniform they
wore. Thomas excelled at his task, reaching his goal of twenty African American regiments by the end of 1863, and seventy regiments by
war's end.[50]

The path to equality was not linear. The government accommodated
racism by organizing segregated units, with black troops serving under
white officers and not receiving the bounties offered to white enlistees.
Democrats blocked efforts to establish equal pay as degrading to white

soldiers—where the latter received $13 a month, blacks earned just $10. New York's Governor Seymour refused to allow the enlistment of blacks under state authority. The state's black volunteers bypassed the governor and gained permission from the War Department to enlist under federal authority, quickly filling three regiments.

The racists feared that respect for black troops would spread with news of their heroism, and indeed, that's what happened. When the 20th U.S. Colored Infantry marched down Broadway on March 5, 1864, huge crowds cheered them. In the very city where rioters had viciously attacked blacks just the year before, a reporter now saw white and black women waving their handkerchiefs together in support of the troops, while white merchants left their businesses to cheer the soldiers. As the journalist asked, "Ain't that a victory?"[51]

The Union's African American forces first experienced significant combat on May 27, 1863, at Port Hudson on the Mississippi. The performance of the Louisiana Native Guards that day would change the minds of many white soldiers, as well as those of civilians reading newspaper reports of the battle. One white lieutenant commanding a unit of "contrabands," runaway slaves, admitted that he had had very low expectations for his troops. But when the order to advance came, his unit moved "forward cool as if Marshaled for dress parade, under a most murderous fire from the enemies guns." His sergeant "fell wrapped in the flag he had so gallantly borne," and his force held the position under fire until reinforcements arrived. They then twice charged under heavy artillery fire, never swerving from their duty or giving the least hint of cowardice. Their "coolness and daring" was widely observed; General Nathaniel P. Banks, the commander of Union forces at Port Hudson, wrote that any skepticism of the courage of black troops had been completely dispelled.[52]

All the officers of these first black units were white, many of them prone to the general racism of their day. The war changed them. For example, Captain M. M. Miller of the 9th Louisiana Colored Regiment wrote his wife back home in Illinois about the victory at Milliken's

Bend, which he described as bloodier than Shiloh. In June 1863, Confederate forces struck at the federal forces at Milliken's Bend in an effort to lift Grant's siege of Vicksburg. Though outnumbered, the black troops counterattacked, engaging in vicious hand-to-hand fighting, suffering a 62 percent casualty rate. Miller lost far too many "brave, noble men" to the Confederate attack, he said; "I never more wish to hear the expression, 'The niggers won't fight.'" He challenged anyone to "come with me, a hundred yards from where I sit, and I can show you the wounds that cover the bodies of sixteen as brave, loyal, and patriotic soldiers as ever drew bead on a rebel." His anger with the casual racism so common in America increased as he described the battle. He wished everyone could have seen the steadiness and heroism of his troops. "I can say for them that I never saw a braver company of men in my life."[53]

Many white soldiers replicated Miller's experience, having their racial prejudices shattered by the living evidence of black troops in combat. Official reports, letters, and memoirs by white soldiers are filled with expressions of stunned admiration for the contributions of African Americans, enlisted and civilian. Charles Dana, the assistant secretary of war, joined the troops at Milliken's Bend and reported that "the bravery of the blacks . . . completely revolutionized the sentiment of the army with regard to the employment of negro troops." Dana heard officers who had previously "sneered at the idea of the negroes fighting" now expressing themselves "as heartily in favor of it."[54]

One of those officers was Colonel Robert Cowden, who had been initially contemptuous of the former slaves under his command in Tennessee. His raw recruits appeared docile and beaten down by slavery. But as the men trained and gained confidence, he found them steady and cool in battle, and he declared them the "bravest of the brave." Another officer wrote a friend after seeing a black regiment in combat: "You have no idea how my prejudices with regard to negro troops have been dispelled." The black soldiers "behaved magnificently and fought splendidly," and appeared "far superior in discipline to the white troops, and just as brave." Comparisons aside, the essential fact was that black and white soldiers shared the experience of war, which tends to create powerful bonds of camaraderie.[55]

The courage of the 54th Massachusetts Regiment at James Island and Fort Wagner gained national recognition, removing lingering doubts about the capabilities of black troops. On July 16, 1863, the 54th, commanded by Colonel Robert Gould Shaw, repulsed a Confederate attack on James Island, south of Charleston. Black corporal James Henry Gooding witnessed the shifting attitudes of white troops when "a regiment of white men gave us three cheers as we were passing them." Just two days later, the 54th led a direct assault on the Confederate stronghold of Fort Wagner on Charleston harbor, suffering 40 percent casualties, including the death of Colonel Shaw. Sergeant William Carney, repeatedly wounded, retrieved the regimental flag as the survivors retreated, becoming the first of twenty-nine black soldiers to receive the Congressional Medal of Honor during the Civil War. The nation could not, and did not, ignore this heroism.[56]

Neither, it seemed, could some Confederate soldiers. Occasional truces between Confederate and black Union troops led to friendly banter and the exchange of goods, with the opponents treating one another as soldiers rather than men of different stations. There were also instances when Confederate soldiers refused to carry out orders to slaughter black prisoners of war. An outraged General Edmund Kirby Smith reprimanded his subordinates when he learned they had taken black prisoners. He hoped his troops "recognized the propriety of giving no quarter to armed negroes and their officers," and ordered them killed. Given the treatment black prisoners of war received—35 percent of all black POWs died in Confederate prison camps, double the rate for white POWs—there appeared to be ample opportunity to carry out such orders.[57]

The attitude of white Union soldiers to their black compatriots had long-term effects on the United States. As we shall see, veterans repeatedly used their influence to promote an extension of human rights, holding up their wartime experience as the essential justification for rethinking America's hostility to equality. General George H. Thomas, a Virginian who remained loyal to the Union, reluctantly accepted black troops in his Army of the Cumberland, certain that they would not fight. But he changed his mind after the battles at Dalton and Nashville, in which, in Colonel Thomas Morgan's words, "colored soldiers had fought side by side with white troops. They had mingled together in the charge. They had supported each other. They had assisted each other from the field when wounded, and they lay side by side in death." Thomas joined his white troops in cheering the 14th Colored Infantry, and after Nashville he told his staff, "Gentlemen, the question is settled; negroes will fight."[58]

Similarly, General James B. Steedman, a Democrat who had supported Breckinridge in 1860 and opposed the use of black troops, wrote after the Battle of Nashville: "I was unable to discover that color made any difference in the fighting of my troops; all, white and black, nobly did their duty as soldiers." General Grant wrote a private letter to President Lincoln in August 1863 in which he gave the further recruitment of black soldiers "my hearty support." The deployment of black troops "with the emancipation of the negro, is the heavyest [sic] blow yet given the Confederacy." He thought they made good soldiers, but even more than that, "taking them from the enemy weakens him in the same proportion they strengthen us." Or, as an Iowa private bluntly told his wife, "they will stop Bullets as well as white people."[59]

Attitudes with which white men began the war withered or became irrelevant in light of events on the ground. William T. Sherman, seen as a great liberator by millions of people, acknowledged that he was part of a revolution transforming the country. Sherman had numerous friends among the southern elite, had never spoken out against slavery before the war, and did not think blacks equal to whites. But he also grasped that black soldiers would not willingly accept subservient status. The irony for Sherman lay in the fact that everything he did as a military leader hastened not just the end of slavery but the enhancement of equality. Sherman recorded a conversation he had with an elderly black man in which he asked the slave if he understood the nature of the war. To Sherman's surprise, the man stated that while he knew the government "professed to be fighting for the Union, he supposed that slavery was the cause, and that our success was to be his freedom." Sherman asked if all the "slaves comprehended this fact, and he said they surely did." Sherman further fed that revolution with Special Field Orders No. 15, breaking up coastal plantations and giving the land to freed slaves, promoting the idea that the slaves deserved some recompense for their long labors that had enriched the nation.[60]

African Americans too believed their military service would win them respect and rights. Those serving shared the certainty that, in the words of James F. Jones of the 14th Rhode Island Heavy Artillery, "we will make all people respect us." Repeatedly black soldiers wrote in astonishment of white troops cheering them on. Some of the signs of self-worth appear minor to the modern reader but carried enormous symbolic weight at the time. For instance, another member of Jones's regiment wrote of joyfully walking the streets of New Orleans. Being a pedestrian hardly seems a major triumph, but this soldier was amazed, as it was the first time in his life that he could imagine walking "fearlessly and boldly through the streets of a southern city!" A black man in the uniform of the U.S. Army walking freely in a southern city did indeed offer proof that the old order was crumbling. But even more powerful was an event such as the 3rd U.S. Colored Cavalry routing the attacking Texans at the Battle of Yazoo City in March 1864 and pushing them into disordered flight. Shattering Confederate pride gave the troops involved a sense of self-esteem and strength, of personal value.[61]

It is a compelling indication of the growing sense of self-worth among black troops that they resented Lincoln's decision to allow no black officers and to pay black soldiers less. The president did not bother to justify the pay differential, but he reasoned that no white soldier would take orders from a black officer and that such an exercise of military authority would destroy the army's morale. Faced with such obvious bias, black recruiters, including Frederick Douglass, reluctantly extolled the virtue of patience. Douglass insisted that allowing blacks to enlist at all was "a great concession" that should be embraced by black men, as serving in the army would quickly overcome prejudice.[62]

But black soldiers resisted being consigned to second-class status as soldiers. They demanded equality, refusing to take their inferior pay and rejecting offers from Massachusetts to make up the difference. As one member of the 54th Regiment wrote, their need for necessities could not "outweigh our self-respect." This disparity ended on June 15, 1864, when Congress equalized the pay of all military personnel and offered the same bounty regardless of race. Widespread celebrations greeted the news that the black regiments would finally receive their full back pay, which they saw as a victory for equal rights. The growing confidence of black soldiers slowly found its match in the attitude of their white comrades.[63]

Encountering the realities of slavery changed the minds of many Union soldiers. Most northern whites serving in the military came from rural areas and had never even seen a black person before the war. Two characteristics of the blacks most surprised whites: their work ethic and their piety. For decades the apologists of slavery had described blacks as lazy and barbarous. What northern soldiers witnessed as the fleeing slaves entered their lines were deeply religious people happy to work long hours to aid the Union cause. These people sought not, as racists had long proclaimed, indolence and bare necessities, but rather freedom and an education. "I never before saw children so eager to learn," wrote one volunteer.[64]

The Union Army provided a great service to both the previously enslaved and poor whites by bringing education to the intellectual wasteland of the South. The southern states had never before promoted public schools, the elites refusing to pay taxes to educate the children of poor whites. During the Civil War, public education moved south in the wake of Union forces. For instance, in March 1864, General Banks established a Board of Education for the Department of the Gulf, setting up the first public schools in the region. The freedmen of

Little Rock established the first public schools in Arkansas with support from volunteer Union soldiers. Elsewhere in the South, formerly enslaved women such as Susie King Taylor set up the first schools for black children.

In the midst of war, many Union soldiers volunteered to teach former slaves to read, finding enthusiastic students of all ages, including among their fellow soldiers. Colonel Thomas J. Morgan, commander of the 14th U.S. Colored Infantry, felt that his black recruits—many of them former slaves—needed first to learn self-respect. He found teaching them to read a quick route to that end, and established a school in every company. Morgan praised them as fast learners who took their books with them everywhere and demonstrated pride in their developing skills. Writing a quarter century after the war, James Monroe Trotter, one of the first black officers in the army, awarded "all honor" to those white comrades who gave such essential aid to the black troops. A large percentage of the black soldiers were illiterate when they enlisted, taking their first lessons from fellow soldiers. White Union soldiers saw and responded to inequality, some feeling an obvious sense of shared guilt for what had been done to the slaves.[65]

Repeatedly, white soldiers of all ranks wrote home that they had once thought nothing of slavery and hated the abolitionists for raising all that fuss. But once they saw what slavery actually did to people, their opinions shifted firmly to the camp of abolition. As John Russell of Illinois put it in a letter to his sister in 1862, "There is a mighty revolution a going on in the minds of the men on the niger question." One of his fellow Illinois privates, Amos Hostetter, stated that he still did not like blacks, "but we hate his master worse." As a consequence, "I am henceforth an *Abolitionist* and I intend to practice what I preach." Union soldiers routinely intervened to prevent the mistreatment of slaves and to aid runaways—they recognized their allies and slowly came to admire their courage.[66]

In stark contrast, the southern elite appeared to learn nothing from the Civil War. They saw any diminishment of their power as total defeat, acknowledging but two options: complete control of other humans or the end of civilization. James Henry Hammond, a self-righteous planter who had sexually abused his own nieces, refused to give any food-stuffs to desperate Confederate soldiers because to do so would be the equivalent of "branding on my forehead 'Slave'," as feeding soldiers ren-dered him a servant of the state. Repeatedly, slave owners preferred the defeat of their cause over giving up one whit of their authority. Thus every attempt by the Confederate government to employ slave labor met resistance from slave owners who rejected any interference with the use of their property. North Carolina planter Catherine Edmondston saw government appropriation of her slaves' labor as akin "to an aboli-tion of Slavery." Confederate assistant secretary of war John Campbell complained that "the sacrosanctity of slave property in this war has operated most injuriously to the Confederacy." The ideology of racism played a key role in defeating the Confederacy.[67]

On the night of May 12, 1862, Robert and John Smalls, enslaved sailors working on the steamer *Planter* in Charleston harbor, perceived an opportunity to escape to freedom while aiding the Union cause. The ship, loaded with ammunition and artillery, would sail the following day to make deliveries to Forts Sumter and Ripley. During the night the brothers' families and a friend boarded the ship, which Robert Smalls guided away from the wharf at 3 A.M.

Demonstrating coolness under pressure, Smalls blew the signal whistles and moved slowly toward Fort Sumter, as though on the sched-uled delivery. As soon as he passed the fort, Smalls and his crew put on full steam, raised a white flag, and headed straight to the blockading federal fleet. In the predawn light, the USS *Onward* was preparing to fire on the approaching Confederate ship when its lookout saw the white flag. As he came alongside the *Onward*, Smalls jauntily shouted to a surprised Captain Frederick Nichols: "Good morning, sir! I've brought you some of the old United States guns, sir!" The United States gained

more than ordnance; it also had another heroic reminder of the hollowness of southern racist ideology. Smalls went on to serve with distinction during the war, eventually becoming captain of the *Planter* when
its white commander deserted his post under enemy fire.[68]

The longer the war continued, the more the concept of equality
gained acceptance. That cause gained support from the mobilization
of African Americans not solely as a military force but also as a political one. Up until the Civil War, many northern and western states
had "black codes" specifically forbidding blacks from voting, giving
testimony, serving on juries, and fulfilling other duties of citizenship.
Blacks themselves went after these laws, enjoying their first great success in California, which repealed its black code in 1863. In Illinois,
John Jones, a prosperous tailor born in North Carolina, organized an
effective campaign to overturn the state's black code. With every week
of war, his movement gained white allies such as J. G. Andrews, serving in Sherman's army, who wrote Governor Richard Yates that he saw
"the black laws of Illinois as a system of injustice and inhumanity . . .
representative of the dark ages." Andrews wrote "as a Soldier" whose
experience had taught him that "the Negro will make a better citizen"
than the typical southern white. The former was hardworking and
"loyal to his country," while "the latter has been reared in vice and
indolence; is disloyal to his country and a disturber of the peace." In
January 1865, the state legislature overturned the restrictive legislation.[69]

Similar black-led movements challenged racist laws throughout the
North, and even within liberated territory such as Louisiana. Their primary goal was the right to vote, an aim that steadily gained Republican
support as the party's leaders came to recognize a powerful untapped
constituency. In 1864, African Americans organized the Ohio Equal
Rights League, demanding united action by blacks in the political realm
to take advantage of the fact that "American society is in a state of
Revolution." They observed that much remained to be done to make
the United States truly the land of liberty, starting with legislation to

ensure "that there shall be no distinction on account of color in all our broad land."[70]

African American unity on equality lacked the cautious nuance preferred by most Republicans. As Sherman's army turned north from Georgia into South Carolina, the majority of the party moved toward support for legal but not social equality and strove to convince white Americans that the former did not threaten their supremacy. One formulation of this position—which closely aligned with Lincoln's—came from New York representative Thomas T. Davis. Fascinated by the new science of natural selection, Davis maintained that the fossil record showed that they lived in "a progressive world" where "advances are slow but sure." Society evidenced the same progressive nature as the physical world. Davis predicted that future explorers of American history would be astonished to find "deep buried in the strata of political geology, a monster fossil": slavery. Emancipation, while an important step in human progress, would not elevate blacks to equality with whites. Nonetheless, said Davis, "I would make every race free and equal before the law, permitting to each the elevation to which its own capacity and culture should entitle it, and securing to each the fruits of its own progression."[71]

Lincoln may have agreed with Davis, but he avoided discussing the future of the freedmen for fear of giving fodder to the Democrats. The president did appreciate that freedom and military service would have an impact on the African Americans themselves. In responding publicly to Illinois Republican James C. Conkling, Lincoln made clear the emerging education of warfare: "You say you will not fight to free negroes. Some of them seem willing to fight for you." Lincoln reminded Conkling that these blacks risked their lives for the most powerful of reasons: "The promise of freedom. And the promise being made, must be kept."[72]

But Lincoln recognized that most Democrats and many Republicans insisted that the Constitution prevented the government from completely ending slavery. As Frederick Douglass complained, "Between the black race and its freedom, the constitution is interposed. It always is." The war changed all that, with black troops becoming the single best argument for equality.[73]

Events on the battlefield altered policy, and ending slavery seemed obvious. Slavery had caused the war; getting rid of it would justify the losses. As the editor of the Cincinnati *Catholic Telegraph* wrote, "We must have some compensation for the blood and treasure which we have been forced to spend, this we find in the abolition of slavery." Battling to preserve the Union meant destroying the institution of slavery and respecting the rights of those who joined in that struggle. The growing hatred of the slave-owning elite drove the vast majority of Union supporters to desire an end to the primary prop of their dominance. After the widely reported heroism of the 54th Massachusetts Regiment at Fort Wagner in July 1863, Angelina Grimké asked a friend, "Do you not rejoice & exult in all the praise that is lavished upon our brave colored troops even by Pro-slavery papers?"[74]

Northern white attitudes shifted rapidly in the years 1863 and 1864, which was remarkable given the complete ossification of racism into the American character prior to the war. Indiana representative George W. Julian acknowledged as much early in 1865 in apologizing for Congress's failure to recognize slavery as a crime against humanity. Now was the time to correct that moral error and repeal all legislation, state and federal, intended to injure black men, and see to "his absolute restoration to equal rights with the white man as a citizen as well as a soldier." It is telling that Julian referred to the "restoration" of rights, recognizing that the Supreme Court had taken away that legal equality.[75]

As Confederate defeat became certain, many southern whites struggled to formulate new means of enforcing inequality. In March 1864, a meeting in the liberated town of Huntsville, Alabama, sought to work out a formula by which southern whites could return to the Union while maintaining white supremacy. Judge D. C. Humphreys, who had supported secession, admitted that it had destroyed the institution of slavery. Now the time had come to rejoin the Union in a way that would "secure the management" of black labor. He added, "Of course we prefer the old method," so the goal was to find the closest approximation to slavery that would not offend northern sentiments. He therefore favored a negotiated peace accepting the end of slavery but retaining a slavery-like system.[76]

The Confederate government would have none of it. Until the end, Confederate leaders warned that northern victory would bring racial equality. When Governor Zebulon Vance of North Carolina faced a significant challenge from peace candidate William W. Holden in the 1864 election, Vance trotted out every tired cliché of slavery's end leading to black equality, which would of course lead to the end of the white race. His racism paid off in a major electoral victory. No matter the cost, most southern whites would not abandon their bigotry.

Confederate fears of racial equality led to numerous atrocities, most notoriously the Fort Pillow Massacre of April 12, 1864. Confederate troops under General Nathan Bedford Forrest slaughtered some three hundred Union prisoners of war, mostly blacks. Forrest was not alone in feeling that maintaining white supremacy justified any sort of brutality, with many Confederate officers ordering their troops to take no black prisoners. For instance, at Petersburg, Virginia, in July 1864, some five hundred black troops were executed after surrendering. As one Confederate soldier, John S. Wise, recalled the day: "It was the first time Lee's army had encountered negroes, and their presence excited in the troops indignant malice such as had characterized no former conflict."[77]

As the war approached its end, the Confederacy staggered and ultimately collapsed before the sweeping force of equality. In desperation, Jefferson Davis proposed the recruitment of black soldiers with the promise of freedom. His fellow slave owners saw this proposal as an outrageous betrayal, and several state legislatures passed resolutions against using black troops, considering it an abandonment of the whole purpose of the war. General Howell Cobb adamantly rejected Davis's proposal as "the most pernicious idea that has been suggested." He was appalled that General Lee had signed off on the idea: "If slaves will make good soldiers our whole theory of slavery is wrong."[78]

Cobb correctly identified the problem for the Confederates. Black soldiers completely negated the ideology of slavery, which held blacks to be inferior and incapable of the duties of citizenship—after all, many white men rejected women's equality on the grounds that they could not be soldiers. Military service imparted the status of equality, and no one could imagine the conditions under which a black who carried a gun would freely accept subservience.

In many ways the most graphic expression of the danger of black troops to southern racist ideology came on February 18, 1865, when Charleston surrendered to Sherman's forces without a fight. The 21st Colored Infantry regiment led the Union forces into the city where the war had begun, past rapturous crowds of those no longer enslaved. This regiment consisted mostly of former slaves from the southeastern states, and they marched proudly past the notorious slave market under a banner reading simply "Liberty." The dream of the white republic came crashing down, trampled under the boots of black Union soldiers.[79]

The Civil War finally and fully confronted white Americans with the true nature of slavery and of its black victims. *Harper's Weekly* published one of the most famous photos of the period on July 4, 1863, the same day that Vicksburg surrendered to General Grant and that Lee's army met crushing defeat at Gettysburg. A former slave named Gordon sits stoically as the photographer exposes the sickening network of scars on his back that resulted from repeated beatings by Gordon's owner, John Lyons of Louisiana. Gordon escaped from Lyons and made his way to Union lines, where he enlisted and rose to the rank of sergeant, fighting with distinction at Port Hudson. There is a later portrait of Gordon confidently wearing the Union uniform with his sergeant's stripes. Military service offered many former slaves this transformative opportunity, to play a vital role in killing the system that had sought to strip away their humanity and crush their spirit.[80]

Serving in the military has proven one of the great equalizing forces in American history. The government sought to minimize this opportunity, initially keeping blacks out of the military, and then keeping them in segregated units. Despite these efforts, an estimated two hundred thousand blacks served in Union forces, finding a respect and sense of belonging they had never before experienced. As Douglas R. Egerton noted, "An astonishing 74 percent of Northern black men of military age enlisted to fight for a nation that denied them citizenship." In joining the military, blacks became fully equal in the eyes of the law for the first time—though it was military law. These soldiers learned that they were any man's equal.[81]

At the same time, civilian African Americans took justified pride in the emerging professionalism of their compatriots. In the public eye, these soldiers represented the entire race, and their steadiness affected the way whites viewed blacks collectively. Faith, a black woman in Philadelphia, wrote a friend in June 1863 that "public sentiment has undergone a great change in the past month or two, and more especially since the brilliant exploits of several colored regiments." Their victories were hers as well. Slaves still working in the fields were heard singing of the day when African American bluecoats would arrive and they would take their masters to prison. As T. Morris Chester wrote in the Philadelphia *Press*, "It is hardly necessary to inform our Southern brethren that what they consider as chattels, but we regard as men, may be found . . . under the inspiration of martial airs keeping step to the music of the Union." A group of recently freed slaves viewing a parade of black troops in South Carolina burst into "My country 'tis of thee, sweet land of liberty." Suddenly it had also become their song and their country.[82]

The Civil War changed the way Americans viewed one another. Most noticeable were the changed attitudes of so many white soldiers, who moved from unquestioned prejudice to true respect for their black colleagues. That acceptance of equality was not transient and is evident after the war, as these veterans consistently supported the extension of civil rights. The leading veterans' group, the Grand Army of the Republic (GAR), established hundreds of posts, most open to black veterans. The GAR consistently lobbied for voting rights for African Americans, as well as for black veterans to receive the enlistment bonuses denied them earlier in the war. Some branches even named their posts after black heroes. When William Carney applied for admission to New Bedford's GAR, he was immediately welcomed. The white president of the Women's Relief Corps made clear the attitude of this mostly white community when she introduced him: "We have Ft. Wagner's hero here, who round his body wound the flag he bore when wounded and 'it never touched the ground.'" This GAR post would later change its name to honor Sergeant Carney. These white veterans left no doubt that black veterans also deserved the gratitude of a nation saved from destruction. Colonel Thomas Wentworth Higginson summarized attitudes well when he wrote that in 1864 nothing appeared "more remarkable than the facility with which the expected aversion of the army everywhere vanished before the admirable behavior of the colored troops."[83]

Not just black men benefited from the shift in public perception. Those who fought in the Civil War discovered more forms of inequality than just race. Both sides had class-based conscription laws that allowed the wealthy to avoid service. Confederates could dodge service if they paid someone to serve in their stead, and the Confederacy also exempted one eligible man per twenty slaves on a plantation—no one could miss this class bias. Private Ollin Goddin summarized the general attitude in a letter to his state's governor: "The Govt. has made a distinction between the rich man (who had something to fight for) and the poor man who fights for that he never will have. The exemption of the owners of 20 negroes & the allowing of substitutes clearly proves it." He resented fighting for the "rich mans negro" while his family suffered grievous privation. Goddin called on the governor to end these unfair exemptions and pass more equitable military service laws.[84]

Immigrants also helped redefine the United States as a land of equality. While many bore a racist animus toward blacks, they still put their lives on the line to end slavery. About one-fourth of those who served in the Union Army had been born abroad, primarily in Ireland or Germany. Some of these immigrants understood the essential nature of the fight better than many members of Congress. A German miner named Peter Klein wrote his father that the slave owners, "great lords who have a hundred and more serfs," started the war. In order to retain control over their serfs, these aristocrats worked "to overthrow the free constitution of the country and set up a government by the nobility." But Klein assured his father that "we, free men and honest workers, we don't want to put up with that." [85]

The war gave these immigrants a wider understanding of the workings of their new country and also fostered an increased sense of self-respect and even acceptance within American society. Before the war, the Irish and Germans may have been the subject of widespread disdain and the target of a political party devoted to keeping them out of the United States, but the Union Army included a few hundred thousand of each group, and these soldiers would not relinquish their status as full American citizens without a fight.

Women, too, found the war provided an opportunity for increased involvement in the public sphere, freeing many from their domestic confinement. Some women sought to help by nursing, but even here men blocked their way. When Frederick Law Olmsted and Henry Bellows organized the U.S. Sanitary Commission in 1861, they studiously excluded women, who they thought would undermine the "masculine discipline" nursing required. Fortunately for thousands of wounded soldiers, these efforts to limit nursing to men failed miserably, as women formed their own support groups. The New England Women's Auxiliary Association fielded hundreds of women, most famously Clara Barton, while hundreds more women served as government staff workers.[86]

A few adventurous women demanded an even more direct role in the war. Speculation persists about the number of women who disguised themselves as men and joined the army, but the evidence is anecdotal. For instance, the Pennsylvania muster rolls include these tantalizing details:

"46th Pennsylvania, Company D: Charles D. Fuller, detected as being a female; discharged. . . . 126th Pennsylvania, Company F: Sergeant Frank Mayne . . . killed in battle . . . and discovered to be a woman; real name, Frances Day." Several women, such as Sarah Rosetta Wakeman, left sufficient documentation to verify their service in the Union Army. Union spy Emma Edmonds, who enlisted under the name Frank Thompson in the 2nd Michigan Volunteers and saw action at the First Battle of Bull Run, routinely passed as a man, sometimes white and sometimes black, in order to gather information behind Confederate lines.[87]

In many ways the symbol of this new female public activism was the young and astonishing Anna Dickinson. She liked to say, "The world belongs to those who take it," and she seized hold of it with fervor. Dickinson became a prominent abolitionist with the publication of an essay in *The Liberator* in 1856, when she was fourteen years old. She quickly became one of the most famous orators of her day, traveling the country during the war to bolster morale and win support for abolition and full equality for all Americans. The Lincoln administration called on her services to encourage women to volunteer, explain the government's policies, and recruit soldiers. She proved particularly effective in inspiring immigrants to enlist, linking their humanity with that of the four million slaves in the South, making their cause the same battle for equality. The editor of the Hartford *Press*, Charles Dudley Warner, praised Dickinson as the most brilliant woman in America, "sent as from on high to save the state." She was repeatedly compared to Joan of Arc, rallying the people to retake their country from a corrupt elite.[88]

Speaking to wounded soldiers in military hospitals, Dickinson came to see the war in human as well as moral terms, calling on the nation to strive for both victory and humanity. During the 1862 election, Republican leaders credited her speeches with winning over thousands of voters; they even urged their fellow Republicans to not attend her packed speeches in order to make more room for Democrats. As she called not just for an end to slavery but also for the enlistment of black troops, she made the case that the Union was fighting for a new constitution that would enshrine "justice and equality [for] every citizen." For Dickinson, equality was simpler as well as just. "We desire nothing but one common law" that would treat all Americans equally, she said. Hers may have been the first truly influential woman's voice in American history.[89]

Following closely on the heels of the Grimké sisters and Harriet Beecher Stowe, Dickinson rose to become the most renowned woman of the Civil War period. But like every other prominent woman of the nineteenth century, she would eventually find her logic overcome by masculine emotion. In the years after the Civil War, the idea of gender equality met passionate resistance from the defenders of traditional patriarchy.

On April 2, 1865, Union forces marched into the Confederate capital. Among the first units to enter Richmond was the 28th Colored Infantry. Its chaplain, Garland H. White, had been born nearby, though as a boy he had been separated from his mother and sold to a plantation in distant Georgia. His regiment called upon him to speak, and he stepped before a large crowd that included Union soldiers and liberated slaves. He was astounded to find black and white soldiers cheering him loudly as he "proclaimed for the first time in that city freedom to all mankind." Afterward, a woman came up to him and asked where he had been born and if he knew his mother's name. After hearing his answer, the woman introduced herself as the mother he had not seen in two decades, years she had spent grieving the loss of her son. As the Confederacy fell into deserved ruin, freedom united families the slave owners had long divided.[90]

The African American reporter T. Morris Chester was also present at the fall of Richmond and wrote of the thousands of new "American citizens of African descent" who would now help rebuild the nation. He saw a resurgence of hope all around him as the blacks' "forgiving nature" allowed them to absolve the many wrongs they had suffered and work with whites for a more liberal nation: "What a wonderful change has come over the spirit of Southern dreams."[91]

Freedom meant many things to the former slaves. The emotion could be overwhelming, as a long-postponed fantasy became a stunning reality. In Kentucky, Matilda Dunbar, mother of the poet Paul Dunbar, remembered the day she heard of slavery's end. She had been making breakfast. "I never finished that breakfast! I ran 'round and 'round the kitchen, hitting my head against the wall, clapping my hands and crying, 'Freedom! freedom! freedom! Rejoice, freedom has come!' . . . Oh, how we sang and shouted that day!"[92]

For the first time in American history, white people treated black people with true respect. Decades later Eliza Sparks of Virginia recalled her first encounter with Union soldiers. After giving directions to the soldiers, one of them gave her a coin for her son and said, "'Goodbye, Mrs. Sparks.' Now, what you think of dat? Dey all call me 'Mrs. Sparks.'" After a lifetime of slavery, it was the first time she had been so addressed, and she understood immediately that the promise of freedom carried with it respect.[93]

For thousands, freedom meant trying to bring families shattered by slavery back together. Newspapers filled with advertisements by freed slaves requesting information on the location of parents and children who had been sold away. These advertisements told brief, heartbreaking stories of the cruelty of an economic system that thought nothing of the most basic tenets of humanity. Other slaves responded by finally being able to speak freely. Upon hearing the news of Lee's surrender at Appomattox, a slave named Caddie in Goodman, Mississippi, threw down her hoe and reacted to an order from her "mistress" by lifting up the back of her dress and shouting, "Kiss my ass!"[94]

As the United States began the struggle to rebuild, many Americans discovered that they finally grasped what the Declaration of Independence had so hopefully set forth as theory: that all people are created equal. Among those whose views had changed with the war was Abraham Lincoln. As he walked through the streets of Richmond on April 4, an elderly black man, with tears falling from his eyes, removed his hat and bowed, calling on God to bless Lincoln. With great solemnity, the president of the United States removed his own hat and bowed to this former slave. A reporter who was present expressed the shock of many in seeing Lincoln "upset the forms, laws, customs, and ceremonies of centuries," inflicting "a mortal wound to caste."[95]

Calling a black woman "Mrs.," doffing a hat to an elderly black man, thanking a black soldier for his service—these may strike us as minor events. But in small gestures great revolutions reside.

America bore witness to equality, and Lincoln bore the cost. In Lincoln's last speech, delivered to a crowd gathered at the White House on April 11, he hoped that black soldiers and educated blacks might soon gain the vote. Lincoln always saw politics as a form of education, a series of compromises leading slowly toward a desired end. A second-rate actor named John Wilkes Booth standing in that crowd had no patience for dreams of progress. "That means nigger citizenship," he venomously told a friend. He then added, "That is the last speech he will ever make." Three days later Booth shot and killed the president.[96]

The war served its purposes. Slavery, Frederick Douglass observed, would have persisted into the twentieth century had Union armies not killed it. But the war did more than preserve the Union and end slavery; it taught a generation of African Americans that they deserved respect and equality. "Once let the black man get upon his person the brass letters U.S.," Douglass wrote, "let him get an eagle on his button, and a musket on his shoulder, and bullets in his pocket; and there is no power on the earth or under the earth, which can deny that he has earned the right of citizenship in the United States."[97]

Military service gave tens of thousands of blacks a sense of worth that the slave republic had long denied them. Even those who did not serve saw black Union soldiers carrying aloft the banner of their humanity. Now came the difficult tasks of translating these victories into constitutional reality. In this new struggle, the American people would, for the first time, take seriously the concept of equality.

CHAPTER 4

Fixing the Constitution

Or, the elusive nature of
"We the People"

In his debates with Stephen Douglas in 1858, Abraham Lincoln had observed the power of public sentiment in controlling the expansion of slavery: "With public sentiment, nothing can fail: without it, nothing can succeed." Lincoln's words capture the importance of sentiment, of feeling, in American politics. He understood that it wasn't reasoned discourse but passionate engagement that changed people's minds.[1]

In this light, the Democratic Party's effort to deny the humanity of blacks was directly aimed at preparing the American people for the expansion of slavery. The Republican Party, on the other hand, hoped to humanize the slaves and thereby encourage people to question whether human bondage was appropriate in a land where "all men are created equal."

Why did the service of tens of thousands of African Americans in the Civil War matter? Those legions of black soldiers, of slaves who refused to work for the Confederacy, who rushed to aid the Union in any way they could, shattered the central myths of the slave owners' ideology. White Americans saw the truth of the sadistic and rapacious brutality of slavery. They saw the truth of the resilience, resolve, piety, and courage of these wronged people. They saw the truth of the *humanity* of black Americans. The Civil War witnessed the transformation of blacks from slaves to people—people willing to forgive, desperate to learn and to raise their families in peace, and proud to be Americans despite their horrific treatment. With time, many American whites would forget this past. But for a brief period, everything changed, and

Americans demanded the restructuring of their nation along the lines of their professed ideals of liberty and equality.

The Civil War devastated the United States. Modern research places the total number of deaths at more than 750,000. As with so many fatality statistics, it is difficult to grasp the reality of the loss—each one of those deaths represents a family shattered, a loved one lost, possibilities destroyed. Near the war's end, one Union soldier wrote of coming upon the corpses of fifteen Confederate soldiers. Though they had been enemies, Rice Bull could not help thinking "of the sorrow and grief there would be in fifteen homes somewhere; for what had these young lives been sacrificed?"[2]

Thousands of veterans returned home without a limb, addicted to laudanum, haunted by their experiences of war, suffering in ways that would not be diagnosed as PTSD for more than a century. Large sections of the southern part of the country lay in ruins, with abandoned fields and devastated infrastructure. While the North had leapt forward into the industrial revolution, the southern economy faced an uncertain future. The effects of the war would last through the lifetimes of the survivors. Twenty years later, Oliver Wendell Holmes Jr. would write of the dead returning to live with the veterans, haunting their thoughts and dreams: "I see them now, more than I can number, as once I saw them on earth."[3]

Americans, in public and private, expressed relief that the slaughter had ended. Millions of people, especially the nation's African Americans, celebrated the war's outcome. But a dangerously large proportion of the white southern population responded to the war's end with rage and an absolute refusal to take responsibility for the destruction they had brought upon their country.

It is difficult to capture public opinion in the nineteenth century, especially as the majority of people were expected to remain silent. Generalizations about popular sentiment must be taken with a degree of skepticism, as the nation remained deeply divided in the aftermath of a bloody civil war. That division ran not just along the Mason-Dixon

Line but also between genders, races, ethnicities, classes, and ideologies. We must look to what sentiments were spoken, printed, applauded, and circulated, making a best effort to determine the scope and extent of the intended audience. The opinions of native-born white males dominated the press and political discourse, but we do have a number of windows onto the opinions of many marginalized groups.

A debate over the war's meaning began almost as soon as the guns ceased firing. Not surprisingly in the aftermath of a civil war, the nation remained deeply polarized. A surprising number of people, even in the North, wanted to return to the way the world had been prior to the war, just without the legal status of slave, while many other Americans insisted that there was no going back and the country would be best served by celebrating change. The loss of hundreds of thousands of lives had to have some long-term meaning; the deaths of so many must mark some fundamental transformation in American life. As the young Minnesota congressman Ignatius Donnelly asked: "Shall nothing be born of this mighty convulsion, mightier by far than the old Revolution, mightier than all the revolutions of the world?" He insisted that it must be so, that the Constitution itself must be rewritten in light of all they had recently learned. For this generation, the essential question must be to determine if Lincoln had been right in the Gettysburg Address that the war marked a "new birth of freedom." They had no real choice but to accept the need for systemic change, as the Civil War would leave its imprint "upon our Government and laws so long as the nation continues to exist."[4]

Clearly attitudes had changed. In 1860, four presidential candidates won votes in the Electoral College, and not one of them spoke in favor of human equality. Yet just eight years later Congress passed and the states ratified the Fourteenth Amendment, enshrining legal equality in the Constitution. By every measure available, the majority of Americans had a positive opinion of equality—at least in theory. It was certainly the case that every previously excluded group hoped that the war's end would bring them into the national polity.

However, these calls for equality were often limited in scope and occasionally self-serving. For instance, immigrants certainly wanted legal equality for themselves, but many also sought to deny it to others, as did many Irish in leading the effort to exclude the Chinese. This one-sided demand for equality proved counterproductive, leading many progressives, including the prominent cartoonist Thomas Nast, to reject the Irish as unqualified for the status of American citizen. Similarly, many black men battling for equality saw no reason to extend civil rights to women, and many white women, even leaders of the suffrage movement, denied that blacks deserved equality. So long as those fighting for equality would not take the final step of demanding equality for all, the champions of inequality could easily divide and conquer progressives.

When word arrived that Lee had surrendered at Appomattox, General Joshua Chamberlain ordered his troops to cease firing and halt their advance. But Chamberlain saw that after four "crimsoned years" of war, no one could stop their advance. Speaking metaphorically, he described his troops as always moving forward, "forward to the new beginning; forward to the Nation's second birth!" Union soldiers who had fought in the bloodiest battles of the century and who had lost so many comrades would not easily give up the goals that had become associated with the war. Most shared a vision akin to Chamberlain's, that the United States must advance.[5]

Black Americans also felt certain that the United States was in the midst of becoming a new, free nation. Most histories highlight the contest over the legal status of black Americans in the Reconstruction period, running from 1865 through 1877. That perspective is certainly understandable given the need of the legal system to adjust to the presence of four million former slaves. All those slave codes regulating the lives of African Americans now joined the scrap heap of history. The largest question facing the country could be framed as a simple dichotomy: are Americans to be treated as individuals sharing the same rights or as members of groups who are treated distinctly under the law?

A feeling spread that the issue had been largely resolved by the war and that now only congressional action was required to fix these dramatic changes into law. As Robert B. Elliott, the first black commander of the South Carolina militia and a member of Congress, stated, "Equality before the law is now the broad, universal, glorious rule and mandate of the Republic." He confidently expected that no state could violate this new standard and that the United States could truly claim the mantle of democracy. The presence of so many allies in Congress reinforced that confidence.[6]

This hope did not indicate naivety. After all, the Union had just won a bitter civil war, the president had been assassinated by a Confederate sympathizer, vast amounts of treasure had been expended, and thousands had died because some powerful slave owners refused to limit the expansion of their racist institutions and play by the country's political rules. Surely the vast majority of Americans would not forget nor abandon those who had proved their loyalty at every critical turn. The joy African Americans felt over the end of slavery gave them confidence that the United States would make good on its democratic promise.

Establishing democracy meant more than tearing down racial barriers. It is worth remembering that half of the roughly thirty-five million Americans in 1865 were women. As historian Elaine Showalter wrote, the Civil War "created a crisis in gender, turning the world upside down for the sexes as well as for the races." The war brought women into the public sphere, and a great many liked it there. Thousands of women, especially in the North, finally found their work valued and their personal worth validated. The war made clear numerous contradictions in American society, including the ambiguous position of women. The government needed their help in this titanic struggle, and women volunteered in great numbers.[7]

The young writer Louisa May Alcott summarized the attitude of many women during the war: "I long to be a man; but as I can't fight, I will content myself with working for those who can." She volunteered as a nurse, almost died of typhus, and gained national recognition with her book *Hospital Sketches*. After that experience, Alcott showed no interest in behaving according to earlier standards and sinking into domestic obscurity. Instead, she remained a public figure, gained further fame as an author, and never married. Her appropriately titled novel *Work* ends with its protagonist becoming a feminist leader after years of toil. The women's rights movement allows her to join "a loving league of sisters, old and young, black and white, rich and poor," all working toward legal equality for women. The war gave women opportunities never before available to them and left many with a desire for more. Alcott encapsulated the hope of most marginalized Americans in the opening lines of a novel she wrote in 1866: "I often feel as if I'd gladly sell my soul to Satan for a year of freedom." [8]

Another indication of shifting popular attitudes toward social traditions can be found in the popular play *The Spirit of Seventy-Six*, which bore the subtitle *The Coming Woman*. First performed in Boston in 1866 and published in twenty-three editions over the next two decades, *The Spirit of Seventy-Six* imagined an American man returning to the United States in 1876 after ten years in China. He finds that women have gained the vote and are no longer willing to play the role of amusing trifle for the entertainment of men. The modern, political woman is able, forthright, and self-confident. The pace of change appeared so rapid in the aftermath of the Civil War that the authors imagined the final barriers to full equality collapsing within a decade. [9]

A few years later Elizabeth Stuart Phelps, a prolific author and radical reformer who urged women to burn their corsets, wrote a controversial essay, "The True Woman." Phelps insisted that "the earth has never seen" a true woman, as society kept women subservient, silent, and stupid. Only when women enjoyed all the rights of citizenship could they fully be themselves. Phelps insisted that women should stop waiting for men to recognize their humanity and instead should claim their rights. [10]

Nearly every prominent woman in the United States saw the promise of equality arising before them. Harriet Beecher Stowe, who had done so much to change northern opinion toward slavery with her book

Uncle Tom's Cabin, thought that women's time had come. In defeating slavery, "the only obstacle to the success of our great democratic experiment is overthrown," and now "this question of Woman and her Sphere" nears resolution. The women's rights movement was the obvious next step on humanity's progressive path forward. Similarly, Julia Ward Howe, whose "The Battle Hymn of the Republic" inspired soldiers and civilians alike, felt the war had changed everything for women. For most of her life she accepted "the masculine idea of character as the only true one." No woman could attain self-respect if constantly reminded of her inferiority to men. Now was the time for "true womanhood," for women to act as "a free agent, fully sharing with man every human right and human responsibility." The realization that women could be the equal of men was like discovering a new continent, it opened a world of possibilities.[11]

Many other authors weighed in, questioning and mocking the patriarchy and the notion that only motherhood defined women. Marietta Holley, often labeled a female Mark Twain, took a comedic tone, suggesting that many married women looked forward to becoming widows so that they could finally enjoy some alone time. Lillie Devereux Blake shocked contemporaries with her tale of a female cross-dresser. As the title of her 1872 novel, *Fettered for Life*, suggested, Blake saw women as unable to advance in their chosen fields and interests because of male biases. To succeed they must either disguise themselves as men or fight for equality. Her efforts to get women admitted to Columbia College in New York led to the founding of Barnard College.[12]

In many ways, Victoria Woodhull surpassed fictional heroines. One of the ablest and most dazzling personalities of her time, Woodhull ran for president in 1872, asking why a woman shouldn't have the same political rights as men and why a woman couldn't be president. The only thing standing in the way was thousands of years of misogyny. She saw the culture shock of post–Civil War America as "an epoch of sudden changes and startling surprises." What appeared ridiculous to the public at one moment may become acceptable common sense in the next. Writing in 1870, Woodhull noted, "The blacks were cattle in 1860; a Negro now sits in Jeff Davis' seat in the United States Senate." With an additional ten years, a woman could be in the White House.[13]

The point here is that with the war's end, expectations ran high for a reformed democratic society. While Confederate die-hards and racist northern Democrats continued battling every hint of change, there is ample evidence that most Americans looked forward to a more inclusive society. Keeping in mind that women could still not vote, the best evidence of the direction of public opinion after the Civil War is appropriately found in election returns. In the North, majorities continued to support the Republican Party, which pushed for legal equality in every election in the Reconstruction period. Even more notable is the fact that during this period of mostly free elections in the South, the champions of equality won majorities. Returns indicate that a sizable minority of southern white male voters stood with the freedmen. It is extremely unlikely that these candidates, North and South, would have won election had not a majority of the male population shared their views on legal equality.

If equality is a self-evident truth, then those who opposed this trend acted in defense of ignorance. As we shall see, those defending inequality used every weapon available to them. By 1870, reactionaries responded with alarm to reports that in the public schools girls were outperforming boys in every academic category. Additionally, women quickly came to dominate teaching in primary and even secondary education. In the face of this gender crisis, many male commentators warned of the emasculation of American boys, while leading doctors proclaimed that higher education posed medical risks to women, as it caused blood to flow to the brain instead of the ovaries, where it belonged. The war to limit the political participation of black Americans would also rely on pseudo-science. But when it came right down to it, the defenders of bigotry and willful ignorance would return again to their most effective weapons: intimidation and violence. The truth of equality would not be eliminated, but it would be denied and deferred for several generations.

One of the first indicators of a major sea change in the attitudes of white Americans toward equality came in the four border states. The Democratic political leadership of these states had rejected every compromise on slavery right up to Lincoln's 1862 offer to buy the freedom of all the slaves in those four states. Lincoln did the math and found that buying those thousands of slaves would cost the equivalent of eighty-seven days of war expenditures. Since Lincoln vowed not to touch slavery where it existed, it seemed that the country was stuck with slavery.[14]

Then came the 1863 elections. Republicans won majorities in the historically Democratic states of Kentucky, Maryland, and Delaware, while Missouri sent the abolitionist Benjamin Gratz Brown to the Senate. The following year, radical Republicans—ardent opponents of slavery—swept the Missouri state elections, with Colonel Thomas C. Fletcher, a brigade commander under William Sherman, winning election as governor. Delegates at a special constitutional convention in January 1865 voted 60 to 4 to end slavery without compensation. The margin of victory in the referendum on the new constitution came from those serving in the Union Army, who, now able to cast ballots while in service, voted overwhelmingly for ending slavery. The new Maryland constitution also outlawed slavery without compensation, winning victory because Maryland's Union troops voted ten to one in favor of this fundamental change. Repeatedly, Union soldiers proved themselves advocates for emancipation.[15]

The prospect of all those returning veterans, who would show little interest in a political party that persisted in endorsing slavery, sobered the Democratic Party. Recognizing this reality, many northern Democratic leaders moved to abandon the party's long-standing support of slavery. A meeting of Cleveland's Germans expressed the direction of northern opinion with perfect clarity, calling for "a revision of the Constitution in the spirit of the Declaration of Independence," for the latter's "proclamation of equal human rights . . . [is] the only true fundamental law of republican life." Public pressure to repair the Constitution increased through 1864 and 1865, based on the conviction that the Civil War must have been fought for some higher purpose. That need for meaning spelled the end of slavery.[16]

The first efforts to end slavery by altering the Constitution came in 1863. In January, Senator Charles Sumner drafted an amendment making all people "equal before the law," but, certain of defeat, he did not submit it. The first two abolition amendments brought before Congress came from Representatives James F. Wilson of Iowa and James M. Ashley of Ohio in December 1863. Both men had been abolitionists active in the founding of the Republican Party, and both their proposals included enforcement mechanisms granting Congress and the federal courts the power to intervene in protecting the civil rights of freed slaves. These passages vanished by the time the final version of the Thirteenth Amendment came to a vote, leaving the future rights of the freed blacks uncertain and unprotected. In January 1864, Missouri senator John Henderson, a Democrat and former slave owner, proposed an emancipation amendment that avoided any reference to enforcement or rights, simply stating that "slavery or involuntary servitude, except as a punishment for crime, shall not exist in the United States." This formulation served as the basis for the wording of the Thirteenth Amendment.[17]

The debate over the Thirteenth Amendment did not simply fall between those favoring slavery and those opposing its end, and the final version, like most amendments crafted after the Bill of Rights, could not claim a single author. A larger struggle over the wording of the amendment divided Republicans: would it merely end slavery, a position favored by Senator Lyman Trumbull of Illinois, or would it include an enforcement mechanism, as promoted by Representative Ashley, or would it offer some guarantee of legal equality, as proposed by Senator Sumner?

Sumner had been an advocate of true legal equality since at least 1849, when he argued against school segregation in *Roberts v. City of Boston*, warning that racism created a caste system in the North as much as in the South. Though Sumner lost the case, his influence within Massachusetts grew, leading to his election to the U.S. Senate in 1850. Despite the *Roberts* decision allowing racial division, the Massachusetts legislature ended educational segregation in 1855. Trumbull, an opponent of slavery since adolescence, had defended without charge blacks held in slavery in Illinois in defiance of the state's constitutional guarantee of full freedom. In 1845 he won a pivotal case before the Illinois Supreme Court establishing that the Northwest Ordinance of 1787 had freed all slaves and their descendants. As a member of Congress during the war, Trumbull thought Lincoln moved too slowly in ending slavery, and he helped draft the two Confiscation Acts that opened the door to emancipation. However, he did not want to enter into the more controversial subject of legal equality.

The first step in the constitutional battle emerged over which committee would draft the amendment, Sumner's new committee on slavery and freedmen or Trumbull's Judiciary Committee. The latter won, largely because the Senate leadership had grown weary of the former. Trumbull and Jacob M. Howard of Michigan crafted an amendment eschewing any declaration of equal rights and offering only a vague enforcement clause: "Congress shall have power to enforce this article by appropriate legislation." The Judiciary Committee hoped using the language of the Northwest Ordinance of 1787 would appeal to anti-slavery Democrats. They also sought to avoid the appearance of radicalism by rejecting Sumner's language, which carried the potential for gender equality—then the ultimate horror for so many men, regardless of party. Maine senator William P. Fessenden literally silenced Sumner by simply asking him if his logic would lead to the enfranchisement of women. Two years later, Trumbull and Howard both insisted they intended the amendment to protect the civil rights of the former slaves, but they certainly chose the least effective language possible to attain that end.[18]

Despite the drafter's caution, the amendment stalled in the House. An early procedural vote indicated support for the amendment by a majority of 78 to 62—far short of the two-thirds required for passage. At this point, even the Republican-leaning *New York Times* opposed the amendment as handing the Democrats a weapon to use in the upcoming election.[19]

As it developed, politics played a vital and often ironic role in congressional approval of the Thirteenth Amendment. The first Democratic congressional defection to the amendment came in February 1864 from New York representative James Brooks, a Copperhead or "peace Democrat," who had long pushed for a negotiated settlement with the Confederacy. Horrified Democrats had his speech removed from the congressional record to create a façade of unified opposition to the amendment. This front collapsed the following month, when New York's Tammany Hall declared that slavery was no longer an issue that should concern the Democratic Party. Tammany, the most powerful Democratic Party organization in the North, thus provided cover for northern Democrats who abandoned their long-standing defense of the South and slavery, even if they did not come out in support of the Thirteenth Amendment.[20]

Some Democrats saw political advantage in supporting the amendment. Because Lincoln hesitated to support it, many Democrats could get in front of the issue and retain support in local elections, finding an easy vehicle to demonstrate their loyalty to the Union despite having a long history of siding with the slave-owning South prior to the war. They also saw support for a constitutional amendment as a way to attack the Emancipation Proclamation as an unconstitutional exercise of executive power. James Gordon Bennett, the powerful editor of the *New York Herald*, took this latter line in supporting the amendment, while also arguing that it would finally settle "this troublesome question of slavery by removing the institution from the country." The Democratic *New York World* simply pretended that the party had always been anti-slavery and urged support for the amendment as a way of proving that stance.[21]

Given this swelling tide of Democratic support for emancipation, many Republicans urged Lincoln to act with greater rapidity to prevent the other party from claiming credit. But the president would not be rushed. Lincoln read the political situation well: his was a well-organized party, while the divided Democrats lacked effective leadership and remained racist to the core. Barely any of them could open their mouths on any issue approaching slavery without saying something appallingly racist. The *Cincinnati Enquirer* expressed the general Democratic attitude in dismissively assuring its readers that freedom for the slaves would lead to little more than their "starving, dying and rotting by thousands." The inept Democratic Party main office in New York even continued to distribute pro-slavery pamphlets.[22]

As the battle over the Thirteenth Amendment heated up in Congress, African Americans energetically entered the debate. They organized petition drives, held rallies, called on members of Congress, and visited President Lincoln. Blacks demanded not just an end to slavery but also legal equality, universal suffrage, and economic justice through restitution—most particularly with land for the freed slaves. Understanding the limitations of abolition alone, they uniformly demanded the right to vote as essential for the attainment of true equality and as the only way to avoid a new form of enslavement as second-class citizens. In 1864, two leaders of the New Orleans black community, Arnold Bertonneau and Jean-Baptiste Roudanez, toured northern cities to speak on behalf of full suffrage rights, meeting with Lincoln and presenting a petition with one thousand signatures. Impressed, Lincoln wrote Louisiana's radical new governor, Michael Hahn, recommending that black veterans and "the very intelligent" be granted the vote. Hahn dismissed the president's suggestion as too limited.[23]

Republicans did their best to avoid public discussions of black suffrage, fearing a racist backlash in the North. Rather than addressing inconsistencies around legal equality in both North and South, they focused solely on ending slavery. Following Lincoln's lead, Republicans did little to push the amendment through Congress in 1864. But they did use it to unify the party for the upcoming election, putting Democrats in the awkward position of either siding with the Republicans or continuing to support slavery in the midst of war. In the election, many successful Republicans argued in favor of abolishing slavery but against equality. Thus Wisconsin senator Timothy Howe agreed with the Democrats on black inferiority but questioned whether this was "a fact which authorizes you or me to enslave them."[24]

Democratic responses tended to be sarcastic or silly. For example, Kentucky senator Garrett Davis insisted that New England abolitionists caused the war, and therefore he proposed an amendment to combine the six New England states into one so as to reduce their political power. In contrast, Maryland's revered Democratic senator Reverdy Johnson, a former attorney general who had argued against Dred Scott before the Supreme Court, caught national attention by stating that only changing the Constitution could preserve the Union. "A prosperous and permanent peace," he told the Senate, "can never be secured if the institution [of slavery] is permitted to survive." Even more dangerous than slavery was the core Democratic Party belief in states' rights superseding federal power, which Johnson dismissed contemptuously by saying, "There never was a greater political heresy." Reminding the Senate chamber of the preamble of the Constitution, Johnson insisted that the Framers put the peace and tranquility of the nation above any imagined right to property in persons. For Johnson, the proposed amendment was an obvious solution to the great constitutional crisis that had so long divided the nation.[25]

Johnson's speech created a sensation, laying the groundwork for many other Democrats to move away from their stubborn refusal to amend the Constitution. Two days later, Missouri Democratic senator John Henderson announced his support for the amendment. Slavery had caused the Civil War, he told the Senate, and added, "Shall we then leave slavery to fester again in the public vitals?" Amending the Constitution, he observed, would save not only the nation but also the Democratic Party.[26]

Many Democrats responded to Johnson's and Henderson's apostasy with traditional white supremacist logic. "This Government was made by white men and for white men," said Senator Lazarus Powell of Kentucky, and white men must preserve it by rejecting anything that threatened white power.[27]

Since the founding of the Republican Party in 1854, Democrats responded to every proposal of the new party by evoking the specter of interracial sex. Whether the issue was the Homestead Act or a national railroad, the Democrats saw a sexualized social equality behind every Republican policy. From the perspective of the twenty-first century, it is difficult to understand the obsession with interracial sex, yet so great was the commitment of nineteenth-century racists to their conception of whiteness that metaphorical images of the skin's darkening over generations sent them into hysteria. Faced with the abolition of the bulwark against equality, the Democrats repeated all the old pro-slavery arguments, from the will of God to saving blacks from their own inferiority. Emancipation would lead to miscegenation and the end of the white race.[28]

The New York *World*'s editor, David Croly, and one of his reporters, George Wakeman, invented the term "miscegenation" in the midst of the 1864 election. They wrote a pamphlet purporting to be by abolitionists promoting interracial sex. Croly gave a copy to Democratic leader Samuel Cox of Ohio, who railed against it in the House as though it accurately reflected Republican policy. His racist rant led to "Cox's commandment": "Thou shalt not degrade the white race by such intermixtures as emancipation will bring." Frenzied Democrats made up stories of white abolitionist schoolteachers giving birth to mixed-race babies, using the fraudulent pamphlet as proof of a Republican plan to mix the races.[29]

Democrats also relied on pseudo-science to justify their most bizarre statements. California senator James McDougall reminded his learned colleagues that science proved racial differences, and "it is a fact established by science" that the more the two races mixed, the less able they were to reproduce, until finally among "octoroons reproduction is impossible." For Delaware's James Bayard, history proved that when two races lived together, "there is but one of two results—the subjection of the inferior race or its extermination." As a kindhearted man, Bayard did "not desire the extermination of the negro race," so they must be kept as slaves for their own good. Facing an amendment to the Constitution ending slavery, the Democrats turned apocalyptic: the very future of the United States as a nation hinged on keeping slavery alive.[30]

In addition to racism, Democrats trotted out the zany argument that the Constitution and its first twelve amendments had already attained perfection. Using this conception as their baseline, some Democrats wove a convoluted argument by which the proposed Thirteenth Amendment was itself unconstitutional since it would terminate slavery, an institution protected by the Framers in the Constitution. Rejecting the Framers' original position on amendments, these Democrats constructed a constitution impervious to change; no correction of error was allowable. As Kentucky senator Garrett Davis fearfully framed the issue, once they started amending the Constitution, Congress would start a process of "destroying and revolutionizing the whole Government." Davis did undermine his argument a bit by complaining that Congress proposed to take away the property of "a great number of people more loyal than themselves, more true to their Government, more true to the true principles of the Constitution," without any compensation. Trying to convince Congress that those who rebelled against the United States were truer to its principles than those who fought to defend the Union was neither popular nor effective.[31]

The Civil War rendered it obvious that the Framers had made mistakes and that the Constitution needed further work. After seventy years of veneration, this mature perspective indicated a sea change in historical understanding: Americans no longer perceived the Constitution as sacred, having come to see it as a human document. The realities of that experience won over many Democrats. In the midst of these debates, Pennsylvania's Democratic representative Alexander Coffroth admitted he now understood that "it never was intended by the wise men who adopted the Constitution that it should remain unchanged." It was an indisputable fact that times change and the nation's "progress and its advancement will, as time passes, demand new articles and additional provisions." [32]

Proponents of the Thirteenth Amendment put forth a new conception of the Constitution as a living document, one able to change with the times. Prior to the Civil War, even the most ardent critics of slavery perceived the Constitution as a dead letter; they were stuck with it and had no hope of changing it. Anti-slavery forces generally saw the Constitution as either, in William Lloyd Garrison's famous formulation, "a covenant with death" or as a document guided by the light of freedom but marred by necessary compromises. Garrison took the uncomfortable stance of condemning—and even publicly burning—a revered American icon, and his interpretation was thus of limited political utility. The leadership of the new Republican Party assumed that the Framers meant for slavery to die out someday, and until then slavery must be protected in the states but prohibited from the territories. The Thirteenth Amendment moved far from this prewar stance, promising to become the first part of the Constitution to protect Americans from their fellow citizens rather than from the government. It established a right to not be enslaved, a significant limitation on the exploitation of one person by another.

In the midst of the war, several leading intellectuals reformulated the popular perception of the Constitution into that of a document open to change. The Irish immigrant E. L. Godkin, founding editor of *The Nation*, laid out the case in his influential 1864 article "The Constitution, and Its Defects." Godkin dissected the American veneration of the Constitution as a form of irrational idolatry bordering on mass hallucination. In making the Constitution sacred, Americans abandoned both history—failing to appreciate that the Framers themselves perceived numerous flaws in this product of bitter compromises—and morality. Godkin credited the secessionists with opening the public's eyes to the Constitution's flaws. "The spell has been broken by the war," Godkin wrote, introducing the Constitution to criticism and proposals for its alteration. Now the time had come to match the Constitution with "a recognition of the great truth,—not that men are literally born equal, that is, with equal capabilities and advantages,—but that they are born with equal right to turn such faculties as God has pleased to give them to the best account." Anything less than that left the Constitution a mockery of democracy and a tool for tyrants.[33]

Godkin's article impressed the prominent abolitionist Gerrit Smith, who initially opposed the Thirteenth Amendment for acknowledging the pro-slavery nature of the Constitution. Godkin taught him to see a "literal" Constitution and a "historical" one. Smith quoted Judge Joseph Story: "Nothing but the text itself was adopted by the people," and that text began with the promise to "secure the blessings of liberty." Thus the literal Constitution was anti-slavery, but the Slave Power had crafted a "cunning and wicked substitution" that had replaced the original. It is not enough to point out the historical alteration of the original social compact; the good citizen enters the stream of history and helps transform the Constitution to be true to its original intent of respecting human rights. Smith's reading of the Constitution pointed forward rather than back, offering a practical formulation of a living Constitution. To ensure that it would never again be made "the servant of wickedness," the Constitution must be amended to secure equal rights before the law.[34]

Republican lawyers and politicians crafted a compelling intellectual case for the living Constitution, but the most powerful support for this reading of the document was the Civil War. As the war proceeded, ever more Americans recognized, as Godkin suggested, the inherent defect of the Constitution in not identifying who is included under the preamble's rubric of "We the People." Those arguing that the Constitution should not be altered beyond the original intent of the founders—

a position that clearly served the interests of the slave owners—battled against the tide of change unleashed by the war. By the end of 1864 few people outside the Confederacy felt that original intent offered a relevant block to amendment.

The living Constitution argument carried great weight with a public confronting the bloodiest war in American history. Even a few leading Democrats recognized the attraction of this new vision. Based on his careful studies, Democratic senator Reverdy Johnson agreed with the Republicans that the Framers of the Constitution had hoped to see slavery abolished someday. The Thirteenth Amendment therefore fulfilled the Framers' wishes and brought their work back to life. Senator Henderson also returned to the sources, observing that the Framers originally intended the people to make use of the amendment process to effect necessary change. The power of amendment existed so that the people may build on experience and correct errors. No honest person could deny that mistakes had been made; the war put an end to the perfection argument. Fortunately, the Framers had given the people the power to amend; amendments became the law of the land and thus "the safety-valve of our institutions."[35]

By the start of 1865 a sufficient number of Democrats had been moved by the force of events, popular sentiment, and the study of history to accept the Republican interpretation of a living Constitution. Senator Charles Sumner put forth a simple and clear summary of that emerging consensus. The proposed amendment, he maintained, "will give completeness and permanence to emancipation, and bring the Constitution into avowed harmony with the Declaration of Independence."[36]

There was no equality in the visitors' galleries, which were separated by gender, as the Senate considered the proposed Thirteenth Amendment. The women's section of the visitors' gallery on April 8, 1864, overflowed with key figures in the women's petition campaign that had done so much to push forth the amendment.

As the vote approached, Senator McDougall felt called upon to rise and warn that freedom would destroy the black race, much as Native Americans had previously been wiped out. He did not specify what exactly would destroy the blacks but suggested that Congress might as well throw them in the Potomac to drown, for all the good freedom would do them. McDougall's last-minute protest was ignored and the vote proceeded without further comment, passing 38 to 6, garnering eight more votes than the two-thirds required.

As cheers filled the Senate chamber, Delaware's Willard Saulsbury, who had cast one of the votes against the amendment, cried out, "I now bid farewell to any hope of the reconstruction of the American Union." McDougall laid the basis for future criticism of the amendment by objecting that the vote did not include all the states—referring to the Confederate states. Vice President Hannibal Hamlin dismissed this objection by noting that it was more than two-thirds of those present.[37]

Senators voting for the Thirteenth Amendment did so for a variety of reasons. Most understood that the amendment alone would not resolve key legal issues, such as how to free the slaves, or what the legal status of the freed slaves might be, or the process by which the amendment would become part of the Constitution, or whether the seceded southern states would be included in the ratification process. Having voted for the amendment, the Senate passed it on to the House of Representatives, whose entire membership faced reelection in November.

The House took up the amendment in mid-June 1864. Thomas Shannon of California argued for ratification as the surest way to destroy the cause of the Civil War, slavery. For too long the nation had given in to the desires of the slave owners, calling every concession "compromise." The Slave Power had used and abused the Constitution to enhance its control at both the state and federal levels. Now the majority of Americans could repair the Constitution and reclaim their country. To do otherwise would mean that their "terrible sacrifices" had served no higher purpose.[38]

Most Republicans repeated Shannon's argument. They hammered home that the Framers sought to promote freedom but had planted a flaw in the Constitution in allowing for the continuation of slavery; that the slave owners had abused that constitutional error to expand their power; that they had repeatedly bullied the nation into accepting slavery's expansion; that Congress could now correct the Framers' mistake; and that to do otherwise would mean that those scores of thousands of brave soldiers had died for no reason.[39]

House Democrats stuck to their traditional counterargument, that ending slavery would lead to racial equality, interracial sex, and then somehow the end of Western civilization. William Holman of Indiana went further, warning that the Republicans' "visionary fanaticism" would lead them to deploy federal troops to enforce social equality. Pennsylvania's Samuel J. Randall once more charged the Republicans with "endeavoring to make the African that which God did not intend—the physical, mental, and social equal of the white man." The best recourse was to acknowledge the different interests of the states and let them decide on slavery. Randall closed with a plea: "Let the Constitution alone. It is good enough."[40]

While hardly the most rousing battle cry, "good enough" appealed to many Democrats. Ignoring the still-raging war, New Hampshire's Daniel Marcy agreed that the Constitution worked just fine. His constituents held that "if there is sin in slavery, they would leave it wholly to the conscience of the southern people and to their God"; they did not care what became of the slaves. Marcy predicted that when the Republicans lost to "the conservative party" in November and the Democrats restored white government, they would have to satisfy their lust for "miscegenetic beatitude" by emigrating to Africa.

As often in American political history, the two competing sides repeated the same arguments. Every time Democrats accused Republicans of "miscegenetic" lust, the Republicans reminded them that southern rape culture led to miscegenation. As Illinois representative John

Farnsworth mockingly observed, "Some of the best blood of the Democracy of Virginia may be found in the contraband village at Arlington," home to hundreds of runaway slaves. At that point the supporters of slavery would insist upon the purity of southern white manhood and accuse the Republicans of projecting their sexual desire onto the noble cavaliers of the Confederacy. So the cyclical controversy continued.[41]

However, a new element had entered the debate. The long-standing pro-slavery argument weakened before a paradigm shift: respect for blacks, especially for black soldiers. A particularly dramatic example of these changing attitudes occurred on the House floor in June 1864. When a Democrat asked fellow representative John Farnsworth, a Union veteran, whether he thought whites and blacks equal, Farnsworth shot back, "That is a silly question." Farnsworth had served with blacks in combat and learned to throw aside racial stereotypes. He witnessed white troops cheering on black soldiers as they charged Confederate lines. "Upon every battle-field where the black troops have had any chance to show their gallantry and bravery," he pointed out, "they have vindicated the high estimation which has been placed upon them." Serving together, Union forces had come to rely on one another, regardless of color. Mentioning a black spy who had repeatedly crossed enemy lines with valuable information, Farnsworth turned on the Democrats, charging them with wanting to return such a man to slavery rather than reward him for his heroism. "Was he not better entitled to respect from the white men of this nation than any man now in the rebel ranks?" Farnsworth made the leap from ending slavery to equal rights as the African Americans' due. The country must not just terminate the institution that had caused the war—and "no child is so simple as not to know that slavery is the cause of this war," in Farnsworth's words—but had to correct the Constitution and do what is right.[42]

That sense of justice—of moving beyond the correction of a constitutional error to awarding humanity and citizenship to those who had stood with the Union in its great crisis—motivated many Republicans.

The nation's political language changed as Americans spoke of the Constitution's flaws and of blacks with respect.

But the question of the exact meaning of equality remained contentious. Many Republicans followed Lincoln's early lead in framing equality in terms of the freedom to enjoy the fruits of one's labor—in other words, to hold a paying job. In the House, Ebon Ingersoll of Illinois drew upon a shared language in supporting the Thirteenth Amendment as securing the black man in "his natural and God-given rights . . . to till the soil, to earn his bread by the sweat of his brow, and enjoy the rewards of his own labor." William D. Kelley of Pennsylvania agreed that the Thirteenth Amendment sufficiently secured equality for blacks by protecting "the dignity of labor" and required no further legislative action. The Constitutional Convention had erred in making a compromise with evil, but this amendment would mend that rent in the Constitution. After this repair job, "I will trust the freed negroes to the care of God, under our beneficent republican institutions." This faith that the states would respect legal equality once slavery was abolished is almost touching.[43]

On June 15, 1864, the House voted for the Thirteenth Amendment 93 to 65, with 23 representatives not voting. No applause greeted the results, which fell thirteen votes short of the necessary two-thirds majority. Only 4 of the 72 Democrats voted for the amendment.

Faced with defeat, James Ashley, the amendment's sponsor, switched his vote to the negative. Through this clever parliamentary maneuver, Ashley allowed the House to reconsider the measure after the November election. The Republicans determined to kick the ball a little further down the road, in hopes that the voters would have the chance to weigh in and change the minds of a sufficient number of Democrats to pass the amendment.[44]

Lincoln gave cover to this postponement in a rambling letter to the Kentucky Unionist editor Albert G. Hodges. "I am naturally antislavery," the president assured Hodges. But he had taken an oath to defend the Constitution, which took precedent over his personal sense of morality. When General Frémont sought a "military emancipation" in the war's first year, Lincoln had countermanded the order as not guided by necessity. Lincoln relied on this standard of military necessity to preserve the Union when he had to decide upon appropriate actions; military necessity drove him to arm blacks and issue the Emancipation Proclamation. He confessed that he did not guide events so much as the war's course determined his actions. As president, he responded to the forces attempting to destroy the Union, and the war led the nation in unexpected directions. God alone could claim credit for what came next, and it now obviously appeared to be God's will that the nation align itself on the side of justice. In a rhetorical sleight of hand, Lincoln transferred responsibility for the expansion of human equality to God.[45]

While it is well and good to await God's further actions, the political parties followed their own agendas. At their national convention in Baltimore in June, the Republicans—temporarily labeled the National Union Party—called for a constitutional amendment ending slavery. However, the convention ignored the issue of equal rights. This was a good indicator of how the war had only partially radicalized the North, falling short of embracing equality.

To avoid frightening the racists in their midst, the convention rejected the application of a delegation from South Carolina that included four blacks among its sixteen members—and which would have been the first biracial representation from the South in any political group. Since the delegation included the heroic Robert Smalls, the convention chairman made the minor gesture of allowing the South Carolinians to attend as observers. Radical Republicans voiced their outrage, while the majority sighed with relief that they would not be accused of "race mixing."[46]

Momentum for the Thirteenth Amendment built through late 1864, as four more states joined in outlawing slavery—Maryland, Arkansas, Louisiana, and West Virginia. In early 1865 Missouri and Tennessee followed suit. Lincoln evidenced his own evolution on the issue. When asked if he would negotiate with the Confederacy, he responded that he would do so only if Jefferson Davis agreed to ending slavery and rejoining the Union. In accepting the Republican nomination for reelection as president, Lincoln endorsed the proposed amendment ending slavery as "a fitting, and necessary conclusion to the final success of the Union cause." Lincoln credited black soldiers for changing his mind, as they helped win the war. Though Lincoln did not publicly support the Thirteenth Amendment until seven months after its introduction, he, like so many Americans, confidently expected it to resolve the deep national division.[47]

Warning signs indicated that this effort to heal would itself cause further division, especially as many Americans recognized the futility of freedom without equality. In the war's last year, a growing movement toward legal equality spread throughout the North, much of it emerging from grassroots efforts by women, blacks, and white men inspired by what they saw as a war-spurred democratic renaissance. In October 1864, a convention of black leaders in Syracuse, New York, called for full equality before the law and for the right of black men to vote. Shortly thereafter, the Iowa legislature repealed laws forbidding the migration of blacks into their state; the legislatures of Illinois and Ohio passed similar acts in 1865. Major cities across the country desegregated streetcar systems and public schools in the name of legal equality. Women throughout the North launched major petition drives calling for an end to slavery and for universal citizenship rights. In this final year of military struggle, the more blacks and women participated in public life, the more acceptable that involvement became.[48]

The election of 1864 addressed more than the Thirteenth Amendment, most particularly the conduct of the war, but no one could doubt that the vote could lead to one of two different constitutional futures for America. Casting a ballot for a Democrat translated into a vote for the continuation of slavery, despite the persisting bloodshed of the Civil War. Many voters found that alone a compelling reason to reconsider traditional party loyalties. Once more the Democrats could respond with only a single argument, unleashing the full fury of a feared "race mixing." Pennsylvania Democrat Jeremiah Black charged Republicans with fighting for black "social equality" and labeled their plans for mis-cegenation "too disgusting to be mentioned" before launching into a full description of those plans, which appeared to include forced marriage. In their fervid imaginations, the Democrats crowned Lincoln "King Abraham Africanus I," the monarch of coerced miscegenation.[49]

The Democratic Party, which prided itself on being "the conservative party," quaked in terror before any and all change. The end of slavery, they consistently warned, would unleash all forms of social disorder, though it was often they who seemed unhinged. The Republican press made much of Delaware senator Willard Saulsbury's personal attack on President Lincoln as an imbecile, among other descriptors. Ordered to take his seat, Saulsbury drew a revolver and threatened to shoot the Sen-ate's sergeant at arms. A notorious cartoon titled "Miscegenation: Or the Millennium of Abolitionism" showed numerous prominent Republicans, including President Lincoln, arm in arm with black women, and white women flirting with black men. One of these women is reminding the black man to come to her upcoming election rally, a further nod to the fearful specter of women engaging in public affairs.[50]

In many ways this cartoon exposed the heart of the change Demo-crats, North and South, most feared: the end to their uncontested patri-archy. One of the women pictured in the "Miscegenation" cartoon sitting on a black man's lap was Anna Dickinson. In January 1864, Dickinson, who was just twenty-two, became the first woman to address Congress, earning a standing ovation. In the 1864 election she turned her full energy to Republican victory as the surest route to ratification of the Thirteenth Amendment. Democrats denounced Dickinson as "unsexed," "unwomanly," and in various ways a violator of proper gender norms. The powerful and attractive Dickinson became a symbol to Democrats of an uncertain and horrifying future of gender equality. New York's vile Fernando Wood admonished that the passage of the Thirteenth Amend-ment would lead to the collapse of every social institution, including marriage. Andrew Rogers of New Jersey felt that if slavery could be abolished, then "the marital rights, the rights of husband and wife, of parent and child" would crumble. Democratic men cowered before the horror of women voters.[51]

At the beginning of the war, feminists decided to devote their energy first to winning the war and abolishing slavery, and only then turning to address their own goals. It was a selfless—and, in Susan Anthony's view, foolish—decision. In May 1863 Anthony and Elizabeth Cady Stanton, feeling that Lincoln had not gone far enough with the Emancipation Proclamation, took the lead in organizing the Women's National Loyal League, which became a formidable force in the battle for an amendment to the Constitution ending slavery. Thousands of women attended their meetings; in less than one year, more than two thousand organizers gathered the signatures of four hundred thousand women on the league's petition calling for an end to slavery—the most yet presented on a petition to Congress. In January 1864, Anthony put aside her objections to giving primacy to abolition in a public letter stating that since slavery caused the war, "shame on us if we do not make it one to establish the freedom of the negro."[52]

Angry misogynist legislators responded by rolling back many hard-won gains for women. For instance, in 1862 New York reversed laws passed in 1860 that had granted widows rights to marital property and the guardianship of their own children, asserting that the change was to protect the interests and possessions of men serving in the military. For the advocates of women's rights, there could have been no clearer indication that women needed the ballot as a measure of self-defense.[53]

Ironically, it was primarily Democrats who spoke of equality in the 1864 election—they were against it. Few Republicans wanted to raise the issue as November approached, fearing precisely the sexually tinged attacks favored by the Democrats. While they did not back down from supporting an end to slavery and the need for some sort of legislation to protect the rights of the freedmen, most Republicans avoided the word "equality." Nearly alone among Republican candidates, James Ashley spoke openly of "the great democratic idea of man's equality before the law," and he almost lost.[54]

Lincoln also avoided the language of equality and any reference to the proposed amendment. He won reelection with a substantial 55 percent of the vote and the electoral votes of all but three states (New Jersey, Kentucky, and Delaware). It was a victory not just for Lincoln but for the entire Republican Party, which won every governorship except in New Jersey and a two-thirds majority in the House of Representatives—sufficient to pass the Thirteenth Amendment without a single Democratic vote. The rhetoric might be muted, but no one doubted where the Republicans stood given the legislation they proposed to pass. In the 1864 election, northern and western majorities sided with the first American political party to promote legal equality.

In November 1864, the voters spoke clearly in favor of significant social change. However, under Congress's archaic structure, the new House would not take office until December 1865. James Ashley did not want to wait that long to amend the Constitution, feeling that the initiative had to be seized in the midst of the war before the return of peacetime inertia. He aimed to build public support for the amendment and persuade his fellow Republicans to speak out in favor of changing the Constitution. At the start of 1865 he counted 108 supporters for the amendment, 14 shy of the two-thirds needed. Ashley targeted nineteen Democrats for aggressive lobbying. The key figure in Ashley's campaign turned out to be the president. After a year's hesitation, Lincoln finally stepped forward as the amendment's prime supporter, giving it more of his energy than any legislation during his presidency.

Like the nation he led, Lincoln had evolved on slavery and equality. Not unreasonably, Lincoln interpreted his 1864 election victory as a mandate for the Thirteenth Amendment and called on the lame-duck Congress to pass the amendment and send it to the states. Upon entering the presidency, Lincoln had offered to change the Constitution to protect slavery. As the war entered its fourth year, he joined those who held that the sacrifices of the nation must lead to the end of human bondage. In a delightful historical irony, he backed up this newfound anti-slavery fervor by appointing his onetime political opponent and champion of equal rights, Salmon P. Chase, to replace Roger Taney as chief justice.

Lincoln made a strong political case for joining Ashley's bid for quick action. Acknowledging that this same Congress had just rejected the amendment, Lincoln observed that the next Congress would certainly pass the amendment. "The voice of the people" demanded change, and the people's representatives must defer to that voice. Then he added a twist: amending the Constitution would serve the common good and maintain "the integrity of the Union" by removing once and for all the cause of the division. Lincoln gently implied that anyone opposed to the Thirteenth Amendment not only resisted the will of the majority but also threatened the survival of the Union.[55]

It is difficult to know the degree to which Lincoln accurately described the direction of public sentiment. Many people joined Lincoln in reading the 1864 election results as solid evidence that the Civil War had convinced a great majority of the nation that the time had come to fix the broken Constitution. It is not surprising that Frederick Douglass celebrated the election as a testament to the public's demand for the Constitution to "be so changed that slavery can never again exist in any part of the United States." It is more startling that a delegation of Louisiana slave owners agreed that the time had come to amend the Constitution to eliminate "the institution to which habit alone wedded them." A number of slave owners stepped forth in support of ending the system of servitude that had for long warped the nation's ideals and laws.[56]

The Republicans thus had every political advantage and enjoyed broad public support as the lame-duck House of Representatives moved to reconsider the Thirteenth Amendment. The shadow of a supermajority Republican House loomed in the near future, the Republican president had just been reelected, Sherman's forces finished their dramatic march through Georgia by taking Savannah on December 22, and the Democratic Party collapsed after the 1864 election, lacking leadership and a clear national agenda. By January 1865, the majority of Democrats recognized that the time had indeed come to accept the end of slavery. Yet even at this late date many powerful figures in the northern Democratic Party, such as James Brooks and Fernando Wood, continued to defend slavery in the House. Eliminating slavery, Wood predicted, would "make the pending conflict yet more intense and deadly," apparently by truly upsetting the Confederacy.[57]

Lincoln and his party demonstrated sustained commitment to getting the amendment passed. Among other moves, they fast-tracked Nevada's admission to the Union, giving the Republicans more votes in Congress and another pro-ratification state. Lincoln welcomed the assistance of New York financier Abel R. Corbin, who promised to bring over some Democrats in return for future favors. We have only Corbin's word for it, but he does appear to have successfully lobbied a number of Democratic representatives.

Ashley, Lincoln, and the other House leaders worked vote by vote to win over the wavering representatives. When two Ohio Democrats, Samuel Cox and Lincoln's former law partner John T. Stuart, promised to support the amendment if the president sincerely sought peace with the Confederacy, Lincoln agreed to Francis Blair's suggestion that he head off to Richmond to negotiate an end to the war with Jefferson Davis. Blair went to Richmond, found that Davis would negotiate only on the basis of Confederate independence, and returned to Washington, personally informing Cox of the failure of his mission. Blair's mission convinced Stuart and a few other Democrats that nothing the North did would placate the slave owners.

Secretary of State William Seward proved a formidable lobbyist for the amendment. Some historians have suggested that Seward dangled "temptations" before the recalcitrant, though no proof of bribery exists. He definitely employed a team of Democratic friends to make the case that their party would ultimately benefit from jettisoning their long-standing support for and identification with slavery.

The effort to pass the Thirteenth Amendment united people with very different agendas. Lincoln hoped to settle the constitutional question once and for all and to avoid postwar divisions that could damage his party and the nation. Seward firmly believed in emancipation, while his cabinet enemy, former postmaster general Montgomery Blair, had a more cynical goal in seeking to unite conservatives into a new party alignment, an ambition he shared with his friend Samuel Barlow, the Democrats' leading organizer. Blair thought passing the Thirteenth Amendment would force the radical Republicans to confront the next great issue, that of black equality, which would impel conservative Republicans to leave the party and look for a new home. Barlow shared Blair's thinking with several Democratic congressmen.

The renewed debate, which began on January 5, 1865, repeated arguments made the previous year, though with some surprising new voices arguing for an end to slavery. The Unionist slave owner James S. Rollins of Missouri had voted against the Thirteenth Amendment the previous June. Now, following a meeting with Lincoln, he switched his vote to support the amendment, insisting that because slavery had caused the Civil War, eliminating it was the one sure path to peace. Rollins astutely noted that the war was changing the political and social structure of the nation, making it more tolerant and open to change, and he confidently predicted that most of the South would be content with ending an institution that had always placed excessive power in the hands of a small elite. Rollins closed with a compelling personal note: knowing he was no longer a slave owner because of the actions of his state in changing its own constitution, "I breathe freer and easier to-day." Liberating the slaves had made him truly free.[58]

Most northern Democrats abandoned their earlier support for slavery in the aftermath of the 1864 election, yet still did not want to eliminate it. Stephen G. Burton of Indiana warned that if three-fourths of the states ratified the Thirteenth Amendment, "the three-fourths adopting the amendment would be a new Union—the other fourth the old Union." Lincoln effectively undercut that argument by allowing various peace missions to proceed to their foregone failure, as the Confederates refused compromise until the end. It was clear that the southern leadership, not the Republicans, had killed Burton's "old Union."[59]

Public opinion overwhelmed the Democrats' efforts to stall consideration of the Thirteenth Amendment until the southern states could return to the Union. Petitions poured into Congress, most organized by women determined to have a political impact even if they did not have the vote, and others directly from state legislatures. Most members of Congress accepted these petitions as an accurate reflection of the public mood, especially in light of the election results.[60]

Democrat Thomas Hendricks of Indiana conceded that popular support for the amendment led him to change his vote to favor emancipation. The two parties had made their positions clear in the election and the people had supported the administration. Like so many Democrats, Hendricks insisted that he had always thought slavery evil but had accepted it to preserve the Union. Neither he nor any northern Democrat bore any "portion of the responsibility" for the war; the fault lay with fanatics in both sections. Now only the complete abolishment of slavery could mend the Union. He warned his fellow Democrats that if they blocked this amendment, they would destroy their party.[61]

While some Democrats framed the Thirteenth Amendment as the first wave in an assault on traditional social structures, Alexander Coffroth of Pennsylvania and several other Democratic representatives argued the opposite, that ending slavery would remove radicalism from America. Slavery had "breathed into existence fanaticism" and threatened the nation's future. Eliminate slavery and the advocates of equality would lose their focus and public support. The best way to prevent more extreme social change was to end slavery.[62]

As Coffroth's argument in the congressional debates suggests, Democratic supporters of the Thirteenth Amendment took pains to insist that no connection existed between emancipation and equality.

Kentucky's George Yeaman, in a long, cautious speech justifying his support for the amendment as a conservative, insisted that ending slavery would calm things down by stealing the thunder from extremists who used anti-slavery sentiment to promote racial equality. But since everyone knew the blacks would die out once freed, this amendment would lead to the "natural, but not painful and violent, diminution" of blacks and thus serve "the white man's interests."[63]

After Coffroth and Yeaman changed sides, Speaker of the House Schuyler Colfax, an astute student of Congress, judged the amendment five votes short of success. Ashley validated this count and agreed to postpone the vote until the end of the month to allow for one final burst of persuasion. Lincoln came through for Ashley and the amendment, turning up the pressure by speaking with wavering representatives. Contrary to popular accounts, there is no evidence that Lincoln made any deals in return for votes, though he did employ his considerable charm and allow Seward and Ashley to make whatever bargains they saw fit.

The Republicans' success hinged, to some extent, on their strategic decision to dodge the entire issue of citizenship. Several key intellectuals and politicians made the case that the Constitution's failure to define citizenship had brought on the war. The Republican leadership knew that raising citizenship in the deeply divided Thirty-eighth Congress would doom the Thirteenth Amendment and decided to postpone that issue until the new Congress, with its Republican supermajority, came into office.

In this context, Thaddeus Stevens's famous refusal to commit to social equality during the debates on the Thirteenth Amendment proved pivotal in unifying support for emancipation. Widely known for his personal relationship with his African American housekeeper, Lydia Hamilton Smith, Stevens came under relentless fire from Cox, who demanded to know if he had given up "his doctrine of negro equality." Stevens answered that he had never declared support for Negro equality—a wary evasion. Cox shot back: "Then I understand the gentleman from Pennsylvania not to hold that all men are created equal?" Stevens crafted a cunning response, "Yes sir, but not equality in all things—simply before the laws, nothing else." Cox repeatedly pressed Stevens, who cleverly parried every thrust, often to laughter from the House.[64]

Leading Democrats slowly, and reluctantly, concluded that their party could no longer afford to be identified as the party of slavery. A Tammany Hall delegation reminded their representatives that they must support the amendment so as to "relieve them from the pro-slavery burden that now ruins the party." Kentucky senator James Guthrie, a former secretary of the treasury and prominent advocate of slavery, reached the same conclusion and urged House Democrats to abandon their opposition to the amendment for the well-being of the party.[65]

On January 31, 1865, the House met to vote on the proposed Thirteenth Amendment ending slavery in the United States. An impressive array of visitors packed the House galleries, including five members of the Supreme Court and several cabinet officers. On the women's side sat numerous leaders of the petition drive such as Laura Julian, daughter of abolitionist Joshua Giddings and wife of Representative George Julian of Indiana. Also in attendance were a large number of African Americans, including Sergeant Charles Douglass, whose father, Frederick Douglass, had played such an important role in making Americans aware of the horrors of slavery. Those present reported deep excitement mixed with abiding anxieties that the vote would prove too close for the amendment's success.

A last-minute drama almost delayed the vote as rumors circulated of a Confederate peace mission heading toward Washington. The rumors were accurate, the results of the senior Francis Blair's machinations. Democrats called for a postponement to avoid alienating the Confederate delegation, headed by Vice President Alexander Stephens. Lincoln met the delegation briefly in Virginia but did not allow them to enter Washington, where he feared they might conspire with congressional Democrats to sabotage the vote on the amendment. But before that encounter, he sent a message to Ashley to share with the House: "So far as I know, there are no peace commissioners in the city, or likely to be in it." Lincoln spoke honestly though not precisely. Ashley used the letter to silence talk of postponement.[66]

Ashley stage-managed the debates well, giving every pro-amendment Democrat a chance to speak. Moses Odell of New York declared slavery a "dead weight" on his party. John A. J. Creswell of Maryland forcefully made the case that slavery had seriously damaged the economy and society of his state, and he drew attention to the heroism of black troops, who had proven that they deserved full citizenship. The parade of Democrats culminated with a stirring speech by Anson Herrick of New York, who demanded to know why his party persisted in defending an evil institution that had brought on the worst war in the nation's history. He pledged his vote to rid the nation of slavery even if it ended his political career, in order to secure "the blessings of liberty" for "my children and my children's children." Herrick's political career did end with this vote, as the Democrats purged every member of Congress who voted for the Thirteenth Amendment—except for John A. Griswold of New York, who joined the Republicans and won reelection.[67]

The drama continued as Samuel Cox stunned the House and broke his promise to the president by voting against the amendment, despite his previous assertions that ending slavery would serve the party's long-term interests. Cox made clear that a racist fear that freedom would lead to social equality determined his vote. On the other side, eleven representatives who had opposed the amendment the previous year now switched to cast affirmative votes. As the tension built toward the final vote and the packed hall did rapid tallies of the totals, Speaker Colfax broke with tradition and asked that his vote be counted, casting his ballot for the amendment. He then announced the total vote as 119 for the amendment with 56 opposed. The Thirteenth Amendment passed with just two votes to spare.[68]

Witnesses reported that a long silence followed the reading of the vote, broken by an explosion of cheers that shook the building. Usually reserved representatives threw their hats into the air and shouted with joy, while in the galleries men and women wept, hugged strangers, shouted, and let loose a long-repressed sense of jubilation that this war might have indeed led, as their president vowed, to "a new birth of freedom." The noisy celebration persisted for a full five minutes before the House adjourned and spilled out into the streets, leaving behind the dejected defenders of slavery who had lost their final battle. Even after the passage of thirty years, George Julian recalled the emotion of the moment: "It seemed to me I had been born into a new life, and that the world was overflowing with beauty and joy." [69]

Others expressed skepticism that the nation had truly achieved equality. Charles Douglass wrote his father that he had never seen white people behave in such an emotional fashion and was deeply moved that they shared the happiness of the country's black people. But he added a significant closing comment to his letter: "I tell you things are progressing finely . . . if only they will give us the elective franchise." The young sergeant understood that there was still much work to be done. [70]

Celebrations of Congress passing the Thirteenth Amendment swept out from the Capitol across the nation, engulfing both races in a sense of triumph. James Ashley celebrated his victory with Edwin Stanton, sending off a telegram from the War Department to his constituents in Ohio: "Glory to God in the highest! Our country is free!" Many former supporters of slavery became caught up in this historic transformation of the Constitution and the nation. In New York, Morgan Dix wrote in his diary, "How strange the changes of time!" as just "4 years ago I was an out and out ultra-Southern and pro-slavery [man]" and now just felt "humble gratitude to Almighty God" that he could witness this event. [71]

Lincoln signed the Thirteenth Amendment in a rare and unnecessary gesture. He apparently intended to counter President Buchanan's signing of the earlier putative amendment that would have protected slavery for all time. Lincoln added to the symbolic significance of his act by inviting Reverend Henry H. Garnet of New York—who had himself been a runaway slave—to speak before Congress.

Standing before an all-white chamber of the nation's representatives, Garnet became the first African American in the nation's history to address Congress. Many of those in attendance on the floor had themselves owned slaves, while several former slaves stood with the overflow crowd in the gallery. Garnet moved beyond the abolishment of slavery and called for equal civic rights for blacks, insisting that the nation's work would not be done until "all invidious and proscriptive distinctions shall be blotted out from our laws." The country would not know true justice until blacks are "equal before the law."[72]

The debate over the Thirteenth Amendment now moved to the states, where it intensified and narrowed as the two parties battled over the meaning of equality. The standard Democratic line remained that abolition was just the first, dangerous step toward racial mixing, social chaos, and the end of white civilization. Some Republican legislators engaged the Democrats by positing different levels of equality. After all, thousands of free blacks lived in the North, most of whom did not enjoy political or social equality—an accurate though rather uninspired rebuttal. Most Republicans compared labor or natural rights with civil or "relative" rights. The first, as one assemblyman put it, granted the opportunity "to live, to be free and to enjoy the fruits of one's labor," while the states regulated the second group of rights, such as voting, office-holding, and jury duty. Legislators referenced the Declaration of Independence in speaking of the first and the Constitution's grant of state power in discussing the second. Recognizing the natural rights of blacks did not mean that you had to grant them equal political and social rights. Another assemblyman urged calm in the face of "the bugbear of negro equality," as no connection existed between ending slavery and ending "legal restrictions against intermarriages with the inferior race." In short, many Republican legislators acknowledged the presence of two classes of citizens in the United States, and they were fine with that.[73]

Many more Republicans did not have a problem with legal equality, since they believed whites superior in every way regardless of what the law said. Thomas W. Bennett of Indiana noted that he "believed the Anglo-Saxon race superior to all others" and was therefore "willing to see all have a fair chance in the race of life." In fact, he thought those most afraid of racial equality suffered from the knowledge that some blacks were better men than they. Black soldiers had certainly proven themselves "the equal of the Northern traitor or the Southern rebel." Republicans framed the Thirteenth Amendment as the natural result of the war and a fitting tribute to their certain victory. The only opponents of abolishing slavery, as one Indiana Republican said, "are the Southern traitors; men who have insulted our flag, trampled our Constitution under foot . . . [and] whose hands are to-day dripping with the blood of our brothers and sons." [74]

Starting with Illinois on February 1, northern state legislatures rushed to ratify the Thirteenth Amendment, while Democrats hoped to stall until the southern states returned to the Union. In Ohio J. H. Putnam offered a resolution requiring legislators to wear mourning as "evidence of their deep sorrow occasioned by the passage of the Constitutional amendment abolishing slavery," which was "the first step towards a centralized despotism." Instead, the House voted overwhelmingly to ratify the amendment and called on the governor to order "a salute of two hundred guns fired in honor of this great event." [75]

Deeply demoralized, most Democrats understood that it was time to move on. Emotions ran so high that even fellow Democrats accused the opponents of the amendment of treason. Democratic representative T. T. Wright of Indiana commented that since "slavery had caused this rebellion, why then should [I] cherish it?" Those who defended it now joined all the traitors who had killed patriotic Americans in the war. Democrats, so long used to defending slavery, had no place left to go and generally just mouthed some racist tripe before giving in to public opinion.[76]

A number of disturbing harbingers of the future riled the ratification debates. In Maryland some representatives put forth a resolution to purportedly "let bygones be bygones" by uniting "all who truly love their country"—by which they meant the Confederates—to preserve "the purity and supremacy of the white race." Doing so would show "the world that we are a nation of free white men, who can overcome our prejudices" in the name of democracy. A bizarre twisting of the meaning of many words, this resolution fell just a few votes short of the requisite two-thirds majority. Among the Union states, only Delaware rejected the Thirteenth Amendment. In Kentucky, as General Clinton B. Fisk put it, "the devotees of barbarism cling to [slavery's] putrid carcass with astonishing tenacity." The legislature ratified the amendment on the condition that Congress agree that the freedmen would be strictly limited in their rights and leave the state within ten years. Congress adamantly rejected such a contingent ratification.[77]

Eighteen of the thirty-six states ratified the amendment by the end of February 1865, and then the process stalled. Following Lincoln's assassination on April 14, Republicans rode the wave of public sentiment as every northern state except New Jersey and Iowa voted for ratification in the next two months. At this point matters became complicated, as the fate of the former Confederate states moved to the forefront of American politics.

The core question facing the country appeared simple but was deeply complicated by the long war: were the Confederate states to be restored to full status in the Union and thus counted toward ratification of the Thirteenth Amendment? If so, then twenty-seven of thirty-six states had to ratify; if not, then just seventeen states were required, and that number had been reached by the end of February. Lincoln had always insisted that the southern states had not left the Union, a position bolstered by the near unanimous ratification of the Thirteenth Amendment in Louisiana, Tennessee, and Arkansas. In contrast, Charles Sumner contended that the southern states had taken themselves out of the

Union and should therefore have to be readmitted. Under that reading, the remaining eight Confederate states should not be counted toward the amendment's ratification—after all, they had not been present when Congress passed the amendment.[78]

While most Republicans agreed with Sumner on an emotional level, they saw the political wisdom of Lincoln's assessment that southern state legislatures would challenge the legitimacy of the Thirteenth Amendment if they did not participate, as he pointed out in his last public address on April 11, 1865.[79]

Many southern and some northern whites continued to oppose ratification even after Lincoln's assassination and the war's end. Confident that slavery could be saved, Stephen G. Burton, an Indiana legislator, blamed God for the crisis, since he had "stamped upon the Negro a mark of inferiority that could not be removed by legislation." Allowing the races to live together in freedom would thus be heresy, leading Burton to predict that there would always be slavery in the United States. Every southern state convention held after Lee's surrender at Appomattox rejected the amendment, certain that if they held firm for slavery long enough the northern people would lose interest and give up.[80]

The former Confederates misread the public temper. The overwhelming majority of those who had remained loyal to the Union demanded an end to the war's cause. Even the new president, Andrew Johnson, himself a southern white supremacist, angrily demanded action from the newly reconstituted state legislatures. Mississippi absolutely refused to go along, its legislature rejecting the amendment. The legislatures of South Carolina and Alabama perceived the futility of further resistance and voted in November for the amendment, but with a resolution maintaining their right to control their former slaves. Regardless of how they voted on the amendment, every one of the former Confederate states quickly passed black codes controlling their freed black population, clearly violating freedom of contract, one of the minimal rights all Republicans felt essential to their formulation of equality.

Sullenly admitting a lack of alternatives, Georgia became the twenty-seventh state to ratify the Thirteenth Amendment on December 6, making it part of the Constitution of the United States. Five of the remaining nine states voted to ratify over the next month, followed by Texas in 1870. Delaware eventually ratified the Thirteenth Amendment in 1901, Kentucky in 1976, and Mississippi, as is its wont, came in last in 2013. With the passage of the Thirteenth Amendment, William Lloyd Garrison declared the Constitution no longer "a covenant with death" but finally "a covenant with life."[81]

The Thirteenth Amendment solved one enormous problem for the United States but left in place the core error in the Constitution: its failure to define citizenship and clarify legal equality. Even before the Thirteenth Amendment passed Congress, some—most notably Franz Lieber and Horace Binney—recognized this defect. Lieber, a German immigrant, rose to prominence on pure intelligence, becoming a key adviser to Abraham Lincoln and joining the cerebral General Ethan Allen Hitchcock in writing the nation's first code of military conduct. His octogenarian friend Judge Binney came from a distinguished Philadelphia family and had witnessed the Constitutional Convention. The two men corresponded often about how to correct the Constitution so as to avoid further crises.

Binney saw a direct path from the Constitution's failure to define citizenship to the *Dred Scott* decision. Simply abolishing slavery, Binney warned, would not resolve anything. Every slave could be freed and still the Constitution would say nothing about legal equality, allowing the Supreme Court to again declare "that the offspring of an African slave, tho' free was not a citizen." Attorney General Edward Bates reached the same conclusion in late 1862 but kept his judgment embedded in unwieldy legal prose that exerted no influence. Lieber followed their reasoning to conclude that without a clear constitutional definition of citizenship, equality remained an ideal rather than a reality.[82]

In December 1865, a new and highly influential journal, *The Nation*, explored the meaning of emancipation for American history and democracy. The Constitution's Framers, giving priority to national unity, had been bullied into allowing slavery to persist, even though they knew it "to be inconsistent with republican principles and a blot upon the national character." As a consequence, the southern elite dominated American politics and manipulated the federal government to expand slavery and impose their beliefs on the whole country. At enormous cost, the Civil War swept away protection for slavery, opening the path for the United States to become a nation truly dedicated to freedom and equality. Yet the ingrained habit of deferring to racist tyrants remained so powerful that the representatives of the victorious Union could not bring themselves to legislate in accordance with their own principles. *The Nation* insisted that the time had finally come to permanently fix the Constitution with language protecting equality.[83]

The Nation understood that legal equality terrified many Americans and entranced others; either way it was not an abstraction. Even uneducated slaves grasped that equality before the law would change every aspect of their lives—from marriage to bodily integrity, from the ability to worship as they saw fit to the ability to move when and where they wished.

Legal equality would also allow them a future. As slaves, they could have no goals beyond those of their masters. Emancipation freed them, but to truly have a future, the law had to protect their rights. The teacher Elizabeth Hyde Botume worked with freed slaves in Savannah shortly after it fell to Sherman's army. She described their quick appreciation for the realities of freedom. They knew "that emancipation had lifted them out of old conditions into new relations with their fellow beings." They understood that they were no longer chattel, the property of others. But to own property, to enter into marriage, to send their children to school, to plan for the future, to be truly "independent creatures with rights and privileges like their neighbors," they must be able to access the law as freely as whites. The promise of emancipation carried hope to every African American, but most saw what few whites would acknowledge: the inadequacy of abolition in the absence of legal equality.[84]

In the war's aftermath, African Americans quickly understood that their main goal had to be legal equality, as slavery could persist under a different name. Members of Congress might think changing the Constitution would end slavery, Frederick Douglass observed, but blacks knew that "slavery is not abolished until the black man has the ballot." James McCune Smith, the first African American to earn a medical degree, summarized a probable future well: "The word slavery will, of course, be wiped from the statute book, but the 'ancient relation' can be just as well maintained by cunningly devised laws." Once freed, blacks must not be fooled again by empty rhetorical promises. As the polymath doctor and lawyer John S. Rock insisted to a company of black soldiers, "We at the North are contending for and shall not be satisfied until we get equal rights for all." The efforts of these black activists and their white allies would soon prove decisive.[85]

CHAPTER 5

Defining and
Defending Citizenship

Or, how racist violence and a call
for consistency led to the
fulfillment of Lincoln's promise

I n one of the most extraordinary cultural shifts in American history, a majority of Americans came to believe in some form of equality. With the passage of the Thirteenth Amendment, Republicans confidently expected southern whites to respect the rights of the former slaves while the workings of the free market ensured their fair treatment. But supporters of the defeated Confederacy refused to abandon white supremacy, leading advocates of equality to seek further congressional legislation.

Ohio's James A. Garfield, an exceptionally intelligent and courageous man, saw the necessity for further action. A classical scholar and college president before the war, Garfield joined the Republican Party in 1858 in response to the expansionist policies of the slave-owning elite. His service as a major general during the Civil War converted Garfield, like so many soldiers, from a mere opponent of slavery's spread to a true believer in human equality. Garfield became one of the first members of Congress to insist that the freedmen deserved the right to vote, rejecting "the absurd and senseless dogma that the color of the skin shall be the basis of suffrage." He reminded his constituents that in the hour of the nation's greatest need, black Americans rushed forth to save their country. "Amid the very thunders of battle, we made a covenant with him, sealed both with his blood and with ours." These black soldiers proved their worth and deserved freedom, which surely meant more than "the bare privilege of not being chained." The United States had a duty to realize the truths embodied in the Declaration of Independence by empowering the freed slaves with the full legal rights of American citizens.[1]

Garfield recognized that the Thirteenth Amendment moved the United States closer to its stated ideals but did not solve the more fundamental problem. The Constitution remained open to further corruption, as citizenship had not been defined, leaving in place Roger Taney's *Dred Scott* decision limiting rights to whites. Congress must secure equality and prevent the resurrection of the Slave Power under some new guise. As Garfield's House colleague Ignatius Donnelly said, "The Constitution will hereafter be read by the light of the rebellion; by the light of the emancipation." The Civil War provided the only justification the Republicans needed for their proposed reforms.[2]

The people of the northern and western states united around the need for further constitutional change because of the attitudes and behavior of southern racists. To them the South had been a foreign country for many years prior to the creation of the Confederate States. Southern governments brooked no dissent and offered a hostile reception to any visitor who failed to celebrate their way of life. After the Civil War, northerners could travel through the South freely for the first time in decades. Without slavery, the South appeared to be a new land, one that many sought to explore. Most notably, Andrew Johnson sent Carl Schurz, the revolutionary immigrant who rose to the rank of major general during the war, through the former Confederacy on a fact-finding mission.

Johnson's request startled Schurz, who had written articles opposing the president's leniency toward former Confederates. He also found it strange that the president wanted him to go alone on his journey, rather than as part of a larger group. The following day Schurz learned from several friends that prominent Republicans had pressured Johnson to acquire information on southern conditions before allowing those states back into the Union. Seeing little alternative, Johnson chose a respected figure who had at least praised Lincoln's proposed policy of reconciliation.[3]

Just a few weeks after the last Confederate forces surrendered, Schurz sailed south with his secretary to Charleston, South Carolina, arriving on July 15. Over the next two months, Schurz traveled widely through the South, meeting governors and field hands, former Confederates and southern Unionists, poor white farmers and freedmen. He saw vast areas devastated by war and peaceful counties untouched by conflict. He spoke with released prisoners of war heading home and former slaves searching for their families. Making routine reports back to the president, Schurz felt that he proceeded as a scholar, allowing those interviewed to speak for themselves.[4]

Upon returning to Washington, Schurz warned the president that former Confederates were moving quickly to establish a "system of terrorism" to control the freedmen and silence Republicans. Schurz then wrote a summary of his travel experiences. At the end of his long life, Schurz would insist that his *Report on the Condition of the South* was the best thing he ever wrote.[5]

Schurz found southern whites unrepentant, bitter, and still willing to use violence to maintain their structures of inequality. Even more surprising, given that they had just cost the nation more than seven hundred thousand lives in an effort to preserve their system of slavery, they expected to be compensated for their freed slaves and planned to pursue this effort as soon as their representatives returned to Congress.[6]

Schurz's report did not find what Johnson wanted—a repentant South happy to be good citizens of a free-labor society—so the president suppressed the document. But doing so only made it more prominent, as Senator Sumner craftily manipulated the administration into publishing the Schurz report as an alternative to reading it into the congressional record. The public grabbed copies as quickly as they were printed, more than 100,000 within a few weeks. The report showed the North that most Confederates believed that they should have won and had no real loyalty to the country, demonstrating the hollowness of President Johnson's program of forgiveness.[7]

Schurz's report found validation in numerous other sources, including the influential pages of *The Nation*, which had become almost the official voice of northern liberals. *The Nation* included a weekly column by John R. Dennett, "The South as It Is." Dennett found southern whites clinging to the connected mythologies of states' rights and white supremacy. The elite had no inclination to accept the war's results and planned to regain power by any means. Lacking alternatives, they ratified the Thirteenth Amendment, but they "were sorry for nothing but their ill-success." Socially, the South remained unchanged "in any important respects from what it was during the war."[8]

The northern press sent a stream of observers to the South, all of whom filed reports on white intransigence. Sidney Andrews of the *Chicago Tribune* attended the Georgia Constitutional Convention, where Confederate veterans mourned their defeat and tried to convince Andrews that "but for this little mistake, or that little accident . . . the Confederacy would now be a great nation." Most convention delegates regretted having to return to the Union but were determined to do so on their traditional terms of inequality and state supremacy, and they had no intention of submitting their new constitution to the voters for approval. Similarly, southern white leaders told Schurz that once they got back into Congress they planned to get the federal government to pay for winning the war and abolishing slavery; in the words of one planter, "The Cons'tution makes niggers prop'ty, and go'ment is bound to pay for them." The southern elite had dominated the American political system from the founding of the nation through 1860, and they aimed to reclaim that position. As one southern official told the prominent journalist Whitelaw Reid: "We'll unite with the opposition up North, and between us we'll make a majority. *Then* we'll show you who's going to govern this country."[9]

Most disturbing to these reporters, and to their northern audience, was the willingness of so many white southerners to use violence to get their way and silence dissent. Reid found the white leadership most notable for "their scarcely disguised hostility to the freedom of the press." The editor of the *Charleston Courier* told Reid that he would never publish news hostile to the local elite. Ironically, the *Montgomery Mail*'s editor wanted to send these northern journalists packing, as they "did nothing but misrepresent and slander" the South as lacking basic freedoms. Reporting on death threats against advocates of black rights, Dennett warned northerners thinking of settling in the South that they "would be compelled to restrict [their] accustomed freedom of speech and action and defer to the social and political theories and opinions" of the elite. Andrews had a more immediate experience of such attitudes when a mob chased him out of Albany, Georgia.[10]

Southern whites obsessed over the future of free blacks. Using the racist language he so often encountered, Andrews wrote that whites had "nigger on the brain"—it was all they talked about. No matter what he asked, the answer came back to the blacks: "Let conversation begin where it will, it ends with Sambo." Schurz quoted Colonel Samuel Thomas: "The whites esteem the blacks their property by natural rights," and despite the end of slavery, "they still have an ingrained feeling that the blacks at large belong to the whites at large."[11]

That attitude of ownership mixed with intimidation became evident to the whole nation in the last months of 1865 as the whites-only southern state governments passed black codes, legal barriers intended to control the actions and rights of the region's blacks. These statutes established a criminal code applicable only to blacks, creating a feudal economic structure based on race. The black codes essentially appropriated the black population to the state, allowing the government to coerce blacks into contractual bondage to planters in need of labor and to remove children from black families to be "apprenticed" to whites, with priority given to former slave masters. The state also claimed authority to imprison, beat, and then rent out unemployed blacks, with local officials given plenty of economic incentive to do so.

The black codes reinstituted most of the slave regulations that had constrained the lives of southern blacks. Louisiana required every black person "to be in the regular service of some white person" and to carry passes when traveling away from their places of employment. Laws across the South established curfews for blacks, declared unemployed blacks vagrants, gave sheriffs the authority to imprison these vagrants and to rent out the convicts' labor, forbade blacks from congregating without official permission, from cohabitating with and marrying whites, from owning guns, and in some instances from owning property.[12]

Southern legislatures justified the black codes as clarifying the rights of the freedmen, including the right to marry, buy, own, and sell property, and to testify in court—when all parties involved were black. But the northern press published the codes verbatim, and anyone could read the long list of civic disabilities. As Carl Schurz told President Johnson, the black codes transformed the freedmen into "the slaves of society."[13]

The workings of the "new" southern legal system shocked northern observers and persuaded Republicans that natural rights can only be adequately protected by the rights of citizenship. Just as the Civil War drove most northerners from merely seeking to prevent the expansion of slavery to the stronger position of abolitionism, so the actions of white supremacists moved them closer to placing substantive legal equality in the Constitution. A lawyer who had served in the Confederate Army told Andrews that the legislature intended to use the penal code to force blacks "back into the condition of slavery." They would adhere to the language of the Thirteenth Amendment, which allowed for "involuntary servitude . . . as a punishment for crime," but the legislature would see to it that lots of crimes existed for the blacks to commit. The result "won't differ much from slavery."[14]

The writer John Trowbridge witnessed firsthand the creativity of the southern legislatures. Observing a chain gang of blacks working on the streets in Selma, Alabama, he inquired about their crimes, which included selling farm produce before the official market bell and being unable to pay a fine to "using abusive language towards a white man." Some local whites who enjoyed watching blacks work shouted, "That's the beauty of freedom!"[15] Schurz observed the same developments in his travels, prophetically warning that southern whites appeared intent on creating "another 'peculiar institution' whose spirit is in conflict with the fundamental principles of our political system" and would once more disrupt the Union.[16]

Violence underlay these efforts to restore a race-based coercive labor system. At every turn, white supremacists spoke the language of brutality and consistently acted upon their threats. Many whites continued to treat blacks as though they were still slaves, beating, whipping, and even killing those who refused to work for free. In Texas, a local judge wrote the governor begging for assistance, as a few of his county's wealthiest whites attacked any freedman bold enough to open his own business, administering five hundred lashes to one shopkeeper who refused to leave town. Dennett was stunned by the language of a white shoemaker who insisted that he would "cut a nigger's throat from ear to ear" if the African American so much as contradicted anything he said. Dennett quickly saw that virulence backed by action, as blacks who dared to take freedom seriously fell before the pathological racism of southern whites. Like many northerners, Dennett came to feel that the Confederates sought to reverse the results of the Civil War. The actions of southern whites fed public pressure for Congress to act.[17]

Equality and the definition of citizenship became intertwined for the first time in 1865. The Civil War definitively changed the United States in a myriad of ways, some of which would only become evident in the decades ahead. Many old verities no long applied. For instance, the traditional argument over states' rights evaporated from national political discourse for several years—though it would be reintroduced by Alexander Stephens to retroactively justify secession. Andrew Johnson stated the point clearly in his first State of the Union address: "'The sovereignty of the States' is the language of the Confederacy, and not the language of the Constitution."[18]

For a southern Democrat like Johnson to hold that position marked a sea change, as the majority of Americans looked to the federal government for action on a range of issues from transportation to legal rights. Hundreds of thousands died fighting to define the Union as one nation, to make the verb following the United States "is" rather than "are." Blacks and women gained a sense of agency, if not yet of citizenship. As Julia Ward Howe wrote, many "women found a new scope for their activities, and developed abilities hitherto unsuspected by themselves" during the Civil War. Industrialization accelerated as tens of thousands of immigrants poured in, with transportation between the states improving and local loyalties weakening. In the midst of that series of dramatic alterations, the vision of equality altered.[19]

The most pressing political issue Congress faced in the war's aftermath was the meaning of secession in the context of Republican efforts to build a nation with a single standard of law. Had the states actually left the Union? Was it possible for the United States to actually be a unified country in which a person could expect respect for individual rights no matter where he or she traveled? Conservatives treated secession as a mulligan, one the states could reverse simply by returning their members to Congress. Not surprisingly, many northerners—apparently most, going by election results—found that position unsatisfying. Did more than seven hundred thousand people die so that everything could be restored exactly as it had been in 1860, but without the institution of slavery? Conservatives answered in the affirmative.

Radical Republicans, as they became known, insisted that there had to be a political cost to secession and four years of war, though they did not agree on what that cost should be. After all, the seceded states had taken up arms against the national government. If that was not treason, what was? Here the argument veered in two significantly distinct directions: some members of Congress wanted the southern states to reapply for admission to the Union, while others, led by Thaddeus Stevens, argued that the rules of war made the southern states conquered territories. The former position sought to normalize the process of readmission through standard political processes, while the latter granted Congress the power to make any changes to the conquered states it thought fit. The moderates generally agreed that certain political changes would have to be accepted by the southern state governments before they could return to the Union, while the Radicals hoped to remake southern society, from altering the electoral system to confiscating lands for distribution to former slaves.

The assassination of Abraham Lincoln complicated the process of reconstruction considerably, bringing to office a man temperamentally ill-suited for leadership. As a Tennessee legislator, governor, and senator, Andrew Johnson had supported slavery but opposed the power of the slave-owning elite. His reputation soared in the North because he was the only southern senator to remain in Congress after secession. Despite his ardent pro-Union stance, he remained a venomous racist. Shortly after becoming president, Johnson announced, "This is a country for white men, and by God, as long as I am President, it shall be a government for white men." His alcoholism and dysfunctional personal traits—bitter self-pity and a bizarre narcissism that included comparing himself to both Moses and Jesus—provided further impediments to an effective presidency. Johnson's first speech as president, given the day after Lincoln's death, glided past the martyred president's accomplishments to focus on Johnson's numerous sacrifices and his path to political triumph. Republicans thought it a tasteless exercise in conceit. Rarely has such a flawed personality stumbled into so much power.[20]

Johnson set out to restore the Union on his own terms. Within days of Lincoln's assassination, Johnson indicated ambitions to be elected president in his own right in 1868. Lincoln had brought Johnson, a lifelong Democrat, into the newly minted National Union Party for the 1864 election to promote national recovery. Johnson had no intention of working with his new Republican brethren and pursued his own movement uniting conservative northerners and defeated Confederates. This scheme required the rapid readmission of the southern states under white supremacist governments. In his first month in office, Johnson accepted five southern state governments back into the Union and granted amnesty to the rebels, excepting only the top Confederate officials and wealthiest southerners, who had to apply personally to President Johnson for pardons.[21]

In the summer of 1865, former Confederate generals and officials trooped into Walt Whitman's White House office to fill out applications for pardon. While Johnson surely took pleasure in having members of the southern elite begging him for forgiveness, his goal was the restoration of white supremacy under his leadership, as "white men alone must manage the South." The southerners petitioning for pardon fed Johnson's dreams, assuring him of their loyalty and future support. Journalist Whitelaw Reid observed this charade and doubted the sincerity of these former Confederates, who "cunningly showed him how he could secure the united support of the entire South and of the great Democratic party of the North . . . for the next Presidency." These compliments and promises became a siren's song Johnson could not resist.[22]

Johnson could, however, ignore Congress, which he permitted no role in bringing the southern states back into the fold. At the war's end, the majority of federal offices in the South sat empty, providing Johnson with an astounding patronage opportunity. He filled those offices with southern Democrats, negated efforts to redistribute land to former slaves, and sabotaged the Freedmen's Bureau, which aided poor whites and blacks. He called on the southern states to use their prewar constitutions to create new all-white governments and send representatives and senators to Congress. Much of the nation had learned the value of equality during the Civil War; unfortunately, the president had not.

In December 1865, fifty-five representatives and twenty would-be senators showed up at Congress demanding to be seated. This delegation of former Confederate officers and officials included Confederate vice president Alexander Stephens. Morally outraged, Republicans immediately recognized the political consequence of letting so many unreconstructed secessionists into Congress. Democrats to a man, these southerners would unite with the northern Democrats to effectively block every piece of Republican legislation. In a further bitter irony, ending slavery without giving blacks the vote would hand the Democratic Party a huge advantage. With the three-fifths clause essentially repealed by the Thirteenth Amendment, the southern states would enjoy a major boost to their representation in the House without having to allow any of the freed slaves to actually participate in the political process. Those eighteen additional representatives would also increase the South's power in the Electoral College, which selected the president. Little wonder that President Johnson thought he had acted cleverly in promoting a quick southern readmission to the Union.

The arrival of these representatives from the former Confederate states forced Congress to confront the issue of reconstruction head-on. Republicans understood that accepting these seventy-five southerners into their ranks doomed their legislative agenda, perhaps permanently. Unsurprisingly, the Republicans decided to snub the southern representatives.

The House of Representatives opened its session on December 4 with the Democrats thinking they had a winning strategy. On the first day, just a single southern representative, Horace Maynard of Tennessee, presented himself. Like Johnson, Maynard had stood by the Union during the war. The Democrats reasoned that the Republicans would have to accept such a man. They underestimated the political acumen of the Republicans.

Calling the roll, House clerk Edward McPherson skipped Maynard. The latter jumped to his feet in protest, but McPherson refused to recognize Maynard, since he was not a member of the House. Quickly elected Speaker, Schuyler Colfax clarified the Republican attitude toward the southern states. Congress's "first and highest obligation is to guaranty to every State a republican form of government," as mandated by Article IV of the Constitution. No southern representative would be seated, as the rebellion had overthrown the legitimate state governments. Congress needed to "establish them anew on such a basis of enduring justice as will guaranty all necessary safeguards to the people." The Speaker then offered a novel reading of Article IV as requiring Congress to meet the Declaration of Independence's standard of "protection to all men in their inalienable rights." Republicans interrupted Colfax with loud applause while Democrats sat in sullen silence. Congress rejected the seventy-five southern representatives and senators.[23]

However, the former Confederates found powerful allies in the North. One of the most significant and overlooked events of the immediate postwar period was the reunification of the Democratic Party. Most northern Democrats had distanced themselves from their southern brethren immediately after the war, insisting that they had always opposed slavery and had only gone along with the South in the antebellum years in order to preserve the Union. Yet five years after the southerners had abandoned their party and nation, northern Democrats overlooked that divisive act and the Civil War to welcome their southern adversaries back. Most willingly reunited on the basis of racism, a deal with the devil they sustained for the ensuing century. In 1866, the Democratic Party slogan gained an extra clause: "The Union as it was, the Constitution as it is, and the Negro where he is."[24]

The reunification of the Democratic Party was not a foregone conclusion. In one of the deeper ironies of the post–Civil War period, many southern Democrats felt betrayed by northern Democrats for having supported the Union during the war. As a consequence, numerous observers predicted that the Democratic Party would follow the Federalists and Whigs into oblivion. But northern Democrats rejected the opportunity to reconsider their identity, as doing so would require them to grapple finally with the issue of equality. With the war's end, most sought to turn the clock back to the 1850s, when they shared national power with southern slave owners. Slavery may have ended, but racism remained available as an effective bond. As a mark of white unity, northern Democrats promoted the mythology of slavery as a benign institution, a perspective they maintained at least through the presidency of Woodrow Wilson, with some whites defending this twisted view into the twenty-first century.

Nonetheless, in 1868, some northern Democratic leaders thought it time to break free of the southern alliance and create a new party with new ideas, free of the taint of racism. This movement found particular traction in urban areas, where appeals to economic grievances gained support among Irish and German immigrants. These Democrats, including New York's governor, Horatio Seymour, and August Belmont, the party's leader, attempted to find a presidential candidate who could represent this image of a party reborn. They appealed to General Ulysses S. Grant and Chief Justice Salmon P. Chase, both of whom expressed initial interest. However, the party leadership could not agree on a clear set of economic policies and kept returning to racism as an enduring unifier. This adherence to racism turned off Grant, while Chase hoped to circumvent it with an emphasis on universal suffrage and states' rights—the former stance being far too radical for the Democratic leaders.[25]

There was an opening for a third party. Initially, divisions within the Republican Party prevented the formulation of a clear vision of the future. Many Republicans felt that the former slaves deserved full civil rights—the legal acknowledgment of their personhood—but not political rights. Cautiously between 1866 and 1868, the Republican leadership unified around a platform of political rights for blacks, for there was one aspect of Reconstruction upon which all Republicans agreed: the need to end one-party rule in the South. A two-party system could work only if blacks voted. The South had long since opted out of anything approaching democracy, never having permitted the free exchange of ideas—the concept of free speech had long been considered a threat to public safety. The southern elite might have no choice but to accept the results of the Civil War in ending slavery, but there was no way they intended to allow freedom into their states—not without a fight.

At the start of 1866, congressional Republicans bypassed President Johnson and seized control of the nation's future. They began by setting up the Joint Committee of Fifteen on Reconstruction. The Republican

Party dominated the Thirty-ninth Congress, holding 145 of 191 House seats and 39 of 50 Senate seats. Just three Democrats sat on the committee, including Maryland senator Reverdy Johnson, at seventy the Senate's oldest member, who had often sided with the Republicans during the war. William P. Fessenden, a depressed and sickly but adroit politician, chaired the committee, which included radicals Thaddeus Stevens and Elihu Washburne, the cynical manipulator Roscoe Conkling, who battled every effort at civil service reform, and the formidable constitutional lawyer John A. Bingham.

Bingham brought a particularly significant experience to the Committee of Fifteen. He had lost his reelection campaign in 1862 largely because of his unstinting advocacy of Lincoln's authority to issue the Emancipation Proclamation. To reward his loyalty, Lincoln appointed Bingham as a judge advocate general in the army, a position he continued to hold after his return to Congress in the 1864 election. Secretary of War Edwin Stanton named Bingham to the special commission investigating Lincoln's assassination. That inquiry convinced Bingham that the Confederate government had planned the attack and that Jefferson Davis had personally directed it. Though the commission held back from prosecuting Confederate officials in the name of national peace, Bingham remained suspicious of any move to restore power to the southern elite—a group that, in his eyes, had attempted to destroy the Union, launched four years of bloody war, and assassinated the president.[26]

Bingham quickly emerged as the committee's pivotal advocate for further amending the Constitution. His pursuit of equality had deep roots, dating to his college days in the 1830s, when he had befriended Titus Basfield, a former slave who became an influential minister and lifelong friend and adviser, including during Bingham's work on the Committee of Fifteen. Bingham's constitutional creativity came from a unique understanding of Article IV, Section 2, which promised that the "Citizens of each State shall be entitled to all Privileges and Immunities of Citizens of the several States."

Most of Bingham's contemporaries read this passage, known as the comity clause, as indicating only that visitors to a state would be treated the same as its own citizens. In February 1859, Bingham formulated an alternative reading in response to Oregon's application for admission to the Union. The new state's proposed constitution took upon itself the authority to determine who would enjoy the rights of citizenship within its borders, explicitly excluding black people from even settling in the state. This "infamous atrocity" aroused Bingham's ire. Citing Article IV, Section 2, Bingham found no limit on the protection of citizens' rights; the citizen of one state is a citizen of the United States and therefore entitled to all the privileges of citizenship. Oregon had no authority to exclude any U.S. citizen, nor could it mar the Constitution by the insertion of "any word of caste, such as white or black, male or female." Bingham went where few other political leaders dared in openly supporting true equality: "The equality of all to the right to live; to the right to know; to argue and to utter, according to conscience; to work and enjoy the product of their toil, is the rock on which that Constitution rests." Bingham found in the Constitution the protection of legal equality for everyone.[27]

Congress roundly ignored Bingham and admitted Oregon with its racist constitution. But the Ohio representative laid the foundation for a great rethinking of the Constitution, one that protected the rights of all Americans regardless of race, ethnicity, class, or gender. In a remarkable 1863 congressional debate, Bingham mocked the Democrats and their cry of "the Constitution as it is and the Union as it was." He reminded the Democrats that their southern brethren had seceded because they refused to live under the Constitution as it is. To protect those "conspirators," the northern Democrats had rushed to change the Constitution to make slavery inviolate, and now they insisted that no one could change it in order to promote democracy. The Confederates and their northern supporters sought to change, in Madison's words, that "great charter of human liberty" into a "written despotism." But,

Bingham insisted, freedom would triumph with a revised Constitution based on equality.[28]

Bingham first put forth his radical proposal to alter the Constitution in December 1865, immediately upon his return to Congress. His initial wording granted Congress the power to make any laws it thought necessary to secure the rights of all citizens in every state. This amendment would arm Congress "with the power to enforce the bill of rights" nationally, ending the notion that states could contravene the Constitution in the name of states' rights. Allowing states to negate the promises of the Bill of Rights mocked the very idea of the United States as a nation. Bingham closed his argument for the Fourteenth Amendment with a stirring call: "One people, one Constitution, and one country!"[29]

Bingham's formulation had a powerful political component in that he intended to bury for good what he saw as the absurdity of states' rights. The states had no inherent powers; their authority originated from and was dependent on the federal government. Though the supremacy clause required the states to respect citizens' rights, the Constitution failed to give Congress the power to enforce that legal equality. He aimed to clear up once and for all the constitutional ambiguity on citizenship and personal rights by inserting into the supreme law of the land a precise statement of equal citizenship and rights that applied the Bill of Rights to the states. It proved a difficult task, but one that was repeatedly aided by the violence of white supremacists.

Those rejecting Bingham's constitutional reform never came right out and said that they opposed the Bill of Rights, though they most certainly did. Instead they wrapped together the same pair of ideas that had buttressed secession: states' rights and racism. Democrats insisted that states must have the power to police their black population, especially to prevent them from voting and marrying whites. The extensive debate filled the congressional record, with Democrats equating equal rights with tyranny and Republicans insisting that they just sought to fulfill the Constitution's core intention. Caught in a repetitive loop, the

House voted to postpone consideration of the amendment. Bingham's version was shelved but not forgotten.[30]

The Committee of Fifteen held its first meeting on January 6, 1866. Even the committee's three Democrats were determined that the southern states not return to Congress under a system that allowed these states to effectively run the country. They began by hearing secret evidence on the current situation in the South from white and black southerners, as well as Union officers serving in that part of the country. That testimony highlighted the intransigence and violence of the former Confederates. The committee's response to this information was guided by Thaddeus Stevens and John Bingham, who also influenced each other.

Stevens picked up on Bingham's use of Madison's Federalist No. 10 and No. 51 to persuade the committee that diversity promoted national strength and freedom. The United States was emphatically not a "white man's country"; ensuring the rights of blacks avoided Madison's feared tyranny of the majority. In return, Bingham adopted Stevens's "Dead States" theory, under which the southern states had essentially committed political self-negation by seceding and must now go through a territorial condition before returning to full participation in the Union—and under Article IV, Section 3, only Congress could determine when these states deserved readmission. Since they were "defunct states," Congress had a duty to create new governments for them, and under Article IV, Section 1, it must ensure their republican form.

Stevens went further than Bingham in one regard: he made clear the political dimension of establishing legal equality. Bluntly stated, amending the Constitution to secure equality for all people would fulfill the Framers' democratic intentions and also "secure perpetual ascendency" for the Republican Party. In protecting equal rights, a citizenship amendment would ensure the black vote, which would allow the Republicans to compete in the South.[31]

Few Republicans stated the political goal of an expanded electoral base quite so baldly, but they did agree on three core principles. First, the previous constitutional system had given too much power to the slave owners and must be scrapped. Second, the danger of southern states increasing their whites-only representation in the House of Representatives by claiming to represent blacks while denying them the vote had to be reversed. Third, the federal government must protect the civil rights of the freed slaves.

Despite Stevens's bold assertion of their political interest, Republicans did *not* move to immediately grant blacks the right to vote. Some, racists themselves, thought blacks unqualified by nature for full citizenship rights. Others thought the freedmen not yet ready to vote, being uneducated, and called for public education as a first step. A few Republicans accepted the slave owners' myth of loyal slaves and feared that whites would control black voters. Further complicating Stevens's plan for an inclusive amendment was the embarrassing fact that many northern states denied blacks the vote. In fact, in 1865 three northern states with small black populations (Wisconsin, Connecticut, and Minnesota) held referendums on extending the franchise and rejected the proposal, as did the more heavily black District of Columbia.

The Committee of Fifteen reversed the logic. Rather than give blacks the vote, they would take away representatives from states that denied blacks the vote, with the number taken away based on the number of voters denied—an approach that would have the greatest impact on southern states. Roscoe Conkling summarized their reasoning with precision, noting that if they failed to amend the Constitution, then the former Confederate states would gain an additional twenty-eight seats in the House of Representatives and Electoral College, even while denying all rights to the freedmen. These twenty-eight additional votes would be controlled by the traitors who had brought on the Civil War.[32]

This short amendment failed, but the debate paved the way for what ultimately became the Fourteenth Amendment. Initial opposition to the amendment rehashed old arguments. New Jersey's Andrew Rogers offered the usual racist terror of blacks being equal to whites, with some added aspersions against Lincoln as a tyrant who trampled the

Constitution by robbing the slave owners of their property—a charge that won few allies.[33]

A more effective Democratic objection to this first draft of the Fourteenth Amendment came from the mischievous James Brooks of New York. He pointed out that they all behaved as though only southern blacks were denied equal rights. What about the Chinese, Japanese, and Indians out west? Brooks forced Stevens to admit that the proposed amendment would cost those states representation if they denied equal rights to these groups. Then Brooks played his trump card: what about the half of the population that had never enjoyed equal rights? Congress had before it numerous petitions from women demanding the vote, to which he added a new one penned by Susan B. Anthony and Elizabeth Cady Stanton calling for universal suffrage on democratic principles, ending taxation without representation, and acknowledging that women too are citizens. Playing to the galleries, packed with women hoping for the vote, Brooks spoke on "behalf of fifteen million of our countrywomen, the fairest, brightest portion of creation, and I ask why they are not permitted to be represented." The Speaker gaveled down Brooks's effort to insert the word "sex" after "color" and warned the women to not interrupt their deliberations with further applause.[34]

Numerous political and cultural currents buffeted the drafting of the Fourteenth Amendment. For instance, Brooks had never supported legal equality for women; he used the principle to undermine Republican efforts in the same way he wielded racism. He and his fellow Democrats perceived the Republicans' greatest weakness as the country's persistent racism, followed closely by fear that all this talk of equality could inspire the women's movement to reach for full legal equality. The evidence is fairly overwhelming that most men in the United States at this time had no interest in giving up their traditional gender privileges. At the same time, women had organized the largest petition drives in American history in favor of abolishing slavery and extending equality to all citizens. All but the most progressive Republican congressmen saw the inclusion of equal rights for women in a constitutional amendment leading to its rejection by the nation's all-male voters. With the danger of gender equality safely shelved, the amendment passed the House by a vote of 120 to 46. It was then sent on to the Senate, where Republican unity collapsed.[35]

Personalities always loomed large in the Senate. Charles Sumner, who saw himself as the nation's preeminent democratic voice—as well as the handsomest senator—found fault with the proposed amendment for not going far enough. In a lengthy speech, Sumner demanded equal rights for all, extending equality to include economic opportunity and power. Sumner challenged Congress to take the next logical step in seeing "that all relics of slavery should be removed, including all distinctions of rights on account of color." He proposed an alternative amendment that would outlaw monopolies and oligarchy, as well as requiring the federal government to ensure that everyone living in the United States "shall be equal before the law." Using the classic standard of no taxation without representation, Sumner demanded the extension of full civil rights to all Americans, chiding his fellow Republicans for leaving their work "only *half done*." Yet Sumner himself did not finish the work; though he called for "universal suffrage," nowhere in his speech does he mention the inequalities of gender.[36]

The moody and disdainful William Fessenden, who had risen to national prominence as a highly effective anti-slavery lawyer, did not avoid the issue of gender, wielding it as a cudgel against Sumner. The plain meaning of words demanded that universal suffrage would include women, and if they used no taxation without representation as their standard, then, once more, women should gain the vote. He demanded that Sumner "tell me why every female that is taxed ought not to vote." For once, Sumner remained silent.

Having raised the specter of women voting, Fessenden reassured his fellow senators that they could rest easy, since voting should not be considered a civil right. Fessenden was not a proponent of gender equality; on the contrary, he wanted to make certain that Sumner's sweeping rhetoric did not mislead the public into supporting universal suffrage.

In Fessenden's creative assessment, the voter served as an officer of the state; like a juror, the voter temporarily fulfills an office required by republican government. The state may choose to limit that office to men, or to white men. With slavery ended, the country must move cautiously in the face of massive social change. The proposed amendment, Fessenden submitted, encouraged states to do the right thing, which was more effective than forcing them to move toward greater democracy.[37]

Reverdy Johnson delivered the Democratic response to the Committee of Fifteen's proposal. A master of misdirection, Johnson focused on Sumner's proposal—and his emphasis on universal suffrage—rather than discussing the actual amendment. Johnson drew laughter for suggesting that by Sumner's definition no state, including Massachusetts, had ever been republican, since women could not vote. More importantly, Johnson crafted an argument that would become a cornerstone of Supreme Court reasoning: the previous existence of slavery in no way justified the expansion of equality, since the Thirteenth Amendment had abolished slavery and so it no longer existed. Johnson twisted his logic further: since slavery no longer existed, the time had come for complete reconciliation. Fessenden's frustration boiled to the surface when Johnson demanded that former Confederates be welcomed back into Congress, asking how Grant and Sherman, who had shown leniency, dealt with their defeated enemies. Fessenden responded tersely: "They do not put them in command of the Army."[38]

Democrats based their response to the proposed amendment on their core belief in white supremacy. Indiana's Thomas Hendricks, a future vice president, took umbrage at the praise heaped upon black troops for their service during the Civil War, denying that they had thus earned the rights of citizenship. In a first draft of what would prove a successful rewriting of history, Hendricks continued, "The colored soldiers did not accomplish much," and he found it distasteful that they received any of the honors that belonged solely to the white soldiers who won the war. He wanted nothing to do with black voters "because I think we should remain a political community of white people."[39]

Republicans felt pressure on their other flank from those such as Frederick Douglass who thought the proposed amendment yet another capitulation to white supremacists. Yes, the amendment promised to punish states denying blacks the vote, but Douglass had no confidence in its enforcement. Black leaders petitioned the Senate to oppose any amendment that did not grant blacks full citizenship rights. In an accurate forecast of the future, they warned that the southern states would deny blacks the vote while Congress did nothing.[40]

With Sumner and seven other Republicans joining the Democratic opposition, the amendment received a bare majority of 25 to 22, well short of the two-thirds vote required by Article V of the Constitution. The matter might have ended there had southern Democrats and the president of the United States kept their private demons under control.[41]

With the failure of the first draft of the Fourteenth Amendment, Republicans made a strategic alteration of the highest significance, switching their focus from the right to vote to civil rights, in an effort to protect the freedmen from the violent hostility of white supremacists. However, civil rights had some fundamental limitations in nineteenth-century America.

With slavery's end, most Americans agreed that everyone had the civil right of free speech and religion. However, most other rights vanished for women, whom men perceived as dependent on men and therefore lacking the self-sufficiency necessary for full citizenship. This formulation of distinctive gender rights found its basis in the notorious concept of "coverture" put forth by William Blackstone in his seminal *Commentaries on the Laws of England* of 1765. Blackstone imagined a married couple becoming "one person in law." A woman loses her legal existence along with her name, as her civic identity is "consolidated into that of the husband; under whose wing, protection, and cover, she performs every thing." It did not matter if a woman did not marry, was widowed or abandoned—in which case she was a "relict," something that survived from an earlier age—or held a job—for her wages belonged legally to her father or husband. Women lacked political identity and legal rights.[42]

Racists, some of them Republicans, perceived African Americans as being like women—dependent and thus unworthy of citizenship. Since the days of Andrew Jackson, the Democratic Party had limited the political community to white men as the only truly independent Americans. In 1866 Republicans took the radical step of passing the nation's first civil rights act to move black men out of the dependent status to enjoy civil—if not political—equality.

Senator Lyman Trumbull, who played an important role in the passage of the Thirteenth Amendment, gave shape to this limited conception of equality. While he had long fought for an end to slavery and for the basic civil rights of free blacks in Illinois, Trumbull had no desire to admit blacks into the political community of his state or nation. He thought the best course of action would be for the nation's blacks to create their own territory out west. Doubting the probability of that solution, Trumbull saw his duty as protecting blacks from further exploitation and physical violation by southern whites.

As noted earlier, it is vital to understand that attitudes toward equality in the aftermath of the Civil War did not fall into a sharp dichotomy. As Trumbull's opinion demonstrates, Republicans divided over the best path forward. While many leading Republicans clung to white supremacy, others, particularly veterans, had come to believe in racial equality. Just as Lincoln said that a conviction in the primacy of the white race did not translate into support for slavery, so many postwar Republicans insisted that support for legal equality did not require a full commitment to egalitarianism. Many Republicans who did believe in human equality, such as Thaddeus Stevens and James Ashley, announced their adherence to white supremacy in order to retain the support of white male voters.

The Republicans' primary opponent in the battle for a civil rights act and a revised Fourteenth Amendment, President Andrew Johnson, ultimately aided the push for legal equality. Johnson made his animosity to black freedom evident from the beginning of his unfortunate presidency. Shortly after taking office, he brought an end to the efforts of General Oliver O. Howard, the head of the new Freedmen's Bureau, to settle freed slaves on their own small farms, ordering confiscated lands returned to the former enemies of the United States. After General Grant issued orders that the army protect soldiers, Freedmen's Bureau personnel, and pro-Union civilians from state prosecution, Johnson undermined these orders by removing effective commanders such as Philip Sheridan, Daniel Sickles, and John Pope, replacing them with officers friendly to the former Confederates.[43]

In response to the president's reactionary policies, and to protect the safety of the freed slaves, Trumbull put forth the 1866 Freedmen's Bureau Act. Congress created the bureau as a temporary agency to aid freed slaves, confident that southern whites would accept and respect the presence of free blacks. Faced with white violence and a hostile president, Trumbull turned to the enforcement mechanism of the Thirteenth Amendment to make the Freedmen's Bureau a permanent agency to aid blacks and protect their civil rights. The most significant and startling section of the bill was its creation of military courts that operated wherever local authorities denied blacks "any of the civil rights or immunities belonging to white persons." Trumbull enumerated those rights in one of the clearer statements of republican ideology: "the right to make and enforce contracts, to sue, be parties, and give evidence, to inherit, purchase, lease, sell, hold and convey real property, and to have full and equal benefit of all laws and proceedings for the security of person and estate." A few months later this language would become part of the Civil Rights Act of 1866.[44]

The Democrats went ballistic over Trumbull's bill. Senator Hendricks wanted to know how the Civil War had so completely altered the federal government's power to the extent that it was now buying homes for former slaves. Who would "buy a home for a white man?" he asked. Hendricks was proud that his state, Indiana, had voted in 1852 to prohibit black people from settling there and had limited the contractual rights of blacks already living in the state: "We do not allow to colored people there many civil rights." Blacks should be content with no longer being slaves and should not bother the good white Americans with demands of further rights. If passed into law, the Freedmen's Bureau Act would lead, of course and as always, to interracial sex. The end of civilization lay just around the corner.[45]

Trumbull recommended Hendricks calm down and read a little history. The white people of the South could mitigate the bill's impact by obeying the law and abandoning their reliance on violence. If the former Confederates would "do justice and deal fairly with loyal Union men in their midst, and henceforth be themselves loyal," then these states could be restored to the Union "and we shall all be moving on in harmony together." Was that so much to ask?[46]

Senator Fessenden went further, celebrating the Democrats' charge that the Freedmen's Bureau Bill expanded government power. Of course it did, because Congress had no choice but to act in the face of persistent white violence in the South. The Constitution granted Congress such powers as the representatives of the people, the same powers that Justice John Marshall had highlighted in numerous decisions and that President Lincoln had called upon to put down the rebellion. The Democrats' argument boiled down to racism and the contention that the Constitution did not explicitly grant powers "in a case which could not be foreseen, and which the founders of this Government purposely avoided foreseeing or speaking about!" Just because the Framers felt it necessary to avoid talking about slavery did not mean that all future generations must do so. Democrats even objected to the presence of blacks in the gallery, leading Fessenden to mock, "That is unconstitutional, too, I suppose." In short, Fessenden did not care if the Constitution lacked specific language supporting this effort to finish what the war started.[47]

Protecting the freedmen's civil rights evoked a much more positive response from the general public in the North than did efforts to extend suffrage. George W. Curtis, editor of *Harper's Weekly* and no supporter of an extended franchise, applauded the Freedmen's Bureau Bill as "a long step forward" for the entire country. Giving former slaves unoccupied southern land was a positive act for blacks and the South, helping the former slaves gain economic independence while fostering productivity in this blighted region. Absent economic stability, all efforts to help them "will be futile."[48]

Enjoying considerable public support, the Freedmen's Bureau Bill coasted to victory. Every Republican senator voted for the bill, while every Democrat voted against it, leading to its passage 37–10. With one Republican exception, the same pattern held in the House, where the bill passed 137–33.[49]

On February 19, 1866, President Johnson vetoed the bill as unconstitutional and dangerous to the public welfare and to blacks themselves. Johnson's stated concern for the freedmen stood upon the persistent perception of them as an inferior, dependent people. Shortly before his veto, Johnson met with a black delegation that included Frederick Douglass. The president harangued Douglass on the danger of giving blacks the vote on the bizarre logic that the former slaves would unite with their former masters to the detriment of poor whites. In his veto message, Johnson asserted that the Freedmen's Bureau would make blacks dependent on the federal government; they would find a better future as dependents of their employers, who needed their labor. If a freedman does not like his place of employment, he can move. Johnson, the former supporter of slavery, now placed his faith in the free market. "There is no danger that the exceedingly great demand for labor will not operate in favor of the laborer." The president made no reference to the southern black codes.[50]

Johnson added one more curious curve to his peculiar veto message: he was more equal than all others. Members of Congress represent states and localities, but only "the President is chosen by the people of all the States." Since the eleven Confederate states had no representatives in Congress, Johnson must act on their behalf. Given that those states had not participated in the 1864 election and that Johnson had not been elected president, his claim to be the only one able to speak for the seceded states and for the whole nation was both extraordinary and directly contradictory. As the sole embodiment of the nation, he alone would decide on the future of the seceded states and their reconstruction—Congress had no role in the process. It was an astonishing claim of executive power from someone claiming to fear federal tyranny.[51]

Johnson's veto shocked the country. Thomas Nast caught the national mood well in a cartoon showing the president kicking the Freedmen's Bureau down the White House steps. Senators Trumbull and Fessenden had discussed the bill with Johnson before its passage and left the White House convinced that he supported the act. They, and most Republicans, suddenly realized that the president was not one of them. But they fell short of the two-thirds majority in the Senate required to override his veto. Representative James Wilson of Iowa immediately introduced a new Freedmen's Bureau Bill, launching a war with the president.[52]

Though both the Freedmen's Bureau Bill and the first draft of the Fourteenth Amendment had been defeated in early 1866, they laid the foundation for a complete rethinking of the nature of equal rights and a fundamental reformation of the Constitution. Across the country a growing consensus developed that Congress had to do more to forestall the southern elite from replacing one form of racial subjugation with another. Public letters and meetings, speeches and petitions, and newspaper and magazine editorials—even from traditionally Democratic sources—demanded congressional action. Citizen groups and local Republican organizations joined the fray. The National Convention of Colored Men, meeting in Syracuse, spoke for many of these activists with their published defense of legal equality. Inequality, among whites as well as between whites and blacks, had been fostered by the slave owners, who "divided both to conquer each." Now President Johnson sought to "arm the strong and cast down the defenseless" in the name of the status quo. The degradation of blacks would never produce social harmony, which could only emerge from "a state of equal justice between all classes."[53]

Leading Republicans joined in this renewed battle for legal equality. Given a hostile president and the certainty that at some point in the near future the Republicans would lose their large congressional majority, Representative Bingham and Senator Trumbull agreed with black and women activists that the Constitution required another amendment to force the states to respect legal equality. Trumbull crafted a bill that would give the government the power to protect the rights of its citizens, while Bingham charged forward with a stunning proposal to completely transform the Constitution and apply the Bill of Rights to the states.

Meanwhile, Senator Fessenden moved on the political front to keep returning Confederates out of Congress. The Maine senator proposed that Congress not admit any southern representatives until both houses agreed that a state was ready for readmission to the Union—and they, not President Johnson, would set the criteria for that approval. In directly challenging the president, Fessenden activated the majority of both houses in refusing to stand by while Johnson made all the key decisions in the nation's reconstruction. Congress delighted in declaring that they had the power to determine when a southern state could rejoin the Union.[54]

After this assertion of congressional authority, Senator Trumbull pushed the Senate to a rapid consideration of his Civil Rights Act of 1866. This act broke new legal ground in being the first law to define citizenship ("all persons born in the United States") while promising to protect all citizens in their rights, even against state action. The full force of the federal government, including the military, backed this strikingly thorough grant of legal equality.[55]

Democratic opposition to the Civil Rights Act is too tedious to repeat. Extending rights to black men would propel white women into their arms, et cetera—the same argument white supremacists would make for the next century. After dwelling on the danger of "amalga-mation," Senator Garrett Davis of Kentucky insisted that only white men could be citizens and Congress could do nothing about it. Davis weaved and dodged when challenged by New Hampshire's Daniel Clark to show him where the Constitution said that and to explain whether women could be citizens. Finally, an exasperated Clark charged that the Democratic position "only comes back to this, that a nigger is a nigger." To extensive laughter, Senator Davis agreed: "That is the whole of it." [56]

The only new argument the Democrats offered would also become a standard of racist opposition to federal action. Willard Saulsbury of Delaware pointed out that the Civil War had ended nearly a year before, the slaves were free, and "I think the time for shedding tears over the poor slave has well nigh passed." The time had come, Saulsbury said, to worry about the true victims here, white men. It seems that white men suffered from government oppression under the Republicans. Neither Saulsbury nor any other Democrat would respond to Republican challenges regarding what course of action could be pursued when a state refused to treat its citizens equally; they simply refused to admit that a state could or would do such a thing. [57]

These debates demonstrate a persistent chasm within American politics. While the Democrats clung to a prewar racial ideology justifying inequality and violence, Republicans transitioned to a conviction in equality before the law as an essential right. Their earlier theory of labor equality—perfectly expressed by Lincoln in 1858 as everyone's "right to put into his mouth the bread that his own hands have earned"—evolved through the war into the realization that a right to work offered no protection for personal liberty. In introducing the Civil Rights Act, James Wilson assured his fellow representatives that the bill did not break from his party's traditional caution, for civil rights remained narrowly defined along the lines laid out in James Kent's *Commentaries* in 1826: "the right to personal security, the right of personal liberty, and the right to acquire and enjoy property." If the southern states simply respected "the rights of our citizens, there would be no need for this bill."[58]

The Senate approved the Civil Rights Act 33 to 12 and sent it on to the House, which passed it by a substantial majority, 111 to 38.[59]

Everyone, including his supporters, expected President Johnson's signature on the act, especially since he had called for such legislation in his veto of the Freedmen's Bureau Bill. Andrew Johnson, however, never fulfilled expectations. He did not just veto the Civil Rights Act; he did so with a racist denial of black citizenship drawn straight from Justice Taney's *Dred Scott* decision—a source many northerners blamed for the advent of the Civil War. Johnson denied they possessed "the requisite qualifications" for citizenship, without specifying those qualifications, and used their exploitation as slaves as sufficient reason to deny them equal legal status. Johnson found Congress's attempt to establish equality repugnant, as it would "operate in favor of the colored and against the white race."[60]

The clearest indication of how quickly the Republican Party evolved in early 1866 is their response to Johnson's two vetoes. In February they failed to muster sufficient votes to override Johnson's veto of the popular Freedmen's Bureau Bill. Yet in April they negated his veto of the much more controversial Civil Rights Act, which altered the very nature of American law, by a vote of 122 to 41 in the House and 33 to 15 in the Senate (the only Republican voting with the president was Senator James H. Lane of Kansas, who shot himself a few weeks later). Power had passed to a Congress dominated by a radical Republican Party. Within a month they would demonstrate that political supremacy by acting independently to transform the Constitution.[61]

A wide variety of people influenced the shape and passage of the Fourteenth Amendment: freed slaves, powerful senators, female activists, small-town merchants, and a number of foreign-born intellectuals. Among the last of these, the high-energy Robert Dale Owen played a prominent role. Born in Glasgow, son of the world's leading socialist industrialist, Robert Owen, Robert Dale Owen came to the United States in 1825 to help create the New Harmony commune in Indiana. In the next forty years Owen drifted all over the political landscape. In 1861 he was a pro-slavery Democrat when South Carolina militia fired on Fort Sumter. Owen then began another political makeover.

During the war, Owen organized the arming of Indiana's troops and served on the national Ordnance Commission. Like Lincoln, Owen initially promoted the restoration of the Union as the war's sole goal. But during the summer of 1862 Owen's opinion changed dramatically. In a public letter to Lincoln, Owen called for the emancipation of the slaves and proclaimed this a war for freedom. Secretary of War Stanton, another Democrat, named Owen to the three-person American Freedmen's Inquiry Commission.

An unusual and creative idea for its time, the commission examined the condition of slaves and the recently freed, recommending future policies. Owen immersed himself in the history and structure of slavery, touring the front lines to interview runaway slaves. On his own initiative, Owen visited communities of escaped slaves in Canada, where he found that the government had granted them full legal equality and protected them from discrimination. Owen appears to have written the bulk of the commission's 1864 report, which was so startling in its recommendations that Senate Democrats attempted to block its release. The report advised the federal government to support the former slaves in their transition to freedom, from building churches and schools to creating jobs and granting lands to the freedmen. Congress accepted these recommendations by creating the Freedmen's Bureau.

By 1866 Owen had made a whole new group of friends, including Thaddeus Stevens and Charles Sumner. Through them he presented a plan to amend the Constitution to the Senate's Committee of Fifteen. His proposed amendment outlawed state discrimination and limitations on the vote based on race, granting Congress full enforcement powers.

To ensure approval, the "states lately in insurrection" could rejoin Congress only after ratifying this amendment.

Owen's proposal found a receptive audience in the committee. However, details of the proposed amendment leaked and criticisms accumulated. Democrats of course objected to anything suggesting legal equality; more unanticipated was the response of many Republicans, who worried that granting black suffrage would hurt the party in the November elections. The committee therefore removed the expansion of voting rights as well as the section laying out the path for the seceded states to return to the Union. The committee recognized the need for stronger protection of civil rights, adopting some of Bingham's language that they had earlier rejected: "No state shall make or enforce any law which shall abridge the privileges or immunities of citizens of the United States; nor shall any State deprive any person of life, liberty, or property without due process of law; nor deny to any person within its jurisdiction the equal protection of the laws." [62]

The revised Fourteenth Amendment emerged from committee during a wave of white supremacist violence in the South. Dissatisfied with the results of the Civil War, former Confederates sought to intimidate freed blacks back into quiescence. The white riots in Memphis at the beginning of May 1866 particularly caught national attention. The state's erratic and blunt governor, William G. Brownlow—a former minister and pro-slavery Whig who opposed secession, hated the slave-owning elite, and followed the example of his gun-wielding daughter Susan in becoming a radical Republican—succinctly stated the view of many whites: "If there is anything a loyal Tennessean hates more than a rebel, it is a nigger." [63]

The year 1866 had been a time of transition for Memphis, as freed blacks and Irish immigrants fleeing famine poured into the city. Tensions were high already, but the city exploded on May 1 when police led an angry white mob in burning the homes and schools of blacks and shooting unarmed freedmen. The state's attorney general, William Wallace, arrived in Memphis on the second day of the riots, not to quell the violence but to help organize and arm the white mobs. The violence continued for three days before General George Stoneman declared martial law and occupied the city with Union forces. Forty-six blacks and two whites had been killed; four churches, twelve schools, and nearly one hundred homes had been destroyed, the property of hundreds of black residents pillaged, and many black women raped.

The riots horrified the North. *The Nation* quickly pointed out that many of the opponents of the Freedmen's Bureau and Civil Rights Bill had insisted they were unnecessary since "the laws of political economy" would bring security to blacks without federal interference. Memphis demonstrated the limitations of capitalist logic, as white employers preferred intimidating black workers over negotiating with them. As a minimum for self-defense, the freedmen needed legal equality and the right to vote. Surely if local authorities had to respect the interests of black voters, they would not allow the police to randomly attack their constituents.[64]

President Johnson did not agree that white violence was unjustified, since Memphis's whites acted in defense of their way of life. In a cabinet meeting, the minutes of which the president himself leaked to the press, he delivered a monologue denouncing the proposed constitutional amendment as a betrayal of the federalist system and American liberty.[65]

In response to the president's linking of white violence with opposition to the Fourteenth Amendment, Bingham pointed out that the amendment did not take away any power from the states other than the ability to violate the nation's highest moral standards of equality and justice. By finally defining citizenship, the amendment would "protect by national law the privileges and immunities of all the citizens of the Republic."[66]

Most Republicans agreed with Bingham and Stevens that the nation had reached a pivotal turning point that allowed them to remake the Constitution to accord with the egalitarian principles in the Declaration of Independence. With the southern elite temporarily out of the political frame, they could finish the founders' work. The Constitution had failed in limiting the abuse of power by Congress and not by the states. The amendment's goal, Stevens said, is simple justice—"that the law which operates upon one man shall operate *equally* upon all." Stevens warned that they must move beyond the Civil Rights Act, since someday the Democrats would regain control of Congress and undoubtedly repeal the act. Congress must repair the Constitution now and fix equal justice firmly into the nation's charter.[67]

Many progressives perceived serious flaws in the amendment, most particularly its failure to mention the right to vote. Wendell Phillips called it "a swindle," while Frederick Douglass dismissed the amendment for making citizenship "but an empty name." Even more outraged were the nation's female activists.[68]

At just over four hundred words, the Fourteenth Amendment is the Constitution's longest amendment. It also embedded the first mention of gender in the Constitution. The opening use of "All persons" certainly pointed to an easy path forward that would include all Americans. But Section 2 based representation on the number of "male inhabitants," implying the limitation of the franchise to men. Leaders of the women's movement charged a betrayal of their prewar bargain by which they agreed to fight first for the end of slavery and then for female suffrage. When they demanded to know why the word "male" was being inserted into the Constitution, the answer they received was: "Suffrage for the black men will be all the strain the Republican party can stand." Elizabeth Cady Stanton felt they could stand a little more strain. Yet she admitted that women had few options with which to address this step backward by the Republican Party.[69]

Even some men saw the abandonment of equal rights in the proposed amendment. The New York *Independent* labeled the amendment "A Law Against Women." While the Constitution did women few favors, editor Theodore Tilton noted, it had "never laid any legal disabilities upon woman." Now the law of the land directly denied women any political rights. The Fourteenth Amendment had thus become "an obstacle to future progress."[70]

Stanton and Anthony organized a massive petition drive calling on Congress to pass an amendment "that shall prohibit the several States from disenfranchising any of their children on the ground of sex." Tired of being forbidden a civic identity, they called for a new organization to fight for equal rights for women, a movement that they hoped would match the commitment and drive of abolitionism. On May 10, 1866, Stanton opened the Woman's Rights Convention in New York City with a call to "base our government on the broad principle of equal rights to all." The convention approved a resolution written by Anthony demanding universal suffrage.

However, the proponents of equality for all stumbled over a fundamental division that would hinder their efforts for decades: racism. Henry Ward Beecher, the most famous minister in the country with a solid track record of supporting reform causes, emphasized, "It is more important that woman should vote than that the black man should vote." Often in the ensuing years, Stanton and Anthony became so frustrated with their Sisyphean struggle that they lashed out at blacks either for getting priority or for holding back the movement for universal suffrage, a response exploited by the opponents of equal rights. As Stanton said, the insertion of the word "male" into the Fourteenth Amendment undermined the concept of women's citizenship and set back the struggle for equality by a century.[71]

Democrats, stuck on repeat, tried to exploit the progressives' split over gender to defeat the amendment. Andrew Rogers issued the usual warnings about it leading to the ruin of "the pure white blood of the Anglo-Saxon people." He now added that legal equality would force states to treat blacks and whites equally in criminal cases, inflicting "the same punishment upon a white man for rape as upon a black man." Reeling from the horror of equality before the law, Rogers rejected all amendments as inherently bad. Robert Schenck of Ohio, a former Union general, asked him if he opposed "every alteration of the Constitution on the ground that it has a tendency to change the instrument." Rogers replied in the affirmative.[72]

Rogers and his fellow Democrats did not want to change the Constitution because doing so would undermine the essential truth that the United States existed for the benefit of white men. Writing equality into the Constitution would interfere in the "sacred and immutable" right of the states to organize their societies as they wished, forcing every kind of cultural change upon a helpless nation. The Fourteenth Amendment "will prevent any State from refusing anything to anybody" and earn the wrath of an angry and racist God, who had given the United States to white men and stamped blacks with the mark of their inferiority. Rogers stormed, "God save the people of the South from the degradation by which they would be obliged to go to the polls and vote side by side with the negro!" Democrats could not imagine "the people of the South" as anything but fellow white racists.[73]

While the Democrats ranted about the coming apocalypse of multicultural democracy, southern racists accelerated their violent attacks on the freedmen. In Pulaski, Tennessee, a group of Confederate veterans founded an organization whose very name haunts American history, the Ku Klux Klan. They selected as their leader Nathan Bedford Forrest, the former slave-catcher and Confederate general responsible for one of the worst war crimes of the Civil War, the slaughter of Union prisoners of war at Fort Pillow in 1864. Over the next several years the Klan's terror campaign scarred every southern state.

Through the spring of 1866, the proposed amendment moved back and forth between Senate and House committees, with its proponents highlighting racist violence to accelerate the vote in Congress. On May 10, the House of Representatives voted on a draft of the amendment. After so much compromise and so many concessions, enthusiasm was a bit muted compared to that which had greeted the Thirteenth Amendment. Nonetheless, the public galleries were packed with people hoping to witness a significant step toward the establishment of legal equality.

Scornful of Democrats begging for forgiveness from the former Confederates, Stevens pointed to recent acts of violence to demand immediate action. "Let not these friends of secession sing to me their siren song of peace and good will until they can stop my ears to the screams and groans of the dying victims at Memphis."

The Republicans swamped the Democrats, the House voting for the amendment 128 to 37. As applause swept the public galleries, Democratic representative Charles Eldredge angrily objected to this outburst from the "nigger-heads," evoking boos and hisses from the galleries. Stevens changed the mood back to laughter and celebration by asking, "Is it in order for members on the floor to disturb those in the galleries?" The Speaker agreed that "members upon the floor should not insult the spectators."[74]

Two weeks later the Senate took up the amendment. The report of Fessenden's Committee on Reconstruction markedly influenced the debate. After once more chronicling recent racist violence, the committee recommended increased federal authority to protect the rights of the freedmen and their white allies. Slavery had created an "oligarchy adverse to republican institutions," one that was willing to tear the nation apart rather than lose its grip on southern society. Leaving that class in political power could lead to another civil war. The committee marshaled compelling evidence that most southern leaders still defended their right of secession, lacked loyalty to the United States, and remained intolerant of those loyal to the Union, whether white or black. If allowed to reclaim political power without adequate protection for the rights of Union supporters, the southern elites would once more attempt to run the country for their own benefit.[75]

The Senate debate replicated that in the House. With Fessenden out sick, leadership fell to Jacob Howard of Michigan, a former anti-slavery attorney who had predicted a civil war over slavery back in 1850 and had helped found the Republican Party. In finally defining citizenship and applying the Bill of Rights to the states, the Fourteenth Amendment would end the inequality that had plagued the United States from its founding. While favoring "universal suffrage," Howard abided by the committee's recommendation that the time had not yet come for this radical step. Nonetheless, the amendment would force every state to live by the standards of republicanism and ensure equality before the law.[76]

Howard stumbled in admitting that he favored votes for women, a position that still did not enjoy widespread public support. Reverdy Johnson leapt on this slip and engaged in a clarifying exchange with Howard that revealed the limitations of language, the law, and logic. In supporting votes for the freedmen, Howard quoted James Madison on "the vital principle of free government, that those who are to be bound by the laws ought to have a voice in making them." Johnson wanted to know if that generalization included "females as well as males." Howard attempted to wriggle away from the question by correctly noting that "Mr. Madison does not say anything about females." Johnson shot back with that one key word from the proposed amendment: "persons." Howard offered a pedantic response that concluded with a comment reflective of the limitations of liberal thought in the nineteenth century: "Everywhere mature manhood is the representative type of the human race."[77]

While Republicans hoped the amendment would sweep away that "state sovereignty" nonsense, Democrats fought a rear-guard action in defense of the old vision of federalism. Democratic senator Edgar Cowan of Pennsylvania revived the notion that citizenship was a privilege, a gift from the individual states rather than a national right. He seemed genuinely afraid that the Fourteenth Amendment would grant citizenship to "gypsies," dangerous gangs of Romani who wandered his state, telling fortunes and making "things disappear mysteriously." They no more deserved citizenship than did blacks, Chinese, and Indians. Citizenship was a blood right rather than a birthright, open only to white males. The amendment's inclusive definition would lead to non-whites taking over the country.[78]

California's John Conness assured Cowan that his state would manage just fine with some Chinese citizens. The senator had never heard "of the invasion of Pennsylvania by Gypsies." The only invasion of that state with which Conness was familiar had come at the hands of southern rebels, and he thought this amendment would prevent its recurrence. He did not remember that Pennsylvania "claimed the exclusive right of expelling the invaders, but on the contrary my recollection is that Pennsylvania called loudly for the assistance of her sister States." He heard no claims of states' rights from the victors at Gettysburg.[79]

The Democrats only had two arrows in their quiver: states' rights and racism. The Civil War had seriously diminished these interwoven attitudes, but that was all they had. Thomas Hendricks regretted the passage of the Thirteenth Amendment, which extended the ill will generated by the Civil War. If only the North had left slavery in place, the Union could have reunited easily. Now the Republicans insanely wanted to define citizenship to include anyone born in the United States. Appalled that he would share citizenship "with the negroes, the coolies, and the Indians," Hendricks warned that Republicans intended to extinguish the states and establish a despotic federal government.[80]

The Democrats did not hold these positions as a false cover; they sincerely believed in states' rights and white supremacy. They could not grasp the Republican view that the Fourteenth Amendment would create a true union of the American people. As Republican Luke Poland of Vermont observed, the Civil War had unleashed an "unparalleled social revolution" that opened the South to "the influence of free labor and free institutions," allowing it to break free of its self-imposed isolation and poverty. He painted a glowing portrait of prosperous towns brought to life by "commerce and manufactures" and the transformation of the United States into "a homogeneous nation of free men, dwelling together in peace and unity." That vision horrified Democrats, who remained enthralled to prewar ideologies that could not accept the end of slavery and the rejection of a state sovereignty dogma that had cost hundreds of thousands of lives. Completely baffled, Senator Cowan asked what difference Ohio's decision about who could vote made to someone in Pennsylvania. The very idea of national citizenship eluded him, and he could not imagine that a citizen of Ohio might want to enjoy the same rights in whatever state he chose to make home—even Alabama. To suggest that every state should respect the Bill of Rights "is to revolutionize the whole frame and texture of the system of our Government." Somehow he had missed the entire Civil War.[81]

Where Democrats gloomily perceived unhinged radicalism, Republicans saw moderation. The Fourteenth Amendment did not create new rights, such as universal suffrage, but clarified citizenship, protected existing rights, and gave Congress the authority to respond to gross violations of those rights. Voting along party lines, the Senate approved the Fourteenth Amendment, with some minor alteration of language, 33 to 11. The House also followed party lines in approving the altered language on June 13 by a vote of 120 to 32, sending the amendment on to the states for their consideration. Matters would only get more complicated.[82]

Having passed the Fourteenth Amendment, congressional Republicans had little expectation that three-fourths of the states would ratify it. While Republicans controlled a solid majority of the northern legislatures, it was not clear if the southern states could participate in the process. If they did so, would they continue to function with their Confederate legislatures?

Further hindering Republican efforts was the bitter animosity of President Johnson, who denied the legitimacy of recent congressional actions and insisted that southern states had to rejoin the Union before any amendment could go forward. Democrats turned up the rhetorical racism, which meshed well with a growing willingness among northern whites to accept the rapid reintegration of the southern states into the Union, even if they were run by former Confederates. But these former slave owners had a long tradition of getting their way through violence, and they employed it with a vengeance in 1866. Where the Memphis riots in May influenced the passage of the Fourteenth Amendment in

Congress, the bloodbath in New Orleans fired support for its adoption in numerous state legislatures.[83]

On July 30, 1866, Louisiana Republicans convened a constitutional convention at the Mechanics Institute in New Orleans. Rumors spread through the city that the all-white convention intended to write a state constitution that would enshrine universal male suffrage. Just as the meeting came to order, a large mob of angry Democrats attacked the building, killing every black person they saw as well as many white Republicans. The rampage spread through neighboring streets, leading to two hundred casualties, including thirty-eight deaths. The New Orleans police, who owed their jobs to Democratic Party patronage, did nothing to curtail the violence, with many officers participating in the riot. In a widely published report, General Philip Sheridan labeled the riots "an absolute massacre." It soon emerged that the city's mayor had helped organize the attack on the convention and that President Johnson had ordered the military garrison in the city to not intervene. Northern public opinion swung firmly behind the proposed amendment.[84]

Connecticut and New Hampshire ratified the Fourteenth Amendment immediately, on June 30 and July 7, respectively. The third state to ratify was Andrew Johnson's Tennessee. Governor Brownlow and President Johnson despised each other, leading Brownlow, once more influenced by his daughter, to side with the state's radical Republicans. When Johnson's followers in the legislature went into hiding to prevent a quorum, the Republicans sent police to drag two of them back, passing the amendment 43 to 11. Brownlow sent a telegram to John Bingham announcing the vote, adding, "Give my compliments to the dirty dog in the White House." Congress immediately voted to seat Tennessee's representatives.[85]

Tennessee proved the exception in the South, as state after state rejected the amendment, often by unanimous votes. All-white southern legislatures, identifying their refusal to defend the rights of the freedmen as self-defense, charged Republicans with attempting to pass political control to the blacks. In the northern states, the story was the complete opposite, especially after Andrew Johnson's notorious speaking tour in August 1866.

The president intended to rally northern support for a rapid reconstruction by undertaking an eighteen-day speaking tour through twenty-one cities and numerous towns as far west as St. Louis. Johnson did not receive a warm welcome, and he fought with hecklers in a rather undignified manner. When the crowd in St. Louis began shouting "New Orleans," Johnson outrageously accused the radical Republicans of planning the riot. The papers covered every confrontation and increasingly more bizarre statements from the president, including his rather immodest comparison of himself to Jesus Christ. In Indianapolis the crowd grew so angry that Johnson gave up trying to speak.

Despite the obvious lesson of his "Swing Around the Circle," as his speaking tour became known, Johnson attempted to intervene in the highly polarized congressional election of 1866. But every presidential attack only seemed to increase the Republicans' popularity. Even earlier supporters of Johnson, such as General Grant, felt driven to the Republicans. Grant initially traveled with Johnson on his campaign tour but quickly tired of the president, writing his wife, Julia, that he had come to look on Johnson's speeches "as a National disgrace." [86]

Carl Schurz, who would soon become senator from Missouri, had spent the previous year trying to find common ground with Johnson. But by the end of the summer in 1866 Schurz also toured the country, speaking against Johnson's southern policies and in favor of the proposed Fourteenth Amendment. Johnson, champion of the "reactionists," wanted them to forgive their enemies but forget their friends, offering a return to a violent and despotic past. Schurz warned that Johnson's policies would terminate First Amendment rights and hand the country over to mob rule. The United States would again be divided "between the fighting traitors of the South and the scheming traitors of the North." The riots in Memphis and New Orleans proved the need for the Fourteenth Amendment, which would defend the civil rights of all Americans and prevent the rise of another oligarchy. The struggle over this amendment was "the final battle of the war," one that would decide whether justice triumphed.[87]

The election of 1866 may have been the only one in American history to function as a referendum on a constitutional amendment. Democrats campaigned furiously against the amendment, presenting themselves as the defenders of inequality and champions of white male privilege. Most Republicans carefully downplayed the potential radicalism of the amendment and sidelined black activists, projecting an all-white image so as to not frighten voters. The strategy worked brilliantly for the Republicans, who increased their representation in the House from 136 to 173 and in the Senate from 39 to 57—more than two-thirds of each house. Effectively marginalized, both the Democratic Party and the president faded into insignificance as Congress took over Reconstruction. Not only did Republicans control most northern and western legislatures, but now they also could set the criteria for the readmission of the former Confederate states to the Union.

The Republican-dominated legislatures moved rapidly to ratify the amendment. With twenty-eight states required to adopt the amendment, twenty northern and western states plus Tennessee voted their approval by March 20, 1867. At that time, the new Congress voted to require the former Confederate states to ratify the Fourteenth Amendment before being returned to the Union. Even as the southern states held the first moderately democratic elections in their history, leading to ratification by six of these states, some northern legislatures had second thoughts. At the start of 1868, Democrats and conservative Republicans in Oregon, New Jersey, and Ohio tried to revoke their ratifications. The New Jersey legislature insisted that the amendment's goals were "unseemly and unjust" and threatened national harmony. They charged congressional Republicans with being race traitors intent on "reducing to slavery men of their own race" in the South in order to gain political primacy there.[88]

Congress reacted quickly, passing a law denying a state the right to reverse its approval of an amendment. In the ensuing confusion,

Secretary of State William Seward hesitated to confirm the amendment, even though twenty-eight legislatures had now ratified it. Once more Congress took the initiative, declaring the Fourteenth Amendment part of the Constitution on July 21, 1868, pressuring Seward to give his official approval one week later.

For Republicans, the Fourteenth Amendment finally made real the promise of Article IV of the Constitution, that "the citizens of each State shall be entitled to all the privileges and immunities of citizens in the several States." Alexander Hamilton, in Federalist No. 80, had labeled Article IV "the basis of the Union." If people could not travel from one part of the nation to another without enjoying the same rights, could they truly be esteemed free? Was the United States really one nation if geography determined rights?[89]

Prior to the Civil War, a free American, no matter what race or gender, living outside the South could not move to that part of the country and enjoy the rights thought foundational to American liberty. The southern states negated freedom of assembly, speech, and movement, and they did not protect personal safety or respect humanity if it interfered with slavery. In theory, the Fourteenth Amendment changed all that in establishing national citizenship, with its assurance of equal rights before the law. But the essence of law is enforcement; unenforced laws have no meaning. After the passage of the Fourteenth Amendment the great question remained: did the words of the Constitution translate into reality?

CHAPTER 6

Equality for Half

Or, deciding to dodge equality

A decade of democracy reborn followed the passage of the Civil Rights Act of 1866. In the South, coalitions of white and black Republicans won the majority of elections and took over former Confederate state governments. They began instituting the Republican platform of expanded democratic participation and protection of civil rights, public education and internal improvements, and progressive taxation that fell most heavily on the wealthy. For this brief period, the United States experimented with democracy and discovered that it worked.

The freedmen enjoyed wide public support in these years, especially as many former Confederates responded violently to the extension of political rights to former slaves. Racist violence confronted the nation with the reality that market forces and a theoretical equality before the law are insufficient to protect the lives of all Americans. A consensus emerged that the federal government must act to defend democracy in the South.

Frederick Douglass credited Anna Dickinson with being the first person to urge the necessity of a Fifteenth Amendment, in 1866. Dickinson traveled the country arousing crowds with her call for true democracy, galvanizing the North to take the next step toward full equality through the grant of universal suffrage. Douglass and the political leaders who took up her call for action did not seem to realize that Dickinson really meant "universal," including women. As a result, the

Fifteenth Amendment would, ultimately, both expand (for men) and severely limit (for women) the reach of equality.[1]

American political theory is premised on the notion that the vote is necessary both to secure representation of one's interests and to protect one's rights from government overreach. By this premise, the Fifteenth Amendment left women without representation and unprotected in the enjoyment of their basic rights.

Women at the time noticed their exclusion from full citizenship. Leaders of the women's suffrage movement, including Sojourner Truth, opposed the Fifteenth Amendment for excluding women. As male reformers who had once promised their support for women's suffrage settled on democracy for half the nation and called on women to sacrifice their interests to those of black men, Elizabeth Cady Stanton wrote to one former male ally, "We must not trust any of you."[2]

Progressive forces lacked a unified program for the extension of equality, and many of their leaders allowed political calculation to guide them. Some activists, primarily women, thought the next step forward both obvious and easy. Before, during, and after the debate over the Fifteenth Amendment, Anna Dickinson summarized the liberal goal in two words: "universal suffrage." No true democracy existed without every adult encouraged to participate in the political life of the nation. Elizabeth Cady Stanton presented a similarly succinct program for the nation: "Our demand has long been suffrage for all, white and black, male and female, of legal age and sound mind." But this notion of complete legal equality, as represented by the shared right to vote, had only recently gained traction.[3]

Equality burst on the American public during the Civil War, motivating tens of thousands of people to seek greater involvement in their country's governance. However, this novel notion frightened as many people as it energized. Having fought and lost a war for the protection and promotion of racial slavery, large numbers of southern whites violently struggled to limit the consequences of their defeat. In the five years after the Civil War, the United States stepped right up to the unexplored abyss of full legal equality, but then scurried back in terror before an uncertain future. Having established the principle of legal equality in the Fourteenth Amendment in 1868, the country immediately moved to limit its reach before too many people took it seriously. With the Fifteenth Amendment, Congress craftily separated voting rights from legal rights.

In the battle over the Fifteenth Amendment, the Republicans compromised with ghosts. Despite their formidable control of both houses of Congress (they had a 126-seat advantage in the House and a 48-seat advantage in the Senate), the federal courts, most state legislatures, and, with the election of Ulysses S. Grant in 1868, the White House, Republicans often hesitated before the specter of reactionary obstruction. At the time, the Democratic Party was in disarray and their resistance to the Fifteenth Amendment ineffectual.

Republicans could have pushed for universal suffrage, as the party's leadership often claimed they would. Leading members of Congress such as Thaddeus Stevens, Benjamin Wade, John Bingham, and Charles Sumner often spoke in favor of full equality. However, the majority of Republicans saw no political advantage in extending the vote or even legal equality to women, and they enjoyed having power far too much to risk alienating an all-male electorate that showed no interest in giving up their primacy. In containing equality, the Republican leadership divided and fragmented the progressive movement through the end of the nineteenth century, opening the door for reactionary forces to restore racist systems of social control in the South. In brief, having won the Civil War and established a working democracy in the South, the Republican Party passively allowed the defeated Confederates to restore white dominance over every aspect of southern society. Equality flared brightly for a decade, only to be smothered into a smoldering ember.

=

Gender would ultimately prove the major stumbling block for
Republicans, but initially they also agonized over the issue of black
suffrage. They feared that the explicit granting of voting rights to
African Americans would lose them white votes in the North—thus
the careful evasions in the Fourteenth Amendment. In 1866, a number
of northern newspapers warned of the danger inherent in granting
the vote to the uneducated, and former slaves had been denied the
benefits of schooling until liberated by Union troops. On the other
hand, public sentiment in the North demanded that the freedmen
be given the tools necessary to protect themselves from the violence
of former Confederates, and there was widespread faith in the ballot
as the best form of self-protection. The accepted reasoning ran that
public officials would not act too excessively contrary to the interests
of such a large block of voters.

The Republicans' enormous success in the 1866 congressional elections, combined with the nearly ceaseless news of racist violence in the
South, finally emboldened the Republicans to press ahead. The first
indication of this new attitude came as Congress voted for black suffrage in the District of Columbia in December 1866. When President
Johnson vetoed the measure as a dangerous extension of the vote to
people who "cannot be expected correctly to comprehend the duties and
responsibilities which pertain to suffrage," the congressional Republican
supermajority promptly and easily overrode his veto. They followed up
with a bill giving blacks in the territories the vote. This time Johnson
signed the legislation.[4]

The campaign for black suffrage stumbled with the 1867 state elections. As was now the hallmark of their party, Democrats stoked
fears of racial equality in their campaign nationwide. The charge that
Republicans sought social equality for blacks, which would lead to
the promiscuous mixing of the races, propelled electoral victories in
Connecticut, New Jersey, Ohio, and California. Black suffrage referendums in Minnesota, Kansas, and Ohio went down to defeat. While
to some Republicans this indicated a need to back away from talk of

equal rights, to others it produced a different logic: the need for black votes in the North.

At the start of 1868, Thaddeus Stevens presented Congress with an amendment giving black men the vote. Publicly he spoke of equality, but privately he told friends that the Republican Party could only maintain power with the votes of blacks in the North and South. In this regard, Stevens accurately reflected the views of his party, which sincerely fought for legal equality for blacks but gave primacy to sustaining the party's own political power.[5]

In the ensuing debates, the Republicans repeatedly contrasted the nation's loyal black citizens with treasonous southern whites. As Robert Ingersoll of Minnesota stated, "It is our duty to see that no man who had fought for the flag should be under the feet of him who had insulted it." His own state indicated the dramatic shift in northern attitudes, impelled in large part by southern white intransigence. The state held three referendums on granting black men the vote in the aftermath of the Civil War. In 1865, the state's voters rejected universal male suffrage by 14,838 to 12,170, though by decade's end there were still fewer than a thousand black people in the whole state. When the matter came up again in 1867, by which time Union soldiers had returned, twice as many voters participated, with a close defeat for equal suffrage, 28,759 to 27,461. Just one year later, after the state Republican Party threw its support behind the proposal, it passed by a substantial majority, 39,322 to 29,906.[6]

There is other evidence that racial attitudes had evolved significantly by 1868, at least outside the South. Initial reports in northern newspapers of black electoral participation moved from condescending to respectful as observers reported on the serious tone with which the freedmen took their new political equality. Most northern newspapers gave laudatory attention to the first participation of black voters in South Carolina's constitutional convention election of November 1867. Former slaves poured out to exercise their newfound freedom. On the Sea Islands, the vote took place in Beaufort's Hall of Justice, formerly a place where slaves were tortured. Many freedmen became deeply emotional as they cast their first ballots in this place of their former humiliation and pain. In January 1868, the convention opened with a majority of black delegates—accurately reflecting a state that was 60 percent African American—intent on overturning the racist constitution of 1865. Their constitution granted universal male suffrage and protected the right of women to own property in their own name.

The northern press and members of Congress saw cause for celebration in this and several other conventions that overturned slave-era constitutions to produce more truly democratic institutions than had ever before existed in the South. The *Charleston Mercury*, which did not share its northern peers' admiration for these events, responded by labeling the gathering "the mongrel convention," full of ugly "darkies" and other "scum" who might have made good slaves but had no place in the halls of power.[7]

As in most Confederate states, Georgia's white elite hoped to rejoin the Union without making significant changes to their social order. At their all-white October 1865 convention in Milledgeville, they adopted a new constitution that eliminated slavery but denied civil rights to the freedmen. While President Johnson accepted this constitution, Congress did not. In 1867 the U.S. Army took over the process of voter registration, including black men, and ensuring safe and free elections. The Atlanta convention, which was 22 percent black, finished its work in March 1868, and, unlike the preceding convention, presented their constitution to the voters. The following month the voters of Georgia approved this liberal constitution, which extended the vote to all adult males and mandated free public schools, with 56 percent of the vote. It is worth noting that African Americans constituted 45 percent of the state's population and 17 percent of the new General Assembly.[8]

Much the same pattern held in other southern states. The Richmond convention, which concluded in April 1868, also included a significant number of black delegates and offered the voters a progressive constitution similar to Georgia's. Virginia's new constitution received the approval of 95 percent of the 220,000 voters. The Raleigh, North Carolina, convention of early 1868 also produced a constitution upholding universal male suffrage, full civil rights for blacks, and the state's first public education system, passing with 56 percent of the vote. Conventions in Florida, Alabama, Mississippi, Louisiana, and Arkansas in 1868, Texas in 1869, and Tennessee in 1870 produced similar constitutions. Union adherents found validation that the Civil War had been fought for a definite purpose.[9]

As congressional Republicans attempted to rewrite the Constitution into a democratic document, they knew full well that they would face the voters in November. Despite the nomination of the enormously popular General Ulysses S. Grant as the Republican nominee, the 1868 presidential election was very much up for grabs. Chief Justice Salmon P. Chase reacted positively to overtures from Democratic leaders who proposed him as their presidential candidate. But Chase made clear that he wanted the party to break from their racist past and accept "suffrage for all." Despite his firm opposition to Chase's egalitarian views, New York's governor, Horatio Seymour, promoted Chase at the Democratic convention in New York City. Seymour felt that the only way to win against Grant was to ignore race and run Chase, a former Democrat, as someone who could unite conservatives across party lines. Instead, the convention—which included former Confederate leaders such as Ku Klux Klan head Nathan Forrest—was a byzantine mess. Its rule requiring a two-thirds majority extended the process through twenty-two ballots, with the ironic result that Seymour was selected as their reluctant nominee. Seymour's running mate was the former Republican Francis Blair Jr. of Missouri.

The Democratic campaign never rose above disastrous, especially given Blair's vicious racism, which he shared widely as he campaigned across the country. In October, several leading Democrats who valued winning more than ideological purity tried to remove both candidates and replace Seymour with Chase, but that effort again floundered on Chase's support for legal equality. Despite the Democrats' divisions, the election proved a lot closer than expected. In large part, this was because the KKK determined that the only way white racists could win in the South was through violent voter suppression; the terror campaign proved especially effective in Louisiana and Georgia, the only former Confederate states to go Democratic in 1868. In those states, the Klan and their allies killed Republican leaders both white and black, kept black voters away from polling places, and stuffed ballot boxes. *The Nation* charged that the Democrats carried those states through "organized assassination." These tactics would soon be adopted by Democrats in other southern states.[10]

In spite of this intimidation, black voters helped the Republicans carry most southern states, thereby proving their value to the party. Blacks understood that the Republican Congress sided with them. When the Georgia legislature expelled every one of the recently elected black legislators in September 1868, arguing that the new state constitution gave blacks the right to vote but did not explicitly grant them the right to hold public office, Congress intervened and ordered the military to restore them to office.[11]

The southern black vote is estimated to have been a little more than 450,000; Grant won the popular vote by 309,000 out of 5,716,000 votes cast. Additionally, the Republicans won narrow victories in several states where blacks could not yet vote, reminding the party how important those votes might prove in the future. Republican newspapers picked up on this latter point to encourage a constitutional amendment assuring the right of black men to vote.[12]

Such an amendment was necessary because individual states, and sometimes individual polling officers, determined whether black men could vote. Because of the Reconstruction Act and the rush of new constitutions in the South, blacks enjoyed greater voting rights in the South than in the North or West in 1868. Nonetheless, black codes still kept freedmen from voting in several southern states, and in 1865, nineteen of the twenty-four northern and western states prohibited blacks from voting. These prohibitions were not always enforced, but officials in some places, such as Cincinnati, actively kept blacks from the polls. A final motivation for the Republicans to push forward quickly was the certainty that if they allowed the issue to drag on too long, the Democrats would use it as a cudgel in the years ahead. Better to get it over with as soon as possible, preferably well before the 1870 elections. Republican leaders also perceived that they needed to act on the national level rather than state by state.

Republicans did not hide their motives. Sumner bluntly referenced northern states where blacks could not vote and asked if his Republican colleagues would like their votes in the future. Of course, giving black men the vote was morally just, but they should not pretend that political reality played no role in their call for equal suffrage. Sumner saw no reason to delay passing another constitutional amendment: "Party, country, mankind, will be elevated, while the Equal Rights of all will be fixed on a foundation not less enduring than the Rock of Ages."[13]

Grant's victory in the 1868 election set the stage for the Fifteenth Amendment to the Constitution, which would grant black men the right to vote. With Congress still firmly in Republican hands, and with a supportive president in the White House, most advocates of equality expected a smooth extension of rights. But nothing is ever certain or easy in American politics.

Writing in his autobiography years later, Nevada senator William M. Stewart, who played a key role in guiding the Fifteenth Amendment through the Senate, recalled a meeting with President-elect Grant. Grant wanted to know if the vote really served the interests of blacks. "I told him the ballot would be [the black man's] ultimate protection," but Stewart acknowledged that once southern whites regained control of their states through violence and intimidation, "the ballot of the negro would amount to very little." Grant worried that the amendment might be a waste of effort that would just make conditions worse for the freedmen, as white racists tended to use violence rather than argument. Stewart had no doubts that southern Democrats would find a way to exclude the black man, but the revised Constitution "would save him from peon laws and . . . prevent his reenslavement." Stewart conceded that the Republicans would ultimately lose most of the southern states, but he assured Grant that black voters held "the balance of power" in several northern states. According to Stewart, Grant then agreed to publicly endorse the amendment.[14]

As it turned out, the significant barrier to passage of another amendment came not from the South but from the North. As the *New York Times* succinctly stated, the "ability to justify negro enfranchisement throughout the South depends somewhat upon the readiness of the North to abate its own hostility to negro enfranchisement." Democrats therefore helpfully advised the Republicans that they would lose votes in the North if they followed this path. They correctly observed that many northern white men rebelled at the thought of blacks and women voting and would turn on the Republicans if they placed equal suffrage in the Constitution.[15]

The Republican leadership sought to overcome resistance to change by crafting an amendment that fell short of universal suffrage. All men would be protected in their right to vote, but ultimately the states would be left with significant authority to suppress the vote.

Supporters of the amendment pointed to the estimated 146,000 northern black men not yet eligible to vote. Since most southern black men theoretically already had that right under the Reconstruction Act, Republicans presented the amendment as creating a simple uniform electoral system in which all men could participate. In addition, the amendment could limit the ability of southern Democrats to take the vote away from blacks through black codes and revised state constitutions despite the apparent protections of the Fourteenth Amendment. In presenting the amendment, Senator Stewart declared it the "logical result of the rebellion, of the abolition of slavery, and of the conflicts in this country during and before the war." They could not rely on state or national laws to protect equality, for those laws might too easily be reversed and slavery restored under a different name. Real peace required that equality become "the immutable law of the land," and that required that all men have the right to vote. Stewart, like most Republicans, saw this amendment as both doing the right thing and aiding their party's continued electoral success.[16]

Over in the House, Samuel Shellabarger of Ohio was more direct. The racist violence disrupting the South since the end of the Civil War "proves that the master white race will submit to negro enfranchisement not an hour longer than compelled to by Federal coercion." If the Constitution did not guarantee the right to vote, the former rebels would find some way to disenfranchise the freedmen, most likely through literacy tests or poll taxes. For "the ugly fact" is that "the rebel and master race at the South are not the lovers of this Union, but are lovers of the 'lost cause'" of the Confederacy. Congress need look no further than the recent action of the Georgia legislature in expelling every black member for the transgression of being black. Though incredibly prescient on the conduct of white southerners, Shellabarger retained his faith in constitutional corrections—backing that faith with proposed mechanisms to prevent voter suppression. His cynical reading of human nature stopped short of imagining that the white leadership of the South would treat constitutional protections as little more than helpful hints.[17]

On January 30, 1869, the House of Representatives considered three versions of the Fifteenth Amendment. The House rejected both Shellabarger's radical prohibition of special tests for the franchise and a more cautiously worded amendment put forth by John Bingham. For compromise language, they turned to George Boutwell of Massachusetts, who served as the first commissioner of internal revenue and had a reputation for integrity. Boutwell exemplified the shifting attitude of many Republicans. During the secession crisis he had favored compromise with the southern states and served on the Peace Commission. Once the war started, Boutwell favored ending slavery on the condition that blacks remained in the South, recommending to Lincoln that South Carolina and Florida be given to the former slaves as black states. But by the war's end he spoke of the need to make the words of the Declaration of Independence a reality by granting equal rights to blacks. His version, which essentially became the amendment, passively stated that the right to vote could not be denied on the basis of race, but it lacked any enforcement mechanism beyond stating that Congress could enforce the amendment "by appropriate legislation." This much vaguer wording pleased the House, which passed the amendment 150 to 42—once more without a single Democratic vote in favor.[18]

Meanwhile, the Senate considered a draft amendment by Senator Stewart. When the war ended, Stewart had opposed black suffrage and sided with President Johnson in seeking a quick forgiveness of the Confederacy. But southern white violence changed his mind in favor of the vote as the only way blacks could protect their interests and the Republican Party could guarantee fair elections. Stewart went beyond the House version by including the right of all men to hold public office.

Far messier than the House's debate, the Senate's deliberations culminated in a thirty-two-hour marathon on February 8 and 9 that considered seventeen different amendments to Stewart's proposal. The Democrats tried every trick to stop the amendment, but with just twelve senators, they stood little chance. Their sole Republican ally, James Doolittle of Wisconsin, had been a Democrat until 1857 and a loyal Republican during the war. But he was a racist who wanted to see blacks, like Indians, eliminated from America (ironically, Doolittle chaired the Committee on Indian Affairs). For support he cited Thomas Jefferson, who had "proved" black inferiority and warned that the two races could not live together. Defying his party, he warned that Congress must not "enforce this unnatural equality." The following year, Doolittle officially returned to the Democratic Party, losing his bid for governor.[19]

The real threat to the amendment came from a few western Republican senators who feared the amendment would enfranchise Hispanic and Chinese residents of their states. Sometimes it seemed that western whites feared and loathed those two groups as much as southern whites did blacks. Congress tended to side with the western racists, as when it effectively kept New Mexico out of the Union from 1848 until 1912 specifically to avoid a large Hispanic voting population. Similarly, Rhode Island Republicans wanted to maintain their limitations on the Irish vote. But an effort to change the wording of the amendment to grant the vote for "citizens of the United States of African descent" in order to leave out the Chinese, Hispanics, and Irish fell far short of a majority.[20]

A more significant debate arose from a widening sense that Representative Shellabarger might be right about the intractability of southern whites. Several senators wanted to add to the amendment protections against contrived voting barriers such as literacy tests. As with Stewart, white violence altered the perspective of many senators. Senator Oliver Morton of Indiana started the session an opponent of unlimited black voting rights, holding education and economic independence as requisites for the franchise. But he saw white supremacy as an aggressive force that would not dissipate, and swung to support voting rights as a political necessity. Morton wanted to take control of voting away from the states. Like Shellabarger, Morton predicted that once former rebels gained control of the legislatures in the South, they would create ways to disenfranchise blacks unless the federal government oversaw elections. His recommendation that the amendment establish a federal election code proved too radical for the Senate, where even many Republicans feared making the federal government too powerful.[21]

Morton found a more receptive audience for his unease that the proposed amendment only protected race, allowing states to restrict voting in any number of other ways. He pointed out that this amendment told the states that "while you shall not disfranchise a man on account of color, you may disfranchise him because he has not got property," or is not native-born, or is not well educated. Why not simplify the amendment to protect the right of all men to vote?

Massachusetts's Henry Wilson agreed with Morton and took the obvious next step, demanding universal suffrage as the logical outcome of the Civil War: "Let us give to all citizens equal rights, and then protect everybody in the United States in the exercise of those rights." Any other position was indefensible and "dishonorable to the nation." Wilson found support from Senator John Sherman of Ohio, whose attitude toward slavery and black people, like his brother William's, had progressed through the war. He now promoted a new "political creed" based on universal suffrage. Senator Willard Warner of Alabama, a former Union general who had served with Grant and Sherman, shared Morton's view that voters needed protection from potentially hostile state governments, and that included women, who also deserved the right to defend their interests through the franchise. Ultimately, these men could not rouse a majority for a more equitable society. Even most Republicans saw no reason to forbid literacy tests or other barriers to the ballot—especially as they hoped to use such methods to block immigrants from the ballot—nor did they want women voting. They therefore favored a limited amendment that seemingly served the interests of the party while retaining the patina of principle.[22]

As various alternatives sputtered out, the House of Representatives rejected the Senate's version of the amendment and called for a conference committee. The Senate rebuffed the conference proposal, instead passing a shorter version of the amendment that protected black office-holding, which the House version did not. At this point, House Democrats, aiming to sabotage the process, joined the radical Republicans to pass an amendment with more extensive protection of voting rights—including for the Chinese and the Irish. They knew that this would guarantee opposition by anti-immigrant Republicans, especially in New England and California. Supporters of black voting rights from Wendell Phillips to the *New York Times* railed against Congress for putting forth amendments clearly intended to fail.[23]

Embarrassed that they had lost control of the process, Republicans in both houses agreed to a conference committee that included Boutwell and Stewart. On February 24, convinced that a thorough protection of voting rights would not pass, they brought forth a shorter amendment that focused solely on the right of black men to vote. Section 1 of this draft became the final wording of Section 1 of the Fifteenth Amendment, while Section 2 went through some minor changes before taking its final form: "Section 1. The right of citizens of the United States to vote shall not be denied or abridged by the United States or by any State on account of race, color, or previous condition of servitude. Section 2. The Congress shall have power to enforce this article by appropriate legislation."[24]

The amendment's negative wording left suffrage qualifications in the hands of the states, while the enforcement clause was vague. The amendment's authors recognized that racial discrimination could undermine their progressive intentions, but they believed they had laid the groundwork for long-term solutions. Senator Jacob Howard spoke for many of his colleagues when he voted for the amendment, as "it is at present the best that can be obtained." Republicans recognized that the amendment did not confer the right to vote; it only offered a vague assurance that the right to vote should not be denied. The actions of southern whites left no doubt that black rights remained fragile. Despite Republican wishes, the question of equal rights would persist, in Howard's words, "for perhaps all time to come." Wilson agreed, calling the amendment "lame," but he voted for it "without taking any responsibility for it." With such muted support, the Fifteenth Amendment gained congressional approval.[25]

President Grant ended his inaugural address that March by endorsing the amendment, even while acknowledging its inadequacy: "The question of suffrage is one which is likely to agitate the public so long as a portion of the citizens of the nation are excluded from its privileges." He did not mention who constituted that portion—the largest of which were women—but he thought ratifying the Fifteenth Amendment was

the best way to restore some calm to American politics. Grant's predic-
tive powers proved weak.[26]

Republicans mostly thought that women would do what they always
did and go along with the decision reached by men. Republicans generally claimed to support legal equality for women without actually
doing much to attain that goal. After all, women could not vote, so
their opinions did not matter that much. Additionally, those women
working for social reform had no alternative to the Republicans, since
the Democrats perceived no political advantage in supporting women's
rights and had no interest in issues of importance to women.

But it was not the case that women quietly accepted this betrayal.
Like black soldiers, women had proven their value to the Union during
the war and reasonably expected some recognition for their commitment to the cause of freedom. Thousands of women had volunteered
for various forms of service, from nursing to sanitary commissions to
dangerous missions as spies and guides. Women consistently put their
interests after those of the slaves, accepting the mistreatment of blacks
as the greater crime. But the country's most prominent women failed to
see why Republicans should not seize this historic moment and extend
legal equality to all Americans.

The path followed by the talented writer Lydia Maria Child well
represents the experience of many of these early feminists. In 1856
she learned that her husband's signature was required to make any
document, including her will, valid. "I was not indignant for my own
account," she wrote. But she was indignant that all women were treated
as chattel, "perpetually insulted by literature, law, and custom." Yet she
assumed that women's rights could wait. She would not speak of her
own social desires but instead would devote her energies to helping
the slaves attain freedom, certain that the United States would then
acknowledge the liberty of all people: "In toiling for the freedom of
others we shall find our own." Women activists had long put aside their

own goals to focus on ending slavery in America, but with the war over
and slavery ended, it seemed like a good time to claim their freedom.[27]

The Fourteenth and Fifteenth Amendments destroyed these expectations. Having faulted the former for implying a gendered definition
of citizenship, Susan B. Anthony and Elizabeth Cady Stanton refused
to endorse the Fifteenth Amendment for failing to establish universal
suffrage. In focusing on votes for black males, Wendell Phillips famously
stated: "One question at a time. This hour belongs to the negro."[28]

But Phillips answered the wrong question; equality, not suffrage,
was the crucial issue of the age. Stanton derided the idea that suffrage was a gift or a privilege; that was the logic of tyrannies. Phillips's reasoning emerged from the false premise that women and blacks
should receive suffrage "as women and negroes, and not as citizens of a
republic." Stanton could imagine no reason why citizenship should be
divided into categories. By what logic did some rights apply to white
men but not to black men or women of any color? Republicanism, Stanton insisted, is premised on the fact "that suffrage is a natural right—as
necessary . . . for the protection of person and property, as are air and
motion to life." A black person or a female person does not need to
make a special case for the right to vote; it is the right of all adult
citizens.[29]

Many women saw Congress's failure to insert the words "or sex" into
the Fifteenth Amendment as a deep betrayal of a long-standing agreement with abolitionists. Women's suffrage leader Abby Kelley had long
argued that the abolition of slavery must be the reformers' top priority. When the Fifteenth Amendment emerged from Congress defending
solely the right of black men to vote, Kelley accepted the limited version,
writing that she would be "a monster of selfishness" to stand in the way
of black men gaining the vote, even at the cost of political equality for
her own daughter. Lucy Stone refused to give in so easily and wrote
Kelley, "O, Abby, it is a terrible mistake you are making." For thirty
years they fought for justice and equality, but now Kelley and the leading male abolitionists willingly accepted "the poor half loaf of justice for

the Negro, poisoned by its lack of justice for every woman of the land."
As Stone saw the dream of women's rights vanish for another generation, "tears are in my eyes, and a wail goes through my heart akin to
that which I should feel, if I saw my little daughter drowning before
my eyes with no power to help her." Susan B. Anthony emphatically
declared that she would rather "cut off this right arm of mine before I
will demand the ballot for the Negro and not the woman."[30]

Tensions emerged among the reformers in the Reconstruction
period, in part because of the racism of many women in the suffrage
movement and in part because of the sexism of male progressives. Much
of this alienation may have resulted from miscommunication and a failure to properly understand one another. Lydia Child sided with black
male leaders who called on women to wait their turn. In attacking
her old ally Stanton, Child wrote, "The suffrage of women can better
afford to wait than that of the colored people," as though only one of
them could win the vote at a time. The Fifteenth Amendment exac-
erbated divisions, placing a major wedge between black and white
women.[31]

Instead of insisting that everyone deserved the vote, these early
feminists divided over who deserved it more. Frederick Douglass
berated Stanton before the convention of the Equal Rights Association for using the descriptive term "Sambo" and for suggesting that
women should get the vote before black men. Blacks had been treated
worse than women, Douglass insisted, and therefore deserved the vote
first. "With us, the matter is a question of life and death." Women
had only themselves to blame as they just did not try hard enough to
get the vote. In the future they should devote as much energy to that
goal as did black men—though Douglass doubted that they would do
so. Only "when they are objects of insult and outrage at every turn;
when they are in danger of having their homes burnt down over their
heads," will they feel "an urgency to obtain the ballot equal to our
own." When someone pointed out that black women suffered as much
as black men, Douglass responded impatiently that the statement was

true, though "not because she is a woman, but because she is black." He closed by admonishing women to follow the example of Julia Ward Howe, who had declared, "I am willing that the negro shall get the ballot before me."

Anthony gave no ground, responding to Douglass that if the vote could not be given to everyone, then it should go "to the most intelligent first." While she did not suggest how that intelligence would be determined, she implied that white women as a group were smarter than blacks. "If intelligence, justice, and morality are to have precedence in the Government, let the question of woman be brought up first and that of the negro last." Equal rights had sufficient enemies without white women and blacks battling for public attention. The Fifteenth Amendment forced women out of the political arena while making it easy for black men to leave their onetime allies behind.[32]

Douglass did not want to deny women the vote. He would have welcomed their political participation. His position came in response to the political maneuvering of the Democrats, who hoped that the Republicans could be trapped into demanding universal suffrage. If a proposed amendment included legal equality or suffrage for women, Democratic leaders confidently predicted, the country would turn on the Republicans and usher them out of office. Democrats worked hard to link black equality with gender equality even while the two camps fought to separate themselves. Given this effective tactic by the Democrats, leading Republicans moved to silence women. Douglass, Phillips, Sumner, and many others spoke out against female suffrage—and even discussions of women's rights—at this exact time. The advocates of women's suffrage bitterly observed that after a lifetime of training "to self-sacrifice and self-abnegation," women too "readily accepted the idea that it was divine and beautiful to hold their claims for rights and privileges in abeyance to all orders and classes of men."[33]

White feminists did not stand alone in their frustration with the Fourteenth and Fifteenth Amendments. Nearly every prominent black woman activist of the nineteenth century agitated for women's rights, and few shared Douglass's view that black men deserved the vote first. As Fanny Jackson Coppin put it: "During my entire life I have suffered from two disadvantages. First, that I am a woman, second that I am a Negro." Sojourner Truth also denied that black men should take priority over universal suffrage. Speaking to the Equal Rights Association in 1867, Truth maintained that she had every "right to have just as much as a man." She echoed Abigail Adams in observing, "If colored men get their rights, and not colored women theirs, you see the colored men will be masters over the women, and it will be just as bad as it was before." Black women had long experience of hard physical labor, and "if they can dig up stumps they can vote. It is easier to vote than dig stumps." Like so many of these early feminists, Truth attempted to vote, only to be turned away from the polling station because of her gender.[34]

Truth understood the condition of the freedwomen well. Though recently redeemed from bondage, blacks tended to accept gender inequalities as the norm. White missionaries encouraged former slaves to adopt the patriarchal structure common throughout the country, with the man as the head of the family and the community. When these missionaries organized black churches in the South, they set up all-male governing bodies, telling the women to stay home and work. The white missionary Laura Towne found it "funny" to observe the enthusiasm of the freedmen for their newfound domestic power, especially to "rule their wives." They claimed and enjoyed their newly acquired status as head of the household and found support from white men, "who have advised the people to get the women into their proper place." Towne predicted that these newly created patriarchs would be very upset if women got the vote. As *Harper's Weekly* noted, black women quickly learned their new place in the social order, and if one of them forgot, her husband "generally has an extempore sermon on hand from some of Paul's dicta about women."[35]

After the combative 1869 convention of the Equal Rights Association, the division in the movement became irreconcilable. In the midst of the national debate over the Fifteenth Amendment, Stanton and

Anthony, impatient about the blacks-first campaign, organized the National Woman Suffrage Association, dedicated to passing an amendment granting women the vote. Lucy Stone and Henry Blackwell led another group, the American Woman Suffrage Association, which focused its energies on the state level, seeking to win women the vote one state at a time. Sharply divided, the women's suffrage movement began losing allies, as advocates of the Fifteenth Amendment ignored their claims for equality.

The issue of women's rights had come up often in the congressional debates over the Fifteenth Amendment but would appear only rarely as the states considered ratification. Two questions dominated these debates: should black men enjoy the same political rights as white men, and should the federal government have any authority over elections?

The First Reconstruction Act had obliged the eleven Confederate states to institute black suffrage, though they did their best to limit the practice. During the debate over the Fifteenth amendment it slowly dawned on the northern press that the amendment would give between 130,000 and 170,000 blacks the vote in the remaining seventeen states, sufficient to determine close elections in favor of the party most aligned with their interests. Many Republican leaders had already made this calculation but kept it to themselves, preferring to take the moral high ground. But once the amendment went to the states for ratification, politics and morality became closely intertwined, with Democrats charging that the amendment amounted to a power grab by the Republicans.[36]

If one reads the ratifying debates alone, it appears that the Republicans consistently addressed the meanings and limitations of equality, while Democrats wanted to talk about interracial sex. Republicans linked political equality with economic opportunity, as the ballot box best protected private interests. While they avoided suggesting that political equality meant social equality, they did see it as vital for the nation's stability, since the government's legitimacy rested on the consent of the governed—though, again, few extended that logic to include women. Democrats happily mentioned women, especially all those white women who would be having sex with black men if the amendment passed. Repeatedly, Republicans deployed the loyalty and courage of black troops as a trump card compared to the treason of southern white Democrats. Members of the latter party responded with appeals to white unity.

Members of both parties demonstrated amazing faith in suffrage to effect change. Speaking for many Republicans, Wendell Phillips defended the amendment against those who felt it did not go far enough by insisting that it "contains within itself the cure for all its defects," since the ballot made it possible for a man to defend "all his other rights." Democrats lived in terror that once blacks started voting they would take over first the southern states and then the whole country, even though they were seriously outnumbered. Naively or cynically, Republicans promoted the notion that race would cease to be a divisive issue once black men had the vote, while Democrats raised the banner of self-defense with the claim that blacks would replace whites if given the vote. Throughout these debates, blacks remained passive objects rather than active subjects.[37]

Democratic arguments had an air of repetition and exaggerated lunacy born of the certainty of defeat, while Republicans proffered rhetorical flights and appeals to the country's best traditions. The Democratic chair in Connecticut proclaimed black suffrage the primary issue facing the nation but had nothing other than racism with which to oppose it. Republicans carefully downplayed the number of black voters and avoided mentioning the political advantages that would accrue to their party with this amendment. The Democrats' states'-rights arguments had grown tedious and been delegitimated in all but the most sterile brains by the Civil War, while Republicans minimized federal powers by pointing out that the states still controlled the registration of voters and elections under the amendment. State legislatures could still require literacy tests and poll taxes, exclude blacks from offices and juries, and use ethnicity and gender to dismiss voters—making moot fears of women, Chinese, Hispanic, Romani, or Irish voters. Nonetheless, the Democrats would not let go of their only rebuttal. The Ohio humorist David Ross Locke, writing as Petroleum V. Nasby, summarized Democratic arguments as "the minit they give the nigger a vote, their daughters must marry niggers."[38]

Beyond this posturing of the two parties lay a simple fact that the press did not hesitate to discuss: if blacks actually voted, the Republican Party stood to retain national political power for at least another generation. What Republicans presented as a simple clarification of democracy could alter the very structure of the nation. During Reconstruction, Republican administrations in the southern states expanded school budgets and increased taxes, worked to build modern infrastructures and took significant steps toward greater social equality, and uniformly acted to protect the Bill of Rights for all. Northern Democrats feared similar progressive legislation in their states. The Democratic Speaker of the New Jersey House of Representatives bluntly warned that the Republicans had already transformed southern society and "now propose to do [the same] in the North by this amendment." The 1868 Democratic National Convention evidenced the party's resistance to any sort of change by derisively dismissing an equal-suffrage proposal without a vote.[39]

Twenty-eight of the thirty-seven states needed to ratify the Fifteenth Amendment for it to become part of the Constitution. Republicans might insist on the moderation of their proposal, but they also knew they faced fierce resistance from a Democratic Party united by racism and appealing to the public to reject such a dramatic transformation of their "white man's republic."

Ironically, the southern states debated the amendment with the least heat, since black men already voted throughout the former Confederacy. The majority of southern Democrats deviated from the national party in choosing not to fight the amendment. Mississippi, Virginia, South Carolina, and Arkansas ratified with only a few dissenting votes. In Texas, where the vote was 69 to 10 in the House and 24 to 2 in the Senate, one newspaper noted that ratification occurred "without scarcely rippling the gently flowing current of Reconstruction." Some Democrats hoped to compete for black votes in the future, while others saw no point in resisting, since they planned to make it ever more difficult for blacks to vote, either legally or through intimidation. As the *Daily Richmond Whig* confidently asserted, the amendment left "loopholes through which a coach and four horses can be driven."[40]

Southern Republicans, though indignant that the amendment did not do more to protect black voters and their right to hold office, had no alternative but to go along with the national party. Both sides understood the real point of the amendment as bringing the black vote to the North.

Temporarily writing off the South, the Democrats hoped to find the ten states needed to block ratification in the Midwest and West. Since Republicans controlled thirty-two of the thirty-seven state legislatures, stalling seemed the most useful approach. In Indiana nearly every Democrat resigned from the state legislature on March 5, 1869, in order to prevent a quorum, which worked for a few days. But Governor Conrad Baker immediately ordered special elections to fill the vacant seats. The state was narrowly divided, with Baker, a Republican, having won election the previous year by just 961 out of 342,189 votes cast. In the campaign for the vacated seats, the Democrats fought entirely on the issue of black suffrage and won every election. They showed up for the new session but warned their Republican colleagues that they would bolt if the amendment came up for a vote.

With the legislature deadlocked, Senator Morton arrived from Washington with a cunning scheme. He advised the Republican leadership that those who resigned from the legislature were no longer legislators, so a quorum should be based on the total number of active members. When the Republicans called for a vote on May 13, most

Democrats again resigned. But this time the presiding officers of the two chambers declared a quorum of the existing members, and the Indiana legislature ratified the amendment with only a single dissenting vote. Having gained several thousand black voters, the Republicans enjoyed a majority in state elections for years to come. At least in Indiana, principle meshed well with politics.[41]

By March 1869, twelve states had ratified the amendment, every one with a Republican legislature, while three states rejected the amendment, each with a Democratic majority. The pace then slowed, as only eight more states ratified by the end of the year. In Rhode Island, many Republicans opposed ratification because they thought that "race" included Irish and that the amendment would negate their laws limiting Irish voting. Equally confused Democrats also thought "ethnicity" and "race" meant the same thing, and they did not want to alienate their Irish constituents by opposing the amendment's apparent protection of their right to vote. It took seven months, numerous extended debates, and a promise from the Republican House leader that they would put literacy tests in place to limit the Irish vote in order to ratify the amendment.[42]

The ratification effort suffered a major defeat in April when the polarized Ohio legislature rejected the amendment. However, Democrats lost their majority in elections later that year, with the balance of power now held by the Reform Party of Cincinnati. Governor Rutherford B. Hayes pulled out all the stops, including offering several patronage positions, to ratify the amendment. The Democrats responded by making deals with Reform Party members, trying to unseat Republican legislators on various charges, attempting to change the rules, and finally demanding that the amendment be put before the voters, successfully stalling a vote through the end of 1869.

With the tally at twenty states in favor and four against, 1870 began with the New York legislature voting to rescind its ratification, once more setting up a legal challenge. The Republicans turned up the pressure, picking up four more ratifications and then using their congressional majority to require Mississippi to ratify the amendment before it could rejoin the Union. Republicans who had previously opposed black suffrage in Michigan and Kansas fell into line with the national party and voted for the amendment, putting party interest over racism.

Then in mid-January, the Ohio Senate voted 19 to 18 to ratify the amendment, the Reform Party joining with the Republicans in this narrow victory. Democrats in the House attempted to trick some legislators into returning home before the vote occurred, while other Republican legislators battled across flooded rivers in order to reach Columbus. Facing a quorum, and mindful of Indiana's recent experience, Democrats attempted to filibuster until the session reached its mandated conclusion. But black and white supporters of the amendment in the galleries shouted down the Democrats. Order restored, the vote proceeded, leading to a 57–55 victory for the amendment. The two houses of the Ohio legislature offered the closest vote in the country for the Fifteenth Amendment. Not a single legislator was absent during these proceedings, indicating their recognition of the significance of this vote; the members of both parties appreciated the potential power of those thousands of black voters in future elections.

When Iowa ratified it on January 27, 1870, the amendment appeared to be within a single state of being approved—depending on which of New York's competing votes Congress accepted. The following day, the California legislature stunned the nation with a surprise rejection of the amendment due to their fear that Chinese men would be able to vote. The state had 49,000 Chinese and 4,000 blacks out of a population of half a million; nonetheless, the Democrats warned that the amendment would lead both to blacks destroying the white race and to the Chinese conquest of America. Running on a platform of rejection, Democrats won a landslide victory in the 1869 state elections and acted on their promise to reject the amendment.[43]

With California's negative vote, the amendment's fate became uncertain. Democrats in the Georgia legislature took advantage of its black members having not yet been returned to office from their earlier expulsion to reject the Fifteenth Amendment in March 1869. The legislature then applied to Congress for readmission to the Union. But the devious Democrats got their timing backward—they should have applied for readmission first, when they had a Republican majority, and then expelled the black legislators and voted against the amendment. Instead, congressional Republicans charged that the Democrats had corrupted the vote by expelling duly elected representatives, and required the state to reverse its rejection before seating its representatives and senators. Now abandoned by their few Republican allies, the Democrats slipped back into the minority and the Georgia legislature voted to ratify on February 2, 1870.[44]

Congress declared Georgia's second vote good enough to ratify the Fifteenth Amendment, though doing so required the rejection of New York's second vote to rescind its earlier ratification. As soon as Congress declared the amendment part of the Constitution, the Democratic-dominated New York legislature voted again to reject the amendment, threatening a major political and constitutional confrontation. Nebraska averted the crisis with its ratification vote on February 17. With Texas's ratification following the next day, Secretary of State Hamilton Fish felt comfortable issuing an official statement recognizing the Fifteenth Amendment as part of the Constitution.

In an unprecedented act, President Grant issued an official proclamation on March 30, 1870, announcing the new amendment to the Constitution. He began with a dig at Justice Taney, reminding Americans of the Supreme Court's great error in warping history to proclaim that no black had been a citizen at the time of the Declaration of Independence. The Fifteenth Amendment "makes at once 4,000,000 people voters who were heretofore declared by the highest tribunal in the land not citizens of the United States, nor eligible to become so." He hoped black Americans would make wise use of their new right and that whites, whom the laws had previously favored, would assist these new citizens in every way. The amendment "completes the greatest civil change" since the adoption of the Constitution, though Congress still needed to make equality a reality by promoting universal public education. The *New York Times* declared that the Fifteenth Amendment "italicizes every word of the Declaration of Independence, and harmonizes our Constitution with the highest civilization to which we may aspire." A feeling that the country had behaved honorably found expression in nearly every newspaper, even many that had previously opposed extending the franchise.[45]

Not surprisingly, black communities celebrated the passage of this amendment as the fulfillment of so many promises made in the name of democracy. Abolitionist organizations disbanded, convinced that their work had reached its natural completion. The black press, which prospered in the years after the Civil War, praised the Fifteenth Amendment as the fulfillment of their struggle. Editorials celebrated "the political equality of the newly made freemen"—making no reference to the newly freedwomen. Philadelphia's *Evening Telegraph* optimistically predicted that the amendment "forever precludes the possibility of the freedmen being despoiled of their right to the franchise by the reactionary party." In New York, the Reverend O. B. Frothingham led a thanksgiving at Trenor's Lyric Hall, declaring that "the ratification of the Fifteenth Amendment marks an epoch in our civilization," protection for the religious and cultural diversity of the nation, and the first step toward true brotherhood.[46]

There were those who felt differently. The legislatures of Oregon, Tennessee, and Maryland gratuitously voted to reject the amendment after it became part of the Constitution, out of racist pique. Oregon and California finally ratified it in 1959 and 1962, respectively, while several states never did so—and New York never reversed its rescinding vote.

Former Confederates sputtered with frustrated anger as they realized that most northern whites supported political equality for black Americans. George Mason of Virginia articulated the irrational fears of his fellow white southerners in predicting the end of the "noble Caucasian, in whose very look and gait the God of creation has stamped a blazing superiority." He fumed that "a more flagrant desecration of the representative principle . . . is not to be found in the annals of the human race." Such apocalyptic projections evoked much mockery. After Hiram Rhodes Revel took his seat in the Senate, the *Philadelphia Inquirer* reported, "The colored United States Senator from Mississippi has been awarded his seat, and we have not had an earthquake, our free institutions have not been shaken to their foundations, nor have the streets of our large cities been converted to blood." [47]

But neither did the Fifteenth Amendment have the political effects anticipated by Republicans. Supporting ratification hurt many state legislators, who lost reelection bids. West Virginia and Missouri swung from Republican to Democratic in 1870 and 1872, respectively, despite the addition of black voters in both states. Democrats, North and South, did not bother to compete for black votes, proclaiming themselves "the White Man's Party." Far too many progressives thought the great battle at an end and equality attained, as black men had the vote and thus could take care of themselves. These optimists underestimated white violence, mistaking the beginning of the fight for equality as its culmination. That said, a significant step had been taken, as northern blacks won the vote and kept it, unlike their southern compatriots.

The black vote did make a difference in some northern states, such as Indiana, where James Sidney Hinton, a former lieutenant in the Union Army, took his seat as the state's first black legislator in 1881, and Ohio, where George Washington Williams, another Union veteran, became that state's first black legislator in 1880. Connecticut was evenly divided between the two parties in 1871 when black voters swung the state firmly to the Republicans. Some blacks benefited from supporting the Republican Party by receiving patronage jobs. The North witnessed a notable cultural shift that manifested in greater civility toward black citizens. By the end of the 1870s, few northern Democratic politicians felt comfortable using racial epithets, accepting "Negro" as the proper usage. [48]

Taken together, the three Reconstruction amendments not only freed the slaves, fixed the Constitution's most glaring flaw, and extended the franchise but also altered the nation's political structure. The Thirteenth Amendment's enforcement clause made possible the first constitutional expansion of the federal government's power, while the Fifteenth Amendment established the principle of federal election oversight even as it placed the first limitation on the state's authority over the right to vote.

A decade later, James Garfield highlighted the essential accomplishment of the Reconstruction amendments in his inaugural address as president: "The elevation of the Negro race from slavery to full rights of citizenship, is the most important political change we have known since the adoption of the Constitution of 1787." This recognition of human equality had transformed the country, and he promised as president to protect every citizen's rights under the Constitution. He never really got the chance, since he was shot four months into his presidency.[49]

Once more, Congress and much of the North thought they had solved the constitutional crisis. But they made two errors of judgment with lasting effects: inserting the word "male" into Section 4 of the Fourteenth Amendment and assuming that the vanquished white supremacists would accept defeat. The first perpetuated a constitutional conflict into the twenty-first century, while the second resulted in renewed southern violence as white racists fought to win the Civil War by other means. What no one seems to have anticipated is that the Supreme Court would once more intervene to constrain legal equality.

CHAPTER 7

The Supreme Court
Strikes Back

*Or, the American legal system
turns against equality*

W riting in 1871, Walt Whitman spoke for those hopefully looking toward a more egalitarian future. In *Democratic Vistas*, Whitman perceived materialism, and the greed and corruption it generated, fighting to undermine equality. The accelerating desire for ever more stuff divided Americans into competing classes that lacked a shared vision for their country and lived hollow lives devoted to accumulation. But Whitman felt confident that the nation would embrace its highest ideals. "The People, of their own choice," fought and died to defeat the Slave Power, bringing freedom to millions. "Democracy, in silence, biding its time, ponders its own ideals," Whitman wrote, "not of men only, but of women." For Whitman, America's ideals are embodied in its two compacts, the Declaration of Independence and the amended Constitution. These ideals might have become temporarily silent, but they remained active just beneath the surface of daily life and would return to create a truly egalitarian nation.[1]

Whitman presented an eloquent and inspiring portrait of a nation moving inexorably toward ever greater equality and democracy—and he could not have been more wrong. The arc of American history would, in the period Mark Twain so perfectly labeled "the Gilded Age," move in the opposite direction from that imagined by Whitman, Frederick Douglass, Anna Dickinson, Susan B. Anthony, and so many other hopeful proponents of equality. The democratic dream died quickly because of southern violence, northern whites' silence, Supreme Court opposition, and an intellectual reaction to the very concept of equality.

Millions of Americans thought the Civil War had secured the triumph of equality, at least at the most basic and essential legal level. African Americans, women, workers, and immigrants all briefly envisioned a nation premised on true democracy, with everyone's rights respected. They had reason to believe that the Fourteenth Amendment had fixed the American legal system in favor of equality with a simple and direct definition of "citizen of the United States." No legal barriers to full citizenship could stand before its eloquent simplicity: "All persons born or naturalized in the United States, and subject to the jurisdiction thereof, are citizens of the United States and of the State wherein they reside." The amendment also made clear that no state could "abridge the privileges or immunities of citizens of the United States; . . . nor deny to any person within its jurisdiction the equal protection of the laws." What could be clearer? Yet powerful forces quickly gathered to limit the impact of this constitutional promise of equal rights.

As we look through the opposition to equality in the last half of the nineteenth century, we will repeatedly see the same two overriding fears: that legal equality would lead to women becoming masculine and to sex between white women and black men. These were not mere pretexts; indeed, one cannot underestimate the fragility that underlay the racism and sexism of a great many white men in this period. It is evident from their fervid denunciations of legal equality that many men feared that women would abandon femininity at the first crack in patriarchal control and that all women longed to have sex with black men. Only strict social conventions backed by the full force of the state and the threat of violence stood between the civilization white men had constructed and chaos.

These efforts to keep the lid on aspirations for equality found their greatest allies in the nation's courts, backed by a popular understanding of science that perceived strict hierarchies in nature. Progressive Republicans had taken advantage of a unique political moment in the aftermath of the Civil War to force equality into the Constitution without any Democratic support. While a widening circle of Americans accepted equality as a valuable aspect of American society, the nation's intellectual elite—judges, professors, lawyers, scientists, doctors— adopted contrary views, constructing new justifications for inequality that warped and ultimately defeated the positive accomplishments of the Civil War. By the century's end, the United States would return to a caste-based social system, and a foreign observer would be justified in thinking that the Confederacy had won the war.

The Confederacy may have ceased to exist, but those who had fought for a slave republic quickly transferred their efforts to violently reas- serting white supremacy. While some postwar violence was local and spontaneous, a definite pattern of organized efforts at intimidation backed by deadly force quickly emerged. White racists formed groups such as the Ku Klux Klan, gun clubs, all-white militia companies, and Democratic Party chapters to coerce quiescence from the newly freed slaves and their white allies. These racist warriors used every tradi- tional means of social control—nighttime terror attacks, public beat- ings, threats of harm to entire families, and even the eighteenth-century practice of tarring and feathering—as well as some new tactics, includ- ing mass lynchings, masked raiders, massed gunfire from private mili- tias, and lethal mob violence. The white supremacists did not feel the need to conduct their operations in secret; indeed, they publicly pro- claimed their anti-equality ideology and plans for the unrestrained use of violence, and they laid claim to one of the political parties to lend legitimacy to their actions.[2]

With federal troops present in the South at the end of the Civil War, Congress gave the military the task of protecting the rights of the freed- men. Though Union soldiers could not be everywhere, they lent weight to the efforts of the freed slaves to vote. These tens of thousands of new citizens united with many white supporters to hand the Republican

Party victory in most southern states from 1866 until 1876. Frustrated by this emerging democracy, white supremacists ratcheted up the terror campaign they had always used to keep blacks in line, this time to prevent Republicans from voting.

It is important to recognize that southern whites had maintained control over the region's black population for decades through organized terror operations backed by the full force of the state. In many ways, the Ku Klux Klan picked up the tasks and techniques of the older slave patrols to control black Americans. The Klan's first meeting in Nashville in 1867 left no doubt of their aim: "Our main and fundamental objective is the MAINTENANCE OF THE SUPREMACY OF THE WHITE RACE."[3]

In the face of increasing violence and voter suppression in the South, President Ulysses S. Grant demanded legislation to protect civil rights. Congress responded by passing the Civil Rights Act of 1870, which extended the federal government's authority and power to protect legal equality under the enforcement clause of the Fifteenth Amendment. The act forbade state officials from using race as a criterion in voter registration, imposed penalties on anyone seeking to interfere with a man's right to vote, authorized the president to deploy troops to enforce the law, and ordered violations of the act to be heard in federal courts, thus preventing stacked all-white local juries from acquitting the accused. The following year, Congress passed the Ku Klux Klan Act, outlawing all efforts to prevent citizens from voting, holding office, or enjoying the equal protection of the law. Vigorous enforcement of the latter act by the Grant administration led to the conviction of numerous Klan leaders and temporarily lessened white violence.

Southern Democrats, in turn, formulated the infamous "Mississippi Plan"—also known as the "Shotgun Plan" and in South Carolina as the "No. 1 Plan of the Campaign." By any name, Democrats aimed to reclaim political control by any means available, including fraud, inaccurate charges of corruption, intimidation, and violence. The plan called on every Democrat to carry arms and to keep blacks from voting in order to reinforce "that their natural position is that of subordination to the white man." The Democrats acted openly, unconcerned that they would be punished for their activities, no matter how deadly, as northern Democratic Party leaders offered their full support. In calling for murdering political opponents, a prominent South Carolina Democrat concluded that "a dead Radical is very harmless." As Congressman A. S. Wallace said, "Intimidation is the order of the day and terrorism reigns supreme."[4]

Democrats did not just want to win elections; they wanted to transform the South into a region of fourteen single-party states, in which no opposition would be spoken and no resistance tolerated. They spoke openly of plans to create what they called "the Solid South." In Georgia, the Augusta *Constitutionalist* boasted that "a minority of white men, when united in a common purpose, never fails to drive from power a semi-barbarous majority." Democratic clubs promoted a tautology: "This is a white man's country and as such has to be ruled by the white men."[5]

White supremacists deployed a formidable array of illegal methods to destroy democracy in the South, techniques they would employ for the next century. The Democrats' gun clubs, of which there were nearly three hundred in South Carolina alone, had the stated purpose of putting "control of the state government in the hands of the white people." Well-armed and full of Confederate veterans, these clubs served as "the armed wing of the Democratic party" and specialized in night attacks on black communities.[6]

Many southern whites, especially merchants and poor white farmers, supported the Republican Party. Generally they preferred the Republicans' policies, especially school funding and infrastructure development. To combat this multiracial unity, Democrats boycotted businesses operated by Republicans and refused to hire any white member of that party, ostracizing them socially as well. By 1875 they would go even further and expand their murderous rage to include white Republicans, as when white supremacists killed scores of German immigrants in Mason County, Texas.

As Louisiana's Henry Adams succinctly stated, the South had once more "got into the hands of the very men that held us slaves." The Democrats did not hide their willingness to kill; the Mississippi party declared they would not hesitate *"to kill every white Radical in the county."* [7]

Incredibly, southern blacks defied the terror campaign and turned out in record numbers in the 1876 election. However, the Democrats, not in the least shy about their anti-democratic practices, bought votes, prevented Republicans from voting, "forgot" to open polls in black areas, failed to provide sufficient ballots to Republican districts, stuffed ballot boxes while destroying others, and used many other techniques in their campaign to prevent an accurate expression of the people's will. Many Democratic districts in South Carolina had greater than 100 percent voter turnout in the 1876 election. As during the antebellum period, the entire Bill of Rights once more became a dead letter in the South; the First Amendment died an especially ugly death, as only opinions supportive of white supremacy could be publicly expressed. Southern blacks continued their efforts to vote, despite the powerful legal and extralegal forces brought to bear against them. A Senate committee investigating violence during the 1878 election concluded, "The right to vote is a privilege more highly prized by the colored voter than by voters of any other class; and he will make sacrifices to exercise this privilege that few white men will." Yet the tally of dead Republicans kept rising. [8]

By killing hundreds of people, including a number of prominent political figures, employing numerous deceptive and fraudulent election strategies, and threatening anyone who dared speak out for legal equality, white supremacists took over all the southern state governments by the time of the notorious deal in 1877 that allowed Rutherford B. Hayes to claim the presidency in exchange for ending federal protection of civil rights.

By accepting Hayes as president, the Democratic Party in the South regained control of their region for white supremacy, quickly terminating every form of nascent equality. After the Civil War, the Republican

Party became the workingman's party in the South, with thousands of poor whites joining the freedmen to fight for common interests. Democrats curtailed this alliance by instituting poll taxes that prevented the poor—white or black—from voting. In Texas, the *Weekly Banner* celebrated the advantages of a poll tax, which "would work like a charm in the counties where there is a large negro population" while also keeping poor whites from the polls, "without any serious detriment to the public good."[9]

The restored Democratic state governments denied fundamental rights to poor whites as well as blacks, a fact recognized by many of the former, leading to a brief Greenback-Republican alliance in 1878 that captured local and state offices throughout the South. The Democrats responded viciously, attacking anyone who favored this alliance regardless of race, and driving the alliance's leaders, such as Louisiana state senator A. R. Blount, out of the region. One white Republican wrote President Hayes, "I know that if I run on the Republican ticket here I will be killed and I don't propose to put myself up as a target to be shot at." With time, the Democrats won over the majority of poor whites with a combination of fear and racism.[10]

The terrorist campaign of the southern Democrats could not have succeeded without the support of northern Democrats and the acquiescence of northern Republicans. Northern whites had grown tired of the long battle over rights and moved on to other issues, leaving southern blacks to the mercy of former Confederates. Liberals demonstrated their own biases in turning on the southern Republicans.

As early as 1871, *The Nation* editorialized that the Reconstruction experiment had failed, with the southern governments made up of "trashy whites and ignorant blacks." The only solution they could imagine was leaving the people of the South to work out their own mess. If the Democrats insisted on using violence, "we cannot interfere effectively, and had better not interfere at all." These states would pay a price for their bigotry, as they suffered "impoverishment and emigration." Any blacks who did not like their treatment should just leave and seek freedom elsewhere. *The Nation* thus abandoned the idea of national citizenship shortly after the concept's creation. In its next issue, this liberal beacon demonstrated its own bigotry in reporting on its snarky exchange with the Charleston *Daily Republican*. When *The Nation* accused the South Carolina legislature of being controlled by uneducated blacks, the southern newspaper had, in *The Nation*'s view, no response but "the usual burst of rhetoric" about equality and opportunity. The magazine concluded by blaming the mixed-race legislature for driving the Ku Klux Klan to acts of violence.[11]

By 1877, most northern newspapers ceased reporting acts of white violence and a great number of former crusaders for equality gave up, turning their energies to other matters. Throughout the country, white people came to accept the emerging mythology of the Old South as a place of benign slave masters and happy slaves. Abusers of all kinds seek to create a counternarrative that denies the abused their status as victims. In the years after the Civil War, when it seemed that southern whites would be cast in history as the bad guys, a concerted effort emerged to reimagine the slave South as a land of noble white men, elegant ladies, and loyal slaves. Alexander Stephens, who began his vice presidency of the Confederacy by proclaiming slavery the cornerstone of the new nation, now devoted himself to arguing that the real conflict had been an elevated intellectual debate over states' rights. Prominent writers, from the poet/priest Abram Joseph Ryan to the novelists Thomas Nelson Page and Thomas Dixon, poured lies and romance over southern history like molasses. Influenced by these novels, historians such as William Dunning and Woodrow Wilson rewrote the story of slavery as if to prove that the victors do not always write the history. This mythology persisted well into the twentieth century, creeping into the new medium of film.[12]

Not just southerners joined in this revisionist project. The nation's most famous minister and onetime abolitionist, Henry Ward Beecher, insisted that the time had come for all northern Christians to welcome the southern states back under their traditional white leadership and that true Christians should feel sorry for all that the former Confederates had suffered. Beecher minimized their "shocking barbarities" as just an effort to adjust to the new, slave-less environment. They had lost their way of life, requiring northerners to have "patience with Southern men as they are, and patience with Southern opinions as they have been."[13]

Reverend Beecher's sister Harriet Beecher Stowe—author of the phenomenally popular abolitionist novel *Uncle Tom's Cabin*—also decided that she was over blacks. From her winter home in Florida, she observed the racial violence she had once portrayed and condemned, but now she called on her friends to join her in keeping quiet on the subject, so as to not hurt the feelings of southern whites. The woman whose harsh portrayal of southern society had led legislatures to ban her book found her sympathies shifting to her wealthy white neighbors as she accepted the mythology of the Old South. She now described blacks as looking like baboons and "the missing link of Darwin" and as uniquely suited to labor in the hot and humid South. As she wrote several friends, she no longer cared for the political and social issues that riled the North, as she hoped to create her own Florida plantation. The two Beechers helped white Americans North and South to become comfortable with their history by forgiving the white South for its racist violence.[14]

Curiously, former Confederates did not return the forgiveness. Most persisted in their conviction that the Civil War was entirely the fault of northern abolitionists, who had destroyed a superior way of life. For instance, the Methodist, Presbyterian, and Baptist churches had all separated into northern and southern branches in the years prior to the war. With the end of Reconstruction, northern clergymen sought denominational reunification, but the southern religious leadership would have none of it, still angered by their brethren's refusal to support slavery.

In religion as in politics, the South got its way. At the beginning of what is known as the Third Great Awakening, a series of evangelical revivals that swept the country starting in the centennial year, Dwight Moody, a Massachusetts-born white minister, brought his revival to Augusta, Georgia. At first blacks and whites mingled freely. But many prominent white ministers, incensed at this innovation, demanded that Moody build a literal fence between the races, which he did immediately, earning front-page praise from the *Atlanta Constitution*. All revivals in the South until Billy Graham's in the 1950s would remain segregated. But Moody went even further than requested, refusing to condemn slavery, rejecting the concept of equal rights, and lending a Christian veneer to the reactionary effort to reclassify blacks as inferior, all in the name of uniting America's white Christians. It is little wonder that Frederick Douglass called Moody a rank hypocrite. "Of all the forms of Negro hate in this world," Douglass wrote, "save me from that one which clothes itself in the name of the loving Jesus." Moody legitimated segregation years before the southern states institutionalized the practice.[15]

Not surprisingly, southern Republicans felt betrayed by their erstwhile northern allies. In New Orleans, the Committee of Five Hundred Women organized to preserve their newly won rights by leaving the South. The white press mocked this palpable failure to "accept their own situation," which was "that they are a people, ignorant, without money, under a terrible necessity to labor and to wait." But they would not wait, helping to launch the great Exoduster movement that took thousands of blacks west in search of equality and opportunity.[16]

Leaving the South proved more difficult than many anticipated. Although every citizen had a right under the Fourteenth Amendment to travel freely between the states, southern white elites did not want to lose the cheap labor of the freedmen. Their racist ideology carefully maintained the right of whites to determine every aspect of the lives of black Americans, and even many poor whites could not tolerate the negation of their culture represented by the Exodusters. The resulting white terror campaign accelerated the desire of ever more blacks to leave the South for good, with the movement gaining added impetus when the governor of Kansas, John St. John, issued a public welcome. Meeting in secret locations, the Exodusters pooled their meager resources and planned their escape. Lacking any central organization, this spontaneous movement westward speaks volumes on not just the virulent racism of the South, but also the complete abandonment of these loyal citizens by the federal government. As a consequence, an estimated fifty to seventy thousand people joined the Exoduster migration of 1877 to 1881. "Fleeing from oppression and bondage," as former Louisiana state senator Andrew Pollard put it, they found on the prairie a better life, one free from terror and violence.[17]

As Georgia's attorney general, Amos T. Akerman, framed the issue, in ending Reconstruction, Congress responded to "lawlessness by letting the lawless have their own way." George T. Downing, the black businessman who ran the congressional dining room, angrily complained, "We were offered up." The national Republican Party saw no point in continuing to battle the terrorists and wrote off the entire region, often not even bothering to put forth candidates for office. *The Nation* rejoiced that the "Compromise of 1877" ending Reconstruction meant that blacks would disappear from the national conversation: "Henceforth, the nation, as a nation, will have nothing to do with him." This liberal magazine was content that political, social, and economic power in the South had been restored to the white elite, where it belonged. The Republicans' complete surrender persuaded southern white supremacists that violence worked, encouraging them to continue to rely on such methods over the next eighty years.[18]

The North capitulated to the South in 1877 by withdrawing federal troops, accepting the end of Reconstruction, and permitting the region to fall once more to despotism based on white hegemony. Many of those who had once led the battle for equality gave up completely, generally allowing what had once been a carefully obscured racism to rise to the surface. "Let us admit," editorialized the *St. Louis Globe-Democrat*, "that though we staked everything for freedom under the spur of the rebellion, we have not enough of principle about us to uphold the freedom, so dearly bought, against the persistent and effective opposition of the unrepentant and unchanged rebels." Northern politicians and the public they represented turned their backs on the cause of equality in 1877, but an even greater betrayal came from the nation's intellectuals, who once more found assurance of their own brilliance in a racist ideology.[19]

For some thirty years starting in the 1850s, American politicians, scholars, and ministers entered into a sustained debate on the existence and nature of equality. This extended dialogue, which drew upon deep religious and intellectual traditions, had enormous political and legal implications. However, the popularly accepted conclusion to the question of equality relied primarily on a misperception of science known as social Darwinism.

A Darwinian vision swept the United States with the end of the democratic experiment of Reconstruction. Like the Republican Party it represented, the Washington *National Republican* had long favored federal intervention in the economy, but in 1877 it switched its loyalty to laissez-faire, for in the future everything would and should be "decided according to the Darwinian theory, 'survival of the fittest.'" This Republican newspaper accepted only one version of equality, the equal right to battle for survival. Under this new "scientific" perspective, the poor had only themselves to blame for their disadvantages. The successful earned their social positions, while those who failed also got what they deserved.[20]

The absence of a level playing field was irrelevant, for nature determined winners and losers based on each individual's inherent skills and on the objective reality of their race and gender. Inequality was an inescapable fact with which no one should interfere, as abundantly verified by the latest advances in science. The renowned biologist and geologist Louis Agassiz, of Harvard, supported this new pseudo-science of racism. "We should beware how we give to the blacks rights, by virtue of which they may endanger the progress of the whites," he wrote, scoffing at the very idea of social equality for blacks as contrary to science. Similarly, the prominent historian James F. Rhodes rejected as absurd the liberal faith in education, which could not overcome "the great fact of race." The modern age of science proved the validity of racism, and anyone who rejected that knowledge rejected science as well.[21]

This new ideology initially developed incoherently, as Henry Adams observed, in response to the mass slaughter and waste of the Civil War. Following the collapse of Reconstruction, vague notions of objective inequality found a solid intellectual—if not truly scientific—structure. Those looking for a scholarly crutch for their preferred form of inequality turned readily to the twisted extension of natural selection to society popularized by the Englishman Herbert Spencer. American supporters quickly made Spencer's work their own, in 1877 giving it the name social Darwinism.[22]

Perceived as indisputable science, social Darwinism became first a fad and then an obsession among educated Americans. Students at the leading colleges all read and discussed the premier texts, the public attended popular lectures on the subject, and even ministers, who as a group rejected Darwinism, celebrated social Darwinism. The leading liberal magazine of the time, *The Nation*, became an advocate in 1877, promoting the idea that the rich deserved their wealth and that any effort to aid the weak undermined natural selection and thus social progress.[23]

The popularity of social Darwinism, while self-serving for many advocates, speaks to more than just personal interest. The conviction that it is wrong to interfere with the workings of nature performed a valuable service in clearing the consciences of the majority of Americans who could not otherwise remain comfortably inert in the face of substantial social injustice. The voice of this clarion call for inaction was the Yale professor William Graham Sumner.

Generally credited as the founder of American sociology, Sumner deployed statistics to demonstrate that any form of social or economic

engagement by the government disrupted evolution and derailed progress. In the 1870s Sumner emerged as the nation's first superstar
scholar, leading the revival of anti-immigrant and anti-Catholic sentiment as he discovered whole new categories of people to disdain in
addition to blacks and women: the poor, workers, eastern and southern
Europeans, Jews, Chinese, Japanese, Filipinos, Mexicans—basically all
those who were not WASP men. Sumner and his fellow social Darwinists cared little for actual science; their defenses of inequality tended
toward the rhetorical rather than the empirical. They did not care that
evolutionary science actively rejected its application to society, for social
Darwinism was, in philosopher William James's words, "an emotional
attitude, rather than a system of thought."[24]

Appearing before a committee of the House of Representatives in
1878, Sumner insisted that nature demanded social inequality and that
misguided efforts to change the natural order would have disastrous
effects. Sumner assured Congress there was only one alternative to his
vision: "If we do not believe in survival of the fittest, we have only one
possible alternative, and that is survival of the unfittest." The inferior
must bear their lot without complaint and get out of the way of their
superiors as nature's "iron spur" crushed the weak. At no time did Sumner offer any actual scientific evidence for his position, contenting himself with its assertion and the most rudimentary understanding of how
natural selection worked.[25]

By the late 1870s, a great many white Americans wanted to believe
in both progress and inequality. Social Darwinism explained how the
two worked in tandem, negating any perceived contradictions and fore-
stalling any need to work for social improvement. Sumner constructed
a masculine image free of emotional concern for others, which he dismissed as feminine sentimentality. The young William James, a professor at Harvard, received a stern injunction from his mentor: "Stop
your sniveling complaints, and your equally sniveling raptures! Leave
off your general emotional tomfoolery, and get to WORK like men!" Real

men did not care what happened to other people, being too busy fighting the battles that would advance the race.[26]

In such an educational environment, intellectuals of every stripe turned against equality. For example, in 1878 the historian Francis Parkman gained wide attention for his article "The Failure of Universal Suffrage." Parkman despaired for his country if just anyone could vote, drawing particular attention to workers and immigrants who had no sense of the public good and cared only for handouts from the government. Though born in Ireland, E. L. Godkin, editor of *The Nation*, warned of the danger posed by ignorant and self-interested Irish workers who fought for more pay rather than the good of the national economy. Charles Francis Adams Jr. trembled before the prospect of universal suffrage leading to a "government of ignorance and vice" dominated by black, Irish, and Chinese workers.[27]

The Civil War and Lincoln's guiding rhetoric restored equal rights to American consciousness. Yet by the mid-1870s the majority of white men disowned equality, reverting to antebellum standards, though with a veneer of scientific-sounding rationalizations camouflaging their indifference to the rights and needs of others. This shift in intellectual currents marked the end of a period of social reform that had brought the United States to the verge of an equal, democratic society. Fearing social chaos, America's political and intellectual leaders turned to a new set of ideas that happily required nothing of them but their own continued selfish conduct. Social Darwinism served as the intellectual validation for every form of inequality, merging easily with the violent racism promoted by white supremacists. Social Darwinism also functioned as the intellectual bedrock of a series of Supreme Court decisions that neutered the Reconstruction amendments and turned back the clock on American social relations. By 1900, social Darwinism served as the unofficial ideology of the American legal system.

=

Social Darwinism gave primacy to masculine cultural characteristics. Women played little role in this worldview beyond giving birth to the next, improved generation. As the influence of social Darwinism spread through politics and the law, women became steadily less significant in the life of the nation, and the notion of women confined to the domestic sphere became a central tenet of American life. The Fourteenth Amendment's promise of "all persons" enjoying due process of law briefly gave women hope that they might finally gain legal equality. But it quickly became apparent that ideology trumps ideals.

America's first feminists tried every avenue to attain legal equality. As Elizabeth Cady Stanton summarized the situation in 1869, they had "argued their right to political equality from every standpoint of justice, religion, and logic, for the last twenty years." They quoted all the key legal and cultural documents in support of equality, "and although much nonsense has emanated from the male tongue and pen on this subject, no man has yet made a fair argument on the other side." Stanton, like progressives throughout American history, could not understand how any rational person could reject human rights as a core principle. To overcome irrational male fears, women now sought to teach men that women too are human, deserving the same rights as any man would demand for himself.[28]

The first convention of the National Woman Suffrage Association, held in St. Louis in October 1869, turned to the Fourteenth Amendment's promise of citizenship and due process rights to all persons to support their claim for equality. Since the Constitution now denied the states the power to "abridge the privileges or immunities of citizens of the United States," states denying women the right to vote—which was all of them—violated the Constitution. Virginia Minor, president of the Missouri chapter, proclaimed that the Constitution "gives me every right and privilege to which every other citizen is entitled." The states might regulate suffrage, she argued, but they could not prohibit it. She sarcastically observed that all previous actions limiting citizenship to white men, such as the *Dred Scott* decision, had been made by white

men, not by "illogical, unreasoning women, totally incapable of understanding politics." According to the Fourteenth Amendment, women,
as citizens of the United States, enjoyed all the rights of citizenship,
not just a select few. To accept otherwise is to live as non-citizens.
"Disguise it as you may," she wrote, "the disenfranchised class is ever
a degraded class." [29]

Operating on the certainty that the Fourteenth Amendment made
them citizens, women around the country attempted to exercise their
right to vote in the 1870 and 1871 elections. Some actually cast ballots, as local officials accepted their argument of legal equality; most,
however, were turned away. Susan B. Anthony cast a vote in November
1872 and was arrested a few weeks later for violating federal law. She
held that the Fourteenth Amendment gave her, a U.S. citizen, the right
to vote. The local judge disagreed, sentencing Anthony to pay a fine
of $100, which she declined to do. In Washington, D.C., Clara Barton
called for the assistance of veterans: "Brothers, when you were weak,
and I was strong, I toiled for you." Now she asked for the right to vote,
"and as I stood by you, I pray you stand by me and mine." [30]

The suffrage movement did retain many significant male allies during Reconstruction, including in Congress. But too many white men lost
interest in sharing the rights of citizenship with others, and only a few
western states passed the necessary legislation. In 1869, George Julian,
whose daughter Grace became a forceful leader in the suffrage movement, introduced a constitutional amendment in the House declaring
that "the right of suffrage in the United States shall be based on citizenship . . . without any distinction or discrimination whatever founded on
sex." His proposal never even came up for a vote. More typical of the
turn against equality in these years was the attitude of the supposedly
progressive journal *The Nation*, which mocked Victoria Woodhull's
efforts to get Congress to declare that women had the right to vote.
The House Judiciary Committee rejected Woodhull's petition by declaring the franchise a matter for the states. *The Nation* snidely dismissed
efforts to diminish politics with "the passionate longings, the delicate

fancies, the flashing intuitions . . . [of] the Feminine Half of Humanity." Women must stop interfering with the serious masculine affairs of government.[31]

With the majority of Congress contemptuous of women's claim to political equality, the movement turned to the courts, where they received a uniformly hostile response. For seven decades after the Civil War, the state and federal courts crushed any and all efforts to extend legal equality.

The first case to challenge women's exclusion from equal citizenship came in the District of Columbia in 1871. In the April elections that year, a group of seventy women went to cast their votes, only to be denied that right by election officials because of their gender. Since women could not practice law in the nation's capital, they hired two male attorneys to present their case in the District's supreme court on the basis of the Fourteenth Amendment and the traditional legal argument that government "can exercise no power not granted by the Constitution; and that instrument certainly confers no power to limit the right of suffrage."

A unanimous court rejected voting as a right, holding that states and localities could establish suffrage rules without regard to the Constitution's other protections. The court insisted "that the legal vindication of the natural right of all citizens to vote would, at this stage of popular intelligence, involve the destruction of civil government." In rejecting women's right to vote, the court also warned of the horrors of allowing all men to vote, since that level of equality had already corrupted the nation's cities to the point of anarchy. For the court, it was a "fact" that allowing an unfettered right to vote "would be destructive of civilization." The District's highest court thus anticipated the reactionary legal standards that would shortly drive America's judiciary to turn back the clock on every aspect of legal equality. Women brought similar cases in state courts from California to New Hampshire, and all ended the same way, with judges rejecting any logic that saw the Fourteenth Amendment conferring rights on women.[32]

Virginia Minor determined to take the matter to the Supreme Court. She read the Fourteenth Amendment and thought its grant of citizenship to "all persons" and promise to protect their "privileges and immunities" must apply to her. However, Missouri would not let her vote. When the Supreme Court heard her case in 1875, Missouri did not bother to send a lawyer, assuming women's inferior status a settled matter in American law. A unanimous court agreed with Missouri's unstated logic. Chief Justice Morrison Waite dismissed Minor's citizenship as irrelevant. Since the Constitution does not mention suffrage as a mark of citizenship, there is no right to vote, and states get to decide which citizens enjoy the franchise. Waite ignored the Reconstruction amendments and argued that since none of the original states had granted all citizens the vote, and since the Constitution did not originally define citizenship, no connection existed between citizenship and voting. Only another constitutional amendment could change that version of history.[33]

Stalled in Congress and blocked by the courts, women turned their attention to the state level, battling in legislatures and placing the issue on the ballot in many states. They enjoyed some early victories in the territorial assemblies of Wyoming in 1869 and Utah in 1870. The latter vote became entangled with anti-Mormon sentiment in Congress and led, in 1887, to the Edmunds-Tucker Bill, revoking women's suffrage in Utah—though the women of Utah regained the vote with statehood in 1896.

This initial legislative battle for suffrage came to a head in Colorado in 1877, attracting national attention and national leaders on both sides of the issue. Colorado had become a state the previous year and nourished a progressive reputation with its inclusive welcome of immigrants, its liberal constitution, and a large majority for reform Republicans. Women persuaded the legislature to place universal suffrage on the ballot and earned the support of several prominent men, including Governor John L. Routt and the influential Hispanic state legislator Agipeta Vigil. Renowned proponents of the right to vote, including Mary Shields, Lucy Stone, and Susan B. Anthony, traveled the state speaking in favor of the referendum. The campaign saturated the news, with the states' two leading newspapers supporting what they called "simple justice"—and welcoming the political opinions of women in their columns. Women organized Equal Suffrage Clubs and held Suffrage Festivals calling for Colorado "to become a truly free state." A Miss Beecher in Colorado Springs succinctly stated the case for equality: "I am a better judge than any man can be of my own responsibilities and powers." [34]

Opponents of universal suffrage found their voice in two other newspapers, the *Colorado Chieftain* and the *Denver Tribune*. The editors of these papers labeled suffragists "faded and awfully frigid" and "windy fanatics," and they warned that if women voted, "the family will be reduced to chaos; women's whole nature altered; men's feeling toward her changed." The state's leading advocates of keeping women in their domestic sphere were Catholic bishop Joseph P. Machebeuf and Denver Presbyterian minister T. E. Bliss, "the Woman Hater." [35]

The Catholic bishop and the Protestant minister came together in constantly referencing St. Paul's injunction that women should just shut up and that God opposed women's suffrage since he created them to be mothers, and mothers clearly should not vote. Neither minister would debate those favoring universal suffrage, confining themselves to public sermons warning that if women voted, they would either never marry or spend their time arguing with their husbands. On Election Day, women tried to compensate for not being able to vote by showing up at polling places to appeal for justice. In Denver, Bliss got into a shouting match with Lucy Stone that concluded with Bliss knocking Stone to the ground. The Woman Hater won both the bout and the election, the proposal failing 14,053 to 6,612. [36]

The surprisingly thorough defeat in Colorado dealt a crushing blow to the suffrage movement, which did not regain national momentum for another thirty years, as the country moved in the opposite direction by limiting rather than extending the vote. The following year, Anthony crafted a simple version of a suffrage amendment, which California senator Aaron A. Sargent introduced to a yawning silence. The high point of this congressional effort came in 1882, when the House and Senate created select committees on women's suffrage, both of which supported an amendment. However, that amendment did not come up for a vote until 1887, when it was defeated in the Senate 34 to 16, with 26 abstentions.[37]

Just as male voters refused to share their right to vote with women, so the all-male legal profession constructed nearly insurmountable obstacles to women's efforts to gain equal rights. The Supreme Court had long proven itself the enemy of equality, as demonstrated most clearly in the *Dred Scott* decision. Given that by 1872 every justice had been appointed by a Republican, supporters of Reconstruction and the three recent amendments confidently expected the Court to side with their new vision of an expanding democracy, defending freedom with the same enthusiasm with which it had once defended slavery. The *Prigg v. Pennsylvania* (1842) and *Dred Scott* decisions had established the federal government's power to protect slavery; now surely, as Representative James Wilson said in introducing the Civil Rights Act of 1866, the Court would grant the same authority for the protection of freedom.[38]

At first it seemed that the nation's courts would follow the intent of the framers of the Reconstruction amendments. In 1869, the Supreme Court upheld congressional power to set the terms on which the Confederate states could return to full standing in the Union. The following year the influential chief judge of Michigan's supreme court, Thomas M. Cooley, deployed the logic of the Fourteenth Amendment to strike down segregated schools, declaring that all students must be treated equally, as all citizens were equal before the law. That standard must hold even if it meant overriding the democratic decision of the voters. Despite this auspicious beginning, the nation's courts quickly veered in a different direction, guided by social Darwinism and a determinative adherence to inequality.[39]

State courts acted first in attempting to negate legal equality. The supreme courts of Delaware and Kentucky ruled that procedural sections of the Civil Rights Act did not apply to their states' prohibitions on accepting the testimony of black witnesses. Other state courts followed suit in a struggle to prevent the adoption of legal equality.[40]

In 1866, Justice Noah Swayne, sitting as a circuit judge, voided these efforts to retain inequality before the law. Swayne ruled that the Thirteenth Amendment and the Civil Rights Act worked in unison to reform the nation's legal system in the name of equal citizenship. Taken together, they empowered the federal government to protect the rights of all citizens everywhere in the country, while the supremacy clause of the Constitution granted the federal courts authority to override state laws.

In a sophisticated analysis, Swayne insisted on the need for continuing legal oversight precisely because the impact of slavery could not be destroyed simply by terminating the institution. It was vital to recall that slaves had long been subject to "the grossest outrages by the whites," with no legal recourse available to them. The states had done nothing to protect them or free blacks, upon whom were affixed also "the badges of the bondsman's degradation." These same states could not be relied upon to suddenly treat blacks as legal equals. Therefore, the procedural standards in Kentucky and other states that limited the legal rights of blacks as witnesses or litigants had to give way to these new constitutional protections. These changes, Swayne stated, constituted an "act of great national grace."

But when the issue came before the full Supreme Court, they threw aside Swayne's decision and reasoning, limiting the meaning of the Reconstruction amendments in the first case addressing their impact.[41]

Given the Republican background of most of the justices who served between 1870 and 1900, their refusal to respect the efforts of the Republican Congress to reconstruct the nation into a more democratic society can appear baffling. Historians have long debated this seeming contradiction, with some seeing the rebirth of federalism and its fear of a powerful central government, while others argue for more ideological explanations such as racism, misogyny, and social Darwinism, and still others put forth entirely economic interpretations of this judicial retreat from equality. No matter the reason, there is little doubt that the high court's actions in those three decades had profound restrictive effects on all those who did not enjoy the privilege of the correct ethnic, gender, and religious identifier.

Blyew v. U.S. (1871) grew out of the murder of a black woman in Kentucky by a group of white men. There were numerous witnesses to the crime, but they were all black. Under Kentucky law, blacks could not testify against whites, allowing the court to find the white defendants innocent. In his majority opinion for the Supreme Court, Justice William Strong noted the protections of legal equality in the Civil Rights Act and then dismissed them since the victim of the crime was dead and therefore no longer enjoyed any rights, which terminated federal jurisdiction. In their dissent, Justices Swayne and Joseph P. Bradley insisted that the limitation on black testimony violated the rights of the witnesses, arguing that such obvious discrimination formed "a badge of slavery"—the first time that term appeared in a Supreme Court case. While the phrase usually appeared only in dissents, its acknowledgment that the brutal history of servitude implanted a heavy cultural bias persistently battled against a complacent insistence that slavery and its attendant racism were safely buried in the past.[42]

The Supreme Court followed this abdication of federal authority in the protection of equal rights with the confusing and confounding *Slaughterhouse Cases* of 1873. Though originally concerning the authority of New Orleans to regulate slaughterhouses in the name of public safety, these three cases became significant precedents in the legal interpretation of the Thirteenth and Fourteenth Amendments. Writing for a 5-to-4 majority, Justice Samuel Miller framed his decision around the assumption that the people would protect human rights without need for federal action. Miller denied that the framers of the Fourteenth Amendment intended to grant Congress authority over civil rights, which had always been the exclusive jurisdiction of the states, nor in any way to diminish state powers. This logic required Miller to explicitly ignore the formal record of the debates. Historian James Kettner wrote that Miller's deliberate lie "frustrated the intent and narrowed the scope of the amendment and set the development of American citizenship on a tortuous new path." Miller returned to Taney's concept of dual citizenship, establishing a distinction between state and federal rights; the amendment could not affect the rights states chose to grant their citizens.[43]

Even the dissents in the *Slaughterhouse Cases* weakened the Fourteenth Amendment. Drawing on the amendment's privileges and immunity clause, Justice Stephen Fields argued against state interference in the economy. Even though it was a dissent, Fields's reading of the amendment evolved over the next twenty years into a majority interpretation that rejected nearly all government regulation, as the protection of equal rights morphed into an unrestricted liberty of contract. Meanwhile, Justice Bradley's dissent laid the groundwork for reading the due process clause as a further limitation on government action. As historians Harold Hyman and William Wiecek wrote, the logic of the majority and dissenting opinions "stalked through the pages of the *United States Reports* for the next generation, disemboweling federal and state efforts to protect workers from predatory employers in such constitutional monstrosities as *Lochner v. New York* (1905), *Adkins v. Children's Hospital* (1923), and *Morehead v. Tipaldo* (1936)."[44]

The *Slaughterhouse* decision is among the most convoluted, and influential, of the nineteenth century. The justices crafted a narrative of the Reconstruction amendments as doing little more than ending slavery. The court distorted the Fourteenth Amendment further by maintaining that it addressed only federal and state actions, not those taken by private individuals or that were the result of custom. That same day the Court issued another, clearer decision that left little doubt of their hostility to legal equality, this time in a case involving a woman.

Under the standards of English common law, women could not be lawyers because they could never truly be independent. Myra Colby Bradwell begged to differ. Bradwell became an activist during the Civil War, raising funds for wounded soldiers and serving on the Sanitation Committee in Chicago. She also apprenticed with her husband, a prominent attorney and judge. She excelled at the law, founding and editing the *Chicago Legal News*, which she kept going despite her offices burning to the ground in the great fire of 1871. Bradwell played a key role in drafting Illinois's 1861 Married Women's Property Act and the Earnings Act of 1869, limiting the harmful effects of the traditional legal concept of couverture. In the latter year she applied for admission to the state bar, impressing her examiners, who recommended her to the state's Supreme Court. But the court rejected her application on the simple grounds that she was a woman, "that God designed the sexes to occupy different spheres of action, and that it belonged to men to make, apply, and execute the laws." No evidence was required since it was absurd to think otherwise.[45]

Bradwell thought otherwise and appealed to the U.S. Supreme Court. Wisconsin senator Matthew Hale Carpenter represented Bradwell, while Illinois did not bother to defend its position since the idea of a woman lawyer was simply ludicrous. Carpenter presented Bradwell's position as a logical answer to the question of whether a qualified female citizen can "claim, under the XIV Amendment, the privilege of earning a livelihood by practicing at the bar of a judicial court." Carpenter thought the answer obvious: since the Fourteenth Amendment says that no state can "make or enforce any law" that abridges the rights and privileges of a citizen, "it must follow that the privileges of all citizens are the same." As a citizen, Bradwell should have the same right as any man to be an attorney.[46]

The justices could not begin to understand this reasoning. Without dissent, the Court ruled that no one has a right to pursue a specific career and that the word "person" was never intended to include women. Justice Miller simply reversed Bradwell's logic; since non-citizens could be lawyers, citizenship was not a requirement to be a lawyer, and therefore there was no right of citizens to be lawyers.

In his concurrence, Justice Bradley expanded on the common-law and divine roots of inequality. The law and nature instituted separate spheres for men and women. That natural divide is evident in the "proper timidity and delicacy which belongs to the female sex," and which obviously makes women unfit for civil life. The "divine ordinance" left women to function solely in the domestic sphere under male direction. Bradley found it "repugnant" to conceive of a woman having any career other than motherhood. For these reasons, "a woman had no legal existence separate from her husband," and could not hold property or enter into contracts—doing so would make the practice of the law impossible. Bradwell should be content with her paramount "destiny and mission," which was to serve as a wife and mother. All human laws must bend to "the law of the Creator"; any notion of equality between men and women is silly and even dangerous. No wonder that when Charlotte E. Ray completed her law studies, Howard University disguised her gender by putting her forward for the bar in Washington, D.C., as "C. E. Ray." Under that name she was accepted to practice law.[47]

The *Bradwell* decision channeled both sides of a significant cultural shift toward inequality. Christians had long perceived women as the cursed descendants of Eve, collectively tarnished by her guilt in the expulsion of humanity from the Garden of Eden. God made women inferior and subservient to men; proposing otherwise was heresy. The growing acceptance of the theory of natural selection made a literal reading of the Bible unpopular with the educated elites. However, like religion, evolution could be forced into a misogynist track with ease, as gendered divisions followed from the very structure of nature. In the late nineteenth century, an opponent of equality could easily turn to either sacred or secular sources for validation.

Neither these religious nor scientific approaches to inequality went unchallenged. Stanton questioned the theological diminishment with *The Woman's Bible*, while brilliant women scientists challenged the superficial reading of natural selection, beginning with Antoinette Brown Blackwell's groundbreaking *The Sexes Throughout Nature* in 1875. Stanton called on women to study religion for themselves rather than follow the lead of male ministers, while Helen Hamilton Gardner made the empirical case for equality, famously challenging other scientists to determine gender or race by examining human brains. Evolutionary theory allowed women to imagine alternative gender relations, if only because science, unlike religion, is premised on skepticism, evidence, and change. Research over the past hundred years has validated much of Blackwell's and Gardner's analysis, as scientists who have examined the actual workings of the human brain have found similar biological and chemical processes. Men (including some Harvard presidents), being slow learners, rejected the evidence of cognitive equality well into the twenty-first century.[48]

A further sign of the retreat from equality by legal scholars and jurists came with the publication of the *Revised Statutes of the United States* by a congressionally appointed commission in 1874. This work was part of the larger project to create a more professional legal practice, one based on education in elite law schools. Though very thorough, the *Revised Statutes* somehow did not include the Civil Rights Acts. As lawyer and judge Francis Biddle would later write, the new compilation "concealed the whole scheme for the protection of rights" established by the Reconstruction amendments as well as the five congressional enforcement acts. Human equality was not a matter with which a law student must concern himself—and as *Bradwell v. Illinois* clarified, they would all be men.[49]

Starting in 1873, the Supreme Court essentially transformed the Thirteenth and Fifteenth Amendments into fossils, and the Fourteenth into a tool protecting the rich. The framers of the amendments intended to put an end to a caste system and protect the legal equality of all Americans. They did not anticipate reactionary judges deliberately ignoring or misreading the clear language of the amendments.

The Supreme Court's decisions affected every level of legal action. For instance, in 1874 a black man beaten by a group of whites for having the temerity to testify in a trial attempted to attain justice by bringing a lawsuit against his attackers. Following the High Court's guidance, Judge William B. Woods dismissed the case as concerning actions taken by individuals, not by the state or federal government. In 1875 the Supreme Court applied the same logic in the notorious *Cruikshank* decision. A white mob that included several local officials slaughtered some one hundred black men in Louisiana. The unanimous court ruled that murder, no matter what the scale and despite any racial motivation, remained a state matter. The Court therefore determined that the Enforcement Act of 1870, which prohibited conspiracies to deny civil rights, violated the Constitution. The federal government can do nothing if private individuals, even when acting through groups such as the Ku Klux Klan, conspire to take away the lives and rights of others. The national government can only act if a state government actively supports a conspiracy; not even the involvement of state officials offers sufficient cause for federal intervention. The Court acted on the legal fiction that the states will protect all their citizens.[50]

The Supreme Court abandoned Reconstruction entirely in 1876 with *U.S. v. Reese*, in which the court effectively terminated the enforcement of the Fifteenth Amendment. Chief Justice Waite ruled that the federal government can act only to prevent intentional racial discrimination and lacked any authority over suffrage. Incredibly, he argued that "the Fifteenth Amendment does not confer the right of suffrage upon any one," but only protected an individual from having his vote taken away because of race. States are free to deny the vote for other reasons, effectively permitting them to institute a number of subterfuges to limit the black vote and undermine democracy. The Fifteenth Amendment may have given black men the right to vote, but it did not require the states to accept those votes. The federal protection of individual rights practically disappeared—except, as it would soon develop, in the case of large enterprises.[51]

By 1880 the Supreme Court existed in a fantasy world of its own construction. That year, in *Virginia v. Rives*, the Court considered challenges in a Virginia county where no black had ever sat on a jury, and refused to see that exclusion as an act of bias. Not only did the Court find no right to sit on a jury, but it also insisted that the state of course protected the rights of all citizens; for what possible reason would it do otherwise? The Court further undermined any efforts to promote equality with *U.S. v. Harris* in 1883, declaring unconstitutional the part of the Ku Klux Klan Act that made it unlawful to conspire to deprive anyone of the equal protection of the law. Responding to a white Tennessee mob that lynched a black man, the Court reasoned that the Constitution protected blacks from enslavement, not death. In combination with the *Cruikshank* decision, *U.S. v. Harris* illuminated the Court's refusal to allow the government any responsibility in protecting the civil rights—and lives—of American citizens.[52]

To address the Court's rulings and white supremacist violence, Congress made one final attempt to defend equality before the law with the Civil Rights Act of 1875. This act gave the federal government the power to defend the lives and legal rights of all citizens, including their access to public facilities and a right to sit on juries. As Representative Benjamin Butler observed, this legislation sought to correct the Supreme Court's constitutional interpretation that the federal government could protect its citizens anywhere in the world, except in the states.[53]

In 1883 the Supreme Court dashed these hopes by declaring the Civil Rights Acts unconstitutional, allowing southern legislatures to institute legal segregation. Justice Bradley argued that Congress, in trying to enforce the Fourteenth Amendment, had violated the Tenth by extending its reach into private matters. The Court adhered to its earlier logic that the Fourteenth Amendment applied only to state actions, not private ones, while the Thirteenth Amendment had successfully ended slavery and was therefore now moot. Bradley had no tolerance for the "badges of servitude" argument, holding that after eighteen years more than enough time had passed since the end of slavery and now it was time to move on. Any reading of bias or legal limitations was self-imposed, not the result of public policy.

Justice John Marshall Harlan, a former slave owner, issued an insightful lone dissent that reverberated through the courts a few generations later. Harlan charged that the Court overstepped its authority in overturning laws well within the power of Congress, which had the responsibility to enforce the amendments. Further, private discrimination required the support of the law to persist. He charged the Court with sacrificing "the substance and spirit of the recent amendments" by a careful manipulation of language. If the Court took away the power of Congress to protect the nation's citizens, Harlan wrote, then the Reconstruction amendments would become little more than "splendid baubles, thrown out to delude those who deserved fair and generous treatment at the hands of the nation."

For Harlan, the Court had entered upon "an era of constitutional law, when the rights of freedom and American citizenship cannot receive from the nation that efficient protection which heretofore was unhesitatingly accorded to slavery." The Court had thus effectively turned the clock back to *Dred Scott*, if with friendlier language. Taney had denied that blacks could be citizens, while the current Court found that blacks could be citizens without rights. Harlan called the High Court delusional if it believed that the former Confederate states would protect the rights of their former slaves. White southerners feared democracy and hated equality, and they put up a variety of façades, frauds, and falsehoods to justify their racism; by overturning the Civil Rights Act, the Supreme Court validated their lies.[54]

In essence, the Supreme Court amended the Reconstruction amendments into irrelevance, except for business interests. In 1886 the Court heard a challenge to a section of California's state constitution denying railroads the right to deduct mortgage debts from their taxable wealth. Lawyers for the Southern Pacific Railroad argued that corporations should have the same rights as people. Humans could deduct their mortgage payments, and so should corporations. For support, the railroad cited the equal protection clause of the Fourteenth Amendment.

Writing for a unanimous court, Justice Harlan focused narrowly on the railroad's fences, which California had included in its assessment of the railroad's property value. Including the fences led to an invalid assessment, Harlan argued, since California's constitution failed to mention fences. Harlan offered no response to the defendants' Fourteenth Amendment argument. The case might have rested there, as an obscure tax case, had not the court's reporter, Bancroft Davis, a former railroad president, added a headnote implying that the court agreed that "corporations are persons within the meaning of the Fourteenth Amendment." *Santa Clara Co. v. Southern Pacific* thus became an accidental precedent setting the standard for applying the Fourteenth Amendment to corporations, though rarely to people.[55]

This interpretation of the Fourteenth Amendment had an enormous impact on American life. State and federal courts lost sight of the intent of the Reconstruction amendments to end legally sanctioned class or caste distinctions and remove race as a legal category in order to integrate blacks into civic life. The *Slaughterhouse Cases* limited the amendments' applicability, while the *Civil Rights Cases* of 1883 blocked the ability of the federal government to act. Thanks to the Supreme Court, the Thirteenth Amendment ended slavery and nothing more; the Fourteenth Amendment left most rights subject to state control; and the Fifteenth Amendment stood as a hollow promise of a right to vote, its enforcement left to the states. The nation's courts treated people not as individuals, as seemingly required by the Fourteenth Amendment, but as members of groups determined by ethnicity, class, race, and gender. Along the way the very concept of equality vanished.

Emboldened by the courts' indifference to legal equality, southern state legislatures, now firmly in the hands of the Democratic Party, began passing laws to keep the races separated. Starting with Florida in 1887, these Jim Crow laws eventually affected every aspect of southern society, from streetcars to hotels, theaters, water fountains, sidewalks, and marriage. Southern legislatures felt no constraint on their actions.

In 1893, the Supreme Court issued its ultimate insult to the Constitution in *Plessy v. Ferguson*. With *Plessy*, the Supreme Court set a standard of collective group equality—all blacks are treated the same, denied the same rights, and subject to the same legal restrictions.

The facts of the case are rather straightforward. The Citizens' Committee of New Orleans recruited Homer Plessy, who was officially one-eighth black, to challenge Louisiana's recently adopted segregation laws. The local railroad also opposed the law, as it required them to put on extra cars to prevent blacks and whites from riding together. Plessy, who easily passed for white, announced his defiance of the statute and was removed from the car and charged with violating state law.

Plessy's defiance of Louisiana's segregation laws raised numerous legal questions. Most basic was the seemingly simple matter of what makes a person white or black. Just how is race determined, and who gets to decide? The heart of the case was the Fourteenth Amendment. Plessy's attorney, the pioneer civil rights activist Albion Tourgée, reminded the court that the Reconstruction amendments established freedom in the United States, protecting all citizens in their rights of citizenship, making the determination of race not just irrelevant but an insult to the Constitution.

The Supreme Court rejected Tourgée's defense of legal equality 8 to 1. Writing for the majority, Justice Henry Billings Brown admitted that the Fourteenth Amendment did indeed intend to enforce "absolute equality," but surely no one believed that it also "intended to abolish distinctions based upon color, or to enforce social, as distinguished from political equality, or a commingling of the two races upon terms unsatisfactory to either." Brown differentiated between "distinction" and "discrimination," with the former acknowledging reality. He denied that a law establishing "merely a legal distinction between the white and colored races" undermined legal equality. Any perceived inequality had its roots solely in the mind of the individual; surely the state of Louisiana did not treat its black citizens as inferiors. Brown provided no evidence for his insistence that segregation hurt no one; he simply wrote that it "is too clear for argument."

The Court maintained that it acted within the nation's legal traditions, upholding the state's police power, as well as respecting contemporary racial science. The Court must reject laws that "conflict with the general sentiment of the community," though it did not specify what community or how to determine sentiment. The Reconstruction amendments had already done their work, having secured for all citizens equal rights and opportunity, and nothing more needed to be done. Racism and racial distinctions lay beyond the purview of any branch of government, and efforts to effect change would only worsen the situation for blacks and whites alike. Segregation did not violate legal equality since "if one race be inferior to the other socially, the Constitution of the United States cannot put them upon the same plane." Eight justices declared themselves comfortable with "separate but equal" facilities regulated along racial lines.

As in the *Civil Rights Cases*, Justice Harlan filed a biting dissent, highlighting the Court's refusal to address the reality of the nation's long history of racism. The Court's task was to determine whether a law that "regulates the use of a public highway by citizens of the United States solely upon the basis of race" is consistent with the Constitution. Harlan could find nothing in the Constitution that permitted any public authority to even determine the race of its citizens. Creating different racial categories violated the legal equality guaranteed to all citizens under the Fourteenth Amendment, as well as the personal liberty of all Americans.

Harlan patiently attempted to explain to his colleagues why the plaintiff included the Thirteenth Amendment as a justification for challenging segregation. That amendment did not just abolish slavery; it also "prevents the imposition of any burdens or disabilities that constitute badges of slavery or servitude." The Court seemed to have trouble understanding that "the arbitrary separation of citizens, on the basis of race . . . is a badge of servitude wholly inconsistent with the civil freedom and the equality before the law established by the Constitution." Harlan bluntly denied that such a perspective can be justified by anything in the Constitution. The Court had determined that the Thirteenth Amendment "decreed universal civil freedom in this country," while the Fourteenth Amendment followed it up to secure "the dignity and glory of American citizenship" by protecting personal liberty. If enforced, these amendments would protect all Americans in their rights; but the Supreme Court refused to allow that enforcement. Harlan pointed out the obvious: that segregation aimed to protect whites from the company of blacks, not the other way around. The state had no duty nor right to enforce the separation of the races; if whites and blacks sat together, that was their business, not the state's. Harlan correctly predicted that the Court was paving the way for many more acts diminishing the status of blacks.

Moving beyond a demonstration of the error of the majority opinion, Harlan put forth an alternative reading of the Constitution that he thought would protect all citizens. Given the language of the Constitution and its clear intent to promote human freedom, the United States should not have a distinctive ruling class. Harlan offered a powerful and succinct legal perspective premised on the conviction that the Fourteenth Amendment had freed the United States from a caste structure: "Our Constitution is color-blind, and neither knows nor tolerates classes among citizens. In respect of civil rights, all citizens are equal before the law. The humblest is the peer of the most powerful."

The nation's future success linked the two races together, Harlan insisted. The interests of all Americans "require that the common government of all shall not permit the seeds of race hate to be planted under the sanction of law." The southern legislatures sought to overturn the "legitimate results of the war" by undermining the Reconstruction amendments, and they should not be assisted toward this goal by the

Supreme Court. Rather than protecting the rights of citizens, Harlan charged, the Court acted to institutionalize racism through segregation, fostering further racial conflict and perpetuating the damage already done to the country by slavery. The Court evaded its responsibility by simply accepting the persistence of racial bias as unavoidable. Such an attitude was unworthy of the ideals of the Constitution and ignored the considerable social progress made during Reconstruction.

Compared to his colleagues, Harlan was a realist. He dismissed the "thin disguise" of separate but equal as unlikely to ever come into actual practice. The Court erred greatly in validating the state's power "by sinister legislation" to regulate civil rights on the basis of race to the detriment of one group, who are placed "in a condition of legal inferiority." Harlan warned that the *Plessy* decision would be seen as one of the Court's great errors and would "prove to be quite as pernicious as the decision made by this tribunal in the Dred Scott case." [56]

Rarely has a Supreme Court justice so clearly analyzed his contemporary society and correctly predicted the consequences of the Court's actions. *Plessy* stands with *Dred Scott* as one of the worst decisions ever tendered by the Supreme Court. For more than half a century it condemned millions of Americans to second-class citizenship and scarred the United States in profound ways. The southern states played a careful game to avoid upsetting northern whites, denying rights in a way that always seemed to find support in the courts. For instance, they did not explicitly prohibit blacks from voting, so the Section 4 restrictions in the Fourteenth Amendment did not kick in; instead they used numerous subtle and not so subtle ways to prevent blacks from voting.

Reconstruction had briefly promised a democratic vision for the future of America. But opponents of legal equality, seeking to turn back the clock, quickly found a supportive power base in the federal courts. The courts even managed to undermine the Thirteenth Amendment. In 1867 Congress had passed an anti-peonage law to enforce the intent of the Thirteenth Amendment, but the courts blocked nearly every effort at enforcement. As a consequence, the southern states established a debt peonage system that has accurately been labeled "slavery by another name." Into the 1930s, the southern legal system sold thousands of black men and women into a brutal system of coerced labor. As W. E. B. Du Bois wrote, "Slavery was not abolished even after the Thirteenth Amendment."[57]

Plessy served as a powerful bulwark for all these inequalities, leaving it up to the states to work out their social relationships. Yet one phrase would stand out from *Plessy v. Ferguson* as a beacon for the ideal of equality, and it came from Justice Harlan's eloquent dissent: "Our Constitution is color-blind."

The Supreme Court completed the dismantling of the Reconstruction amendments with *Hodges v. U.S.* in 1906, with the majority eliminating protection even for the right of contract when it came to individuals rather than businesses. The case involved three white men who conspired to use violence to prevent a group of blacks from fulfilling their contractual work with a lumber mill. Justice David J. Brewer held that the nation had no interest in protecting jobs or contracts, which were private wrongs that had no bearing on federal rights. Once more Justice Harlan dissented, again pointing out that truly ending slavery meant eliminating the badges of servitude, which had been the intention of the Reconstruction amendments and several acts of Congress aimed at protecting civil rights. He also observed that in the *Civil Rights Cases* the Court admitted that making contracts was a fundamental civil right. The majority did not care about their previous decisions, declaring that state courts held exclusive power to determine violations of the Thirteenth Amendment, effectively circumscribing their own power and allowing slavery to persist.[58]

It is fair to say that for at least half a century after the *Slaughterhouse Cases* the Supreme Court appeared confused about the meaning of the Reconstruction amendments. In 1922 the Court ruled in the *Prudential Insurance* case that "neither the Fourteenth Amendment nor any other provision of the constitution of the United States imposes on the States any restrictions about 'freedom of speech,'" leaving the states free to limit all forms of expression. Yet just three years later, in *Gitlow v. New York*, the same court ruled that "freedom of speech and of the press . . . are among the fundamental personal rights and liberties protected by the due process clause from impairment by the States."[59]

In diminishing the reach of the equality amendments, the Supreme Court adopted the "state action" doctrine, leaving the regulation of citizenship rights entirely in the hands of the states. This reasoning held that the amendments prevented states from denying rights, but it allowed no mechanism for protecting those rights. Social Darwinism had so warped elite ideology that by 1900 the Fourteenth Amendment had become a legal safeguard of corporate capitalism. As Oliver Wendell Holmes Jr. wrote in an acerbic 1905 dissent in *Lochner v. New York*, "The Fourteenth Amendment does not enact Mr. Herbert Spencer's *Social Statics*"—a foundational text for social Darwinists. The reactionaries triumphed; legal equality appeared dead, all were equal in their isolation, and only the powerful prospered.[60]

The betrayals littered the American landscape and blasted the nation's future. Julia Ward Howe, the woman responsible for one of the most stirring patriotic songs of the century, "The Battle Hymn of the Republic," felt that sense of shattered hopes and abandoned ideals. Before the war she had questioned the purpose of a woman's life, asking if in marriage and child-rearing "we lose our own vitality, and sink into dimness, nothingness, and living death." The Civil War saved Howe from the living death of marriage, giving her purpose and work. At the war's end she wrote that in her twenty-two years of marriage, "I have never known my husband to approve of any act of mine which I myself valued." He found every act of hers "contemptible . . . because it was not *his* way of doing things." When equality eluded women, she fought for the Fourteenth Amendment; when that still did not secure women the rights they so clearly deserved, she devoted the remainder of her long life to battling for the right to vote, becoming president of the American Woman Suffrage Association and founding the Association for the Advancement of Women.[61]

Women who had devoted enormous energy to the Union cause felt deeply betrayed by the Reconstruction amendments. As Elizabeth Cady Stanton wrote, when abolitionists and Union leaders "asked us to be silent on our question during the War, and labor for the emancipation of the slave, we did so," giving over all their time and energy to winning freedom and civil rights for black men. With time Stanton came to feel this policy had been "a blunder" of historic proportions. They kept expecting their male allies to fulfill what they thought of as a fair bargain, but it did not happen in their lifetimes.[62]

Similarly, black women expected but did not receive much support from the majority of black men. When Frances Harper spoke in New Orleans in favor of women's rights, *The Louisianan*—edited and published by P. B. S. Pinchback, the first African American governor—declared itself "struck dumb with consternation." Black women were expected to conform to masculine desires, as *The Louisianan* indicated with such poems as "A Woman As She Should Be," which advised: "Submission to her husband's will / Her study is to please him still." Frederick Douglass tried to dissuade Monroe A. Majors from writing his book *Noted Negro Women*, since he did not think any of them that notable. When W. E. B. Du Bois, Paul Dunbar, and Francis Grimké organized the American Negro Academy, they limited membership to men.[63]

Yet many black women did not passively accept male direction. Anna J. Cooper, who was born into slavery in 1858 and received a master's degree in mathematics from Oberlin in 1887, captured the excitement felt by many talented young black women in the aftermath of the Civil War: "Everything to this race is new and strange and inspiring." She felt a sense of excitement and increased consciousness of her own abilities: "I can aspire to that! I can honor my name and vindicate my race!" Cooper would do more than just vindicate her freedom; she would go on to earn a doctorate in history from the Sorbonne and become a prominent scholar. She, too, persisted.[64]

In its early years, the women's rights movement aimed for full legal equality. They assumed that such equality would of course lead to the right to vote, as well as to protection for women's right to bodily autonomy, property rights, the right to hold jobs and public office, the right to enter into contracts and sue, and all the other markers of full citizenship. But those adhering to traditional cultural values found the whole package a threat to the moral and natural order. Female equality, they charged, would lead to free love, the corruption of the institution of marriage, the collapse of the family, and the end of civilization.

In combating these apocalyptic fears, the advocates of women's rights slowly moved to a focus on suffrage alone. They did not abandon their other goals, but they trusted that once women could vote, the other rights would follow. Women leaders, finding their egalitarian arguments gaining no traction, switched to a position based on difference: more moral than men, women would serve as a balance wheel in the polity. This shift appeared less threatening in a general way, as it did not call into question preexisting gender relations. Opponents of women's suffrage took the proponents' argument and turned it back on them: women are more moral and should therefore be protected from the corruptions of the public sphere. As the women's rights movement weakened, so did the public perception of women. The image of the rugged frontier woman or heroic wartime nurse gave way to the fragile flower of the boudoir, weak in mind and constitution, prone to fainting spells and irrational emotions. By the end of the nineteenth century, women's role in popular culture rarely rose above the damsel in distress, and most men thought the suffrage movement had died out.[65]

Many male leaders of the crusade for equality fought on through public indifference. Charles Sumner continued his struggle for civil rights until his death in 1874, just as the North began losing interest. Frederick Douglass reached peak prestige in 1877 with his appointment as the first African American marshal in the nation's history. But at the same time his tension with the women's rights movement intensified. At the 1876 Republican convention in Cincinnati, Sarah Spencer, the nation's first lobbyist for women's rights, confronted Douglass after he failed to mention women's suffrage in his speech, as he had promised. Douglass lamely demurred that he had forgotten to do so. He may have been myopic regarding women's rights, but Douglass recognized the persistent inequality suffered by blacks and bitterly denounced "the So-Called Emancipation as a Stupendous Fraud." He continued to fight for black rights until his death in 1895, though he watched in horror as violence against blacks rose every year.[66]

In 1890, the courageous Ida B. Wells, just twenty-eight, began documenting that racial violence in her journal, *Free Speech*, castigating lynch mobs as an "awful indictment against American civilization." Reporting on blacks burned at the stake by white mobs, Wells wrote, "No other nation, civilized or savage, burns its criminals; only under the stars and stripes is the human holocaust possible." In 1896, the year of *Plessy*, black women met in Washington to organize the National Association of Colored Women. The oldest woman present, Harriet Tubman, introduced Wells as the movement's new firebrand. In passing the torch to a younger generation, Tubman promised that the struggle for equality would continue.[67]

In many ways, Carl Schurz's tour through the South in 1885 best exemplifies shifting attitudes among white progressives. Twenty years earlier, Schurz had condemned the racist intransigence of southern whites and called for federal intervention to protect the freedmen. In 1885 he saw a South rapidly segregating and thought it not such a bad idea. Southern whites reassured him that the blacks just needed more education, which they insisted they were providing. With time all would be well. Schurz fell for their twaddle without question.[68]

At the dawn of the new century, Schurz reconsidered what the southern whites had put in place since the end of Reconstruction. He now recognized that white supremacists had created a despotism that violated nearly every part of the Constitution, and most certainly the Reconstruction amendments. As under slavery, the South had no true freedom of speech or assembly, for either whites or blacks. The southern elites burdened "the Southern people with another 'peculiar institution,' closely akin to its predecessor in character." Once more, most workers, white and black, were "kept in stupid subjection, without the hope of advancement and without the ambition of progress." The repressive society of the antebellum South had been restored, just without the legal institution of slavery. Schurz saw that in 1885 he had been completely fooled by southern whites telling him exactly what he wanted to hear. By 1905 it was too late to change a system that the same whites now insisted was "natural." [69]

The last congressional effort to protect legal equality came in 1890, when the patrician Massachusetts representative Henry Cabot Lodge proposed federal supervision of congressional elections. This bill empowered the president to send in the military to secure free and fair elections if federal monitors found evidence of intimidation, discrimination, or fraud. Lodge insisted that Congress must protect southern blacks in their right to vote. The United States had changed its Constitution to make black men citizens. A government that would not defend its own citizens was weak and contemptible: "A failure to do what is right brings its own punishment to nations as to men." Not a single Democrat voted for the bill, which passed the House only to be subjected to a staggering thirty-three-day-long filibuster in the Senate before Republicans finally dropped the bill as a lost cause. [70]

After Reconstruction came the battle for history, the struggle to craft the narrative that would determine the future. On this field of battle, the Confederacy emerged victorious. In the early twentieth century, advocates of the Confederate rewriting of the nation's history found a powerful advocate in Woodrow Wilson. As a popular historian, Wilson promoted the vision of slavery as a benign institution in a romantic "Old South" and of a corrupt Reconstruction that forced the "Redeemers" to save civilization by organizing the Ku Klux Klan and reclaiming government by and for white males. When he became president in 1913, Wilson set about turning back the clock, segregating the federal civil service and public buildings and ending all federal efforts to protect civil rights. On the fiftieth anniversary of the Battle of Gettysburg, Wilson went to the place were Lincoln had promised "a rebirth of freedom" and assured an all-white audience—no black veterans had been invited— that he would not be so impertinent as to address the war's significance.

Inequality corrupted every aspect of American life. The notion of women as in any way equal to men largely disappeared, as did any pretense that those not blessed with a WASP heritage could ever aspire to the glories of the master race. Communities felt completely justified in punishing those who strayed over the approved lines. The examples are numerous and often violent. In 1911 the state of Maine evicted an interracial community living peacefully on the island of Malaga, subjecting many of these citizens to forced sterilization to ensure that they would bear no more children. The racist science of eugenics justified the routine involuntary sterilization of those identified as less fit, becoming a model cited by Adolf Hitler and upheld by the Supreme Court in *Buck v. Bell* (1927). Popular culture routinely mocked every ethnicity outside northwest Europe while demoting non-white races to subhuman status.

The Civil War engendered government action and a conviction that the nation could solve its problems through legislation. For a brief period it appeared that the government stood firmly on the side of the people. Those seeking equality longed for a coherent and predictable system of law and the security it offered. The Supreme Court effectively alienated them from the law for generations, making the majority of Americans suspicious of law enforcement. Crimes went unreported, witnesses would not cooperate, charges were not pressed, police operated as repressive agents in numerous communities, and the legal system became a stultifying servant of the privileged.

Legal equality is more than just an abstraction; it is a protector of life and liberty. By 1900 that protection applied only to a specific class of Americans within a highly unequal society, creating the nation James Madison had feared, a republic corrupted by the tyranny of the majority—though in this case it was a self-proclaimed rather than numerical majority. Minorities of every kind—and even the majority, who were women—lived at the mercy of the white male "majority." Faced with the negation of their rights and freedoms, minorities had no choice but to turn to their home states for protection. Yet those states not only had no interest in their defense but often were the agents of the very crimes needing redress. A white man who took the life of a black would almost never be prosecuted. Women, Chinese, Hispanics, Japanese, blacks, Native Americans, the poor, the homeless, recent immigrants—anyone whose rights were violated had no place of refuge. Once more, equality had become just a dream, with little hope for its realization. Yet within the Constitution's Fourteenth Amendment the possibility of change lay dormant, just waiting for a society that would recognize the promise of those two words: "all persons."

Epilogue: Overcoming the Tyranny of the Minority

Or, a good idea is hard to kill

Prior to the Civil War, Americans perceived equality as a fine word with little real meaning. The nation's leading thinkers scoffed at the idea that equality had any place in human affairs. After the *Dred Scott* decision, a growing chorus of voices outside the South came to agree with Abraham Lincoln's formulation of an equality of labor, the concept that everyone had a right to the fruit of their work. The Civil War drove the majority of Americans further, to the conviction that democracy requires legal equality, an equal standing before the law and the right to enter freely into every sort of legitimate legal contract. There things might have remained but for the refusal of white racists to accept this change in American governance.

Southern white violence persuaded a majority of Americans to take the next step toward political equality, the right to participate in the nation's decision-making. The Reconstruction period also demonstrated that the federal government needed to step in to protect the civil rights of citizens in the face of hostile local and state governments. The Constitution had created national rights, but slavery took away those rights from millions of people and placed power in the hands of individuals rather than the government. The Reconstruction amendments intended to restore individual rights and establish the principle of equal national citizenship. The next obvious step was a push toward social equality, the recognition of each person as having the same rights and opportunities as individuals rather than as members of a group, protected by their legal and political equality. But the Supreme Court stepped in, effectively curbing the amended Constitution. In a series of significant decisions, the high court made the Thirteenth, Fourteenth, and Fifteenth amendments largely irrelevant in American law except as a defense of liberty of contract against state action.

However, the Reconstruction amendments established the Constitution as a living document, one capable of changing with time—a point many contemporaries understood. Neither "infallible" nor "stationary," the Constitution, in the words of Pennsylvania attorney general James J. Creigh in 1867, "moves with the nation." It serves the people and must change with the times in order to protect "the citizenship of all the people [and] the equality of citizens." It took decades, but eventually that concept became the center of American law and culture.[1]

In the century and a half since the end of the Civil War, differing visions of the Constitution and legal equality have battled for primacy. Both positions developed in the years immediately following the Civil War. On one side the Supreme Court interpreted the Reconstruction amendments as having limited reach; on the other side stood those who argued that those amendments had fundamentally altered the Constitution into the guarantor of legal equality. For much of the period following the end of Reconstruction, the former position held sway, but that never stopped the advocates of equality from pressing their democratic interpretation of rights.

Advocates of equality did not become silent after the end of Reconstruction, but Congress and the nation's leading intellectuals, ministers, jurists, and journalists stopped listening. Voices rose against all forms of inequality, but their efforts to battle the spreading tyranny of America are largely forgotten, probably because those favoring the extension of equal rights generally lost. But these many battles mattered greatly to those involved. Even minor victories could make a great difference in the lives of many people.

For example, Sojourner Truth spoke for most activists when she insisted, "I have been forty years a slave and forty years free, and would be here forty years more to have equal rights for all." She never quit. Encouraged by two white friends, Truth refused to give in to racist conductors; combining political acumen with precise legal arguments, she forced the integration of the streetcars in Washington, D.C. As she wrote another friend, "It is hard for the old slaveholding spirit to die. But die it must."[2]

That racist spirit died, but not quietly. Southern whites enjoyed boasting of their victory in the post-Reconstruction years. In 1890, Mississippi judge J. B. Chrisman, addressing the state's constitutional convention, bluntly described its political system: "Sir, it is no secret that there has not been a full vote and a fair count in Mississippi since 1875." For generations, the Democratic Party preserved "the ascendancy of the white people by revolutionary methods." Chrisman proudly admitted that "we have been stuffing ballot boxes, committing perjury[,] and here and there in the State carrying the elections by fraud and violence." Southern racists saw no need to even pretend that they lived in a democracy.[3]

A debilitating racism distorted the South and the nation for most of the twentieth century. In 1956 William Faulkner explained white opposition to equality as rooted in masculine anxiety. What southern white men most feared was "that the Negro, who has done so much with no chance, might do so much more with an equal one that he might take the white man's economy away from him." This primal terror undermined all logic and proclaimed ideals. Faulkner observed that in every war black soldiers proved themselves as brave as any white, "yet the Southern white man dares not let that Negro's children learn their ABC's in the same classroom with the children of the white lives he saved or defended." The fear of "lesser" people proving themselves the whites' equals drove America's rejection of equality through the century after the end of Reconstruction.[4]

Just as African Americans persisted in their battle against racism, women battled misogyny and inequality. As Carrie Chapman Catt and Nettie R. Shuler summarized the long campaign: "To get the word 'male' in effect out of the Constitution cost the women of the country fifty-two years of pauseless campaign." During those years, women placed 56 referendums on ballots, engaged in 480 legislative efforts to win the vote, and lobbied 47 state constitutional conventions, 277 state party conventions, 30 presidential party conventions, and 19 different Congresses. During those years they raised millions of dollars to support the efforts of thousands of women who devoted enormous energy to effecting change in scores of active organizations in every state, winning over hundreds of thousands of male voters to their cause. They published feminist newspapers all over the country, including in Salt Lake City, where the *Woman's Exponent* gave a Mormon slant to women's rights. In Topeka, the *Farmer's Wife* carried the slogan "Equal Rights to All, Special Privilege to None!" along with the masthead. As Catt and Shuler wrote, "It was a continuous, seemingly endless, chain of activity," that kept women's rights before state legislatures throughout the late nineteenth century—and kept failing.[5]

Meanwhile, social Darwinists extended the stigma of inferiority beyond blacks to include all poor people, workers, Asians, Mexicans, immigrants, and basically everyone who was not a prosperous WASP male. Despite a professed adherence to the notion of natural selection, the social Darwinists found numerous allies among the evangelical clergy. The most effective voice in this Christian attack on equality was that of the Reverend Josiah Strong. In his bestselling book, *Our Country*, Strong held immigrants responsible for "the most noxious growths of our civilization," including most of the crime. The typical immigrant was an uneducated peasant, lacking in morals and intent on a life of crime in the United States. If true Americans did not close their borders to this primal threat, the country would face the ultimate horror: a Catholic president.[6]

The influence of the social Darwinists and their Protestant allies spread into the halls of Congress. Attempting to control the ethnic future of the United States, Congress forbade Chinese immigration in 1882 and, with the 1917 Immigration Act, specified for the first time several categories of "undesirables" barred from entering the United States. Congress extended the reach of inequality with the National Origins Act of 1924, establishing ethnic quotas that favored northwestern Europe over all other possible sources of immigration. The exclusionists did not go unopposed, and numerous groups turned to the Reconstruction amendments in their battles for inclusion, slowly crafting a counternarrative of the United States as a nation of immigrants. As Boston mayor James Michael Curley put it, "The Puritan is passed; the Anglo-Saxon is a joke; a newer and better America is here." The only problem was that the majority of white Americans did not yet perceive the virtues of diversity and equality.[7]

For half a century, many courageous people tried to breathe life into the Reconstruction amendments but were defeated at every turn by the American preference for inequality. Those who favored equality came up against the full force of the state and found their legitimacy denied by leading intellectuals. Even the federal courts, intended as the Constitution's bulwark, turned their backs on those sections of the nation's charter that protected legal equality. Nonetheless, the believers in equality fought on, and that fight is a worthy subject for another book.

The string of defeats came to a rather remarkable end in the late 1930s. Advocates of equality found their greatest victories before a federal court system reborn as a consequence of the many judicial appointments made by President Franklin Delano Roosevelt. Those battling for equality had always relied on the Reconstruction amendments to support their cases, but suddenly it seemed as though the federal judges were reading them for the first time. Those three amendments had lain quietly ignored for decades, only to burst into life in the last half of the twentieth century.

The Fourteenth Amendment gained particular stature with the Supreme Court's 1954 decision in *Brown v. Board of Education of Topeka*. The *Brown* decision has been well explored in several outstanding books. What is significant here is that Chief Justice Earl Warren, speaking for a unanimous Court, held that racial segregation "denies to Negro children the equal protection of the laws guaranteed by the Fourteenth Amendment." Warren supported this assessment with one of the most famous footnotes in legal history, presenting evidence from contemporary research on the harmful effects of segregated schools upon black children. This research left little doubt that state-sanctioned racism denied both an equal education and equal rights to millions of Americans. Warren rooted his decision in the realities of inequality, moving beyond constitutional theory and abstractions to the direct consequences of a previous Supreme Court decision, brilliantly brushing aside precedent.[8]

In the aftermath of *Brown*, the use of the Fourteenth Amendment to extend rights has expanded enormously and can be found in a wide variety of cases. It justified striking down a Massachusetts law preventing unmarried people from buying contraceptives and a Missouri law that denied a widower benefits from his wife's work-related death; the Supreme Court used it to overturn a Virginia law that prevented interracial marriage and to confirm the right of the disabled to sue for access to government buildings; and recently a group of elementary school students in North Carolina called on the equal protection of the law to successfully overturn a dress code denying them the right to wear pants.[9]

At one level, these decisions led to significant changes in the lives of the people involved. It matters that Richard Loving and Mildred Jeter were free to get married and enjoy a long life together despite being identified as belonging to different races. On another level these decisions reflect and reinforce enormous cultural shifts. In striking down an Alabama law that limited alimony to women only, Justice William Brennan rejected the "baggage of sexual stereotypes" and called for "gender-neutral" legislation. It is hard to imagine such language and legal analysis appearing in a Supreme Court decision prior to 1970.[10]

It is vital to avoid the impression that the Supreme Court served as the guardian of progressive change in the United States. The high court did not wave a wand with the *Brown* decision and alter the character

of America. Rather, the nation's court system engages in a subtle inter-
action with public opinion, being influenced by, reflecting, and influ-
encing wider social changes. For example, it was a surprisingly short
journey from *Bowers v. Hardwick* in 1986 to *Obergefell v. Hodges* in
2015. In *Bowers*, the Court confirmed the constitutionality of Georgia's
sodomy law outlawing oral and anal sex. In his majority decision, Justice Byron White complained that the extension of due process rights
under the Fourteenth Amendment had gotten completely out of hand,
"recognizing rights that have little or no textual support in the constitutional language." In a concurring opinion, Chief Justice Warren Burger
warned that "to hold that the act of homosexual sodomy is somehow
protected as a fundamental right would be to cast aside millennia of
moral teaching." Yet just seventeen years later, in 2003, the Supreme
Court completely reversed course, the majority insisting that private
consensual sex fell under substantive due process protections and was
not a concern of the government. Then, in 2015, the Supreme Court
ruled that "the Fourteenth Amendment requires states to recognize
same-sex marriages." The Court did not create this rapid and crucial
cultural shift; rather, it responded to changing public attitudes resulting from an active and compelling gay rights movement that used the
methods, language, and legal strategies pioneered by two heroes of the
civil rights movement, Thurgood Marshall and Pauli Murray.[11]

Nor do Supreme Court decisions go uncontested. Many conservatives hate the use to which the Fourteenth Amendment has been put by
the courts. In 2014 Senator Ted Cruz of Texas angrily denounced the
Supreme Court for "making the preposterous assumption that the People
of the United States somehow silently redefined marriage in 1868 when
they ratified the Fourteenth Amendment." For forty years American
conservatives have united around opposition to *Roe v. Wade* and the
Court's refusal to extend personhood to fetuses—an argument Justice Harry Blackmun explicitly rejected in noting that the Fourteenth
Amendment grants citizenship to all persons *born* in the United States.
In 2016 the Electoral College selected a president who questioned that

central premise of the Fourteenth Amendment: that all persons born in the United States are citizens.[12]

Nonetheless, some conservatives perceive value in the reach of this amendment. Theodore Olson, who acted on George W. Bush's behalf in *Gore v. Bush*, the case that awarded Bush the presidency, and then served as his solicitor general, debated another conservative on Fox News in 2015 on the meaning of the Constitution. "So ultimately," Olson said, "the reason we have a Constitution, the reason we have separation of powers, the reason we have the 14th Amendment, is to provide the courts with the opportunity to override the will of the people, when the will of the people leads to discrimination against a segment of our society." Olson saw the Fourteenth Amendment serving a necessary function of protecting those who might otherwise have no recourse within the usual political mechanisms controlled by a political minority or against the strictures of cultural conformity. Such a position can easily be identified as politically conservative or liberal, depending on the intellectual framing. For many Americans across the political spectrum, the Fourteenth Amendment offers the best hope of securing a meaningful legal equality for all.[13]

The Civil War has often been called America's *Iliad*. If so, then the ensuing search for legal equality constitutes this nation's great odyssey, a journey that continues to this day. The United States is a nation founded on equality; yet the nation's leadership almost immediately turned their collective back on that ideal. For the next 240 years Americans battled to win acceptance for that simple and beautiful truth that all people are created equal. At the beginning of the twenty-first century, historian David Brion Davis wrote that "the United States is only now beginning to recover from the Confederacy's ideological victory following the Civil War." There is some recent evidence that this assessment may be a bit too optimistic.[14]

Equality remains a contested concept at every level of American society. Many Americans persist in denying equality in all forms, while some offer a limited notion of equality, one confined to contract law. Many see equality as a sort of accordion that can be expanded with rhetorical hot air and then compressed when practical issues arise. The majority of male Americans certainly did not want to extend any sort of equality to women through much of the twentieth century, and many women feared the consequences of equality. A few groups organized to extend equality to one particular class of people, whether Catholics, women, blacks, or Jews, but until the 1960s very few people seized hold of the core formulation of social equality and demanded that the logic of the Fourteenth Amendment be read across American law and society. As a consequence, the same arguments made at Seneca Falls in 1848 could be heard at suffragist rallies in 1918, rallies for the Equal Rights Amendment in 1978, and feminist rallies in 2008, as women insisted that they are citizens too, and entitled to equal rights. Similarly, Frederick Douglass's demands for humanity in 1856 resonated through the articles of W. E. B. Du Bois in 1916, the speeches of Martin Luther King Jr. in 1966, and the Black Lives Matter protests of 2016. Far too many Americans find it difficult to accept that equality for all may actually mean everyone.

Since the nation's founding, Americans have relished speaking of equality, but always with exceptions—usually basing these omissions on "common sense" or "nature." The examples are legion. Even great progressive actions such as the Social Security Act of 1935 violated the concept of equality: men received more money than women, while the act excluded agricultural and domestic workers—and more than half of all black workers and most Hispanics fell into those categories. Similarly, the Fair Labor Standards Act of 1938 and the National Labor Relations Act also excluded agricultural and domestic workers. It has taken a massive social revolution lasting seven decades to end the qualified assertion that all men are created equal except for those who are not.

The Supreme Court has certainly proven important in clarifying the nature of American law, but it did not create the cases challenging inequality. Rather, the great victories for human equality came in response to the actions of American citizens demanding inclusion, insisting on their equality. It took the engagement of millions of men and women, Americans of African, Asian, and Hispanic descent, of gays, of people from all faiths, of the disabled, of those who felt marginalized by their society, to proclaim "We are all equal." Their victories were not quickly won, but took decades of sustained effort.

Madison and Tocqueville were wrong—it has not been the tyranny of the majority that the nation needed to fear, but the tyranny of the minority. To be sure, it has been a large minority, but a minority nonetheless. Privileged white males of northern European Protestant descent who insisted that equality applied only to themselves and fought hard to exclude others have dominated much of the nation's political life. Equality did not just happen because people suddenly recognized it as the right thing to do; it resulted from generations of struggle. Contrary to what Thomas Jefferson wrote, equality has never been self-evident; it needed to be discovered, learned, and nurtured by all those persons born or naturalized in the United States.

George Washington may have had a clearer understanding of Jefferson's ideal than Jefferson ever did. In 1790, Moses Seixas of Newport's Touro Synagogue wrote the first president expressing relief at the new nation's tolerance. Washington responded that it is equality, not tolerance, that matters. Tolerance, Washington wrote, implies "indulgence of one class of people" for another in what is in fact "the exercise of their inherent natural rights." Washington spoke to theory rather than practice in stating, "All possess alike liberty of conscience" and the rights of citizenship, as the new constitutional government "gives to bigotry no sanction, to persecution no assistance." To make clear the substance of this equality, Washington employed the language of Micah, from a passage familiar to contemporary Christians and Jews alike: "Every one shall sit in safety under his own vine and figtree, and there shall be none to make him afraid." [15]

At the very beginning of our great experiment, Washington offered a profound understanding of the core value of equality: the right to be left alone to enjoy the fruits of one's own labor. Though the United States persisted in violating that standard, the goal remained unchanged as diverse Americans battled for two and a half centuries to enjoy the right to decide their life's path for themselves. The labor to attain human equality does not cease. The frightened bigots have repeatedly seized the levers of power and found new groups to declare less than human, worthy of exclusion from the grand dream of America as a land of equality. Adherence to that great discovered truth, that we are all equally human, demands the continuation of that struggle.

Acknowledgments

After five years' work, I finish this book in the midst of the imposed isolation of the coronavirus. In many ways, this situation represents little change in the process of writing, which is generally an isolated task. That is not to say that the research and ideas are the product of a single mind. As I hope is evident, I have benefited enormously from the hard work and keen analysis of many scholars, and a complete bibliography can be found on the website for this book. I would, however, like to extend particular appreciation to Rebecca Solnit and Danielle Allen, who have written with such clarity on the issues addressed in this book.

For the past five years my wonderful coworkers have put up with me talking about equality and history. Their perspectives proved as helpful as anything I have read. My gratitude to Rodney Brock, Emilie Greene, Christine Bastian, Shane Hobart, Jamie Strohl, Stephanie Orton, and Susan DiFabbio. Similarly, my good friends Eric and Karen Davison have patiently waited for their cocktails as I launched into another mini-lecture on the failure of Americans to take ideas and science seriously. Equally patient, my daughter-in-law, Chat Ying Wang, has provided valuable technical advice with good humor despite my formidable ignorance. Thanks also to Joe Carl, who made me the desk upon which I write, as solid an act of friendship as I've encountered.

My thanks to Tim Bartlett and his outstanding staff at St. Martin's Press. Their extensive editorial assistance has definitely made this a better book than my limited skills could produce. I hope that their commitment to seeing this book through to publication proves justified.

My greatest debt is to the three people who never let me quit, encouraging me through the dark periods of doubt and the ravages of internet trolls. I am humbled by the love and loyalty of my wife, Nina K. Martin, and daughter, Lilith Acadia. I recognize my good fortune in having such brilliant women in my life, and am the happy beneficiary of their unwavering support and wit. I have also been fortunate in the advocacy of my agent, Dan Green, who has devoted his life to fighting for free speech and intellectual integrity. Having him on my side has made all the difference, and I dedicate this book to him with profound appreciation and gratitude.

Since I first tended bar in 1974, I have listened to many different understandings of human equality. Over those years I have witnessed dramatic cultural shifts as well as stubborn refusals to recognize changed realities. I have learned a great deal from those hundreds of customers who shared thoughtful insights and embarrassing ignorance, deep personal anxieties and unquenchable hopes, intellectual curiosity and ironclad certainty, the full human comedy and tragedy. All that I have seen, read, and experienced confirms my abiding conviction that all people are created equal, and should share an equal opportunity to live their lives in freedom and be able to pursue happiness as they believe fit. That, it seems to me, is the undying promise of America.

Notes

A full bibliography and other ancillary material can be found at: https://www.inventingequality.com.

INTRODUCTION

1 Frederick Douglass, "What to the Slave Is the Fourth of July?," in *Narrative of the Life of Frederick Douglass, an American Slave, Written by Himself*, ed. David W. Blight, 2d ed. (Boston: Bedford/St. Martin's, 2003), 146–71.

2 Frederick Douglass, "The Constitution and Slavery," *The North Star*, March 16, 1849.

3 "Resolution of the Massachusetts Anti-Slavery Society," *The Liberator*, February 3, 1843. Garrison is using the language of Isaiah 28:18.

4 Douglass, "What to the Slave Is the Fourth of July?," 159.

CHAPTER 1: CORRUPTED FROM THE START

1 Max Farrand, ed., *The Records of the Federal Convention of 1787* (New Haven, CT: Yale University Press, 1911), 2:417.

2 Ibid., 2:168–69.

3 Ibid., 2:364, 370–73, 415.

4 Farrand, ed., *The Records of the Federal Convention of 1787*, 1:135.

5 Ibid., 2:221–22.

6 Ibid., 2:222–23.

7 *Return of the Whole Number of Persons Within the Several Districts of the United States* (London: J. Phillips, 1793).

8 Jonathan Elliot, ed., *The Debates in the Several State Conventions on the Adoption of the Federal Constitution* (Philadelphia: J. B. Lippincott, 1866), 2:237–38.

9 Publius, *The Federalist, on the New Constitution* (New York: George F. Hopkins, 1802), 2:46.

10 Elliot, ed., *Debates in the Several State Conventions*, 2:228; Michael Kammen, ed., *The Origins of the American Constitution* (New York: Penguin, 1986),

320; *Debates and Proceedings in the Convention of the Commonwealth of Massachusetts, Held in the Year 1788* (Boston: W. White, 1856), 285–320.

11 Farrand, ed., *Records of the Federal Convention of 1787*, 2:271–72.

12 Ibid., 2:415–18.

13 James Madison, *The Writings of James Madison*, ed. Gaillard Hunt (New York: G. P. Putnam's Sons, 1904), 5:365–66.

14 Wirt to Sec. of Treasury, November 7, 1821, *Official Opinions of the Attorneys General of the United States*, comp. Benjamin F. Hall (Washington, DC: Robert Farnham, 1852–70), 1:507.

15 State v. Crandall, 10 Conn. 339 (1834); Hobbs v. Fogg (1837), 6 Watts 533.

16 Commonwealth v. Aves (1836), 18 Pick. (35 Mass.) 193; Leonard W. Levy, *Law of the Commonwealth and Chief Justice Shaw* (New York: Oxford University Press, 1987), 59–71.

17 Roberts v. City of Boston (1849), 5 Cush. (59 Mass.) 198; Levy, *Law of the Commonwealth*, 109–17.

18 Groves v. Slaughter (1841), 15 Pet. (40 US) 449.

19 Alexis de Tocqueville, *Democracy in America* (New York: Vintage Books, 1990), 1:167; Jefferson to Coles, August 25, 1814, in *The Works of Thomas Jefferson*, ed. Paul Leicester (New York: G. P. Putnam's Sons, 1905), 11:416–19.

20 John Adams, *Familiar Letters of John Adams and His Wife Abigail Adams, During the Revolution*, ed. Charles Francis Adams (New York: Hurd & Houghton, 1876), 149–50, 155.

21 Robert M. T. Hunter, "The Massachusetts Proposition for Abolishing the Slave Representation as Guaranteed by the Constitution," *Southern Literary Messenger* 11 (1845): 458; Fisher Ames, *Works of Fisher Ames: Compiled by a Number of His Friends* (Boston: T. B. Wait, 1809), 230.

22 Rufus Choate, *The Works of Rufus Choate: With a Memoir of His Life*, ed. Samuel Gilman Brown (Boston: Little, Brown, 1862), 1:215; William "Chancellor" Harper, "Memoir on Slavery," *DeBow's Review* 8 (1850): 235–36; John Quincy Adams, *The Social Compact: Exemplified in the Constitution of the Commonwealth of Massachusetts* (Providence: Knowles and Vose, 1842), 13.

23 James Fenimore Cooper, *The American Democrat* (Cooperstown, NY: H. & E. Phinney, 1838), 78–82.

24 George Bancroft, *Literary and Historical Miscellanies* (New York: Harper & Brothers, 1855), 258, 422; "Introduction," *United States Magazine and Democratic Review* 1 (January 1838): 7–8, 11.

25 A Southron, "Thoughts on Slavery," *Southern Literary Messenger* 4 (1838): 742; Dr. Samuel Cartwright, "Diseases and Peculiarities of the Negro Race," *DeBow's Review* 11 (1851): 336; William Harper, *Memoir on Slavery: Read*

Before the Society for the Advancement of Learning of South Carolina (Charleston: James Burges, 1838), 33, 38; *Selections from the Letters and Speeches of the Hon. James H. Hammond, of South Carolina* (New York: John F. Trow, 1866), 318–19.

26 Calvin Colton, *The Junius Tracts, No. 1* (New York: Greeley & McElrath, 1844), 9, 15, 105.

27 Henry Bellows, "The Influence of the Trading Spirit on the Social and Moral Life in America," *American Review: A Whig Journal* 1 (January 1845): 95.

28 *The Politics of Aristotle*, trans. Benjamin Jowett (Oxford: Clarendon Press, 1885), 1:161; Thomas Hobbes, *Philosophical Rudiments Concerning Government and Society* (London: John Bohn, 1841), 7.

29 John Locke, *The Second Treatise of Civil Government* (London: W. Wilson, 1821), 232, 259, 277.

30 *Congressional Globe*, 36th Cong., 1st sess. (1859), 3; Henry Mayer, *All on Fire: William Lloyd Garrison and the Abolition of Slavery* (New York: St. Martin's Press, 1998), 122–23; Laura Bristol Robinson, ed., *History of the Centennial Celebration, Warsaw, Wyoming County, New York, June 28–July 2, 1903* (Warsaw, NY: Warsaw Centennial Association, 1903), 165–66.

31 Alexander Keyssar, *The Right to Vote: The Contested History of Democracy in the United States* (New York: Basic Books, 2000).

32 Hudgins v. Wrights (1806), 1 Hen. & Mun. 134.

33 State v. Post and State v. Van Buren (1845), 20 NJ Law 368.

34 *Annals of Congress*, 16th Cong., 2nd sess., 599; James H. Kettner, *The Development of American Citizenship, 1608–1870* (Chapel Hill: University Press of North Carolina, 1978), 312–14.

35 "Democratic Party Platform of 1840," May 6, 1840, in Gerhard Peters and John T. Woolley, The American Presidency Project, http://www.presidency .ucsb.edu/ws/?pid=29572.

36 Charles Jared Ingersoll, *A Discourse Concerning the Influence of America on the Mind* (Philadelphia: Abraham Small, 1823), 31, 39; Edward Everett, *Orations and Speeches on Various Occasions* (Boston: American Stationers Company, 1836), 12–13, 17.

37 *Herkimer Convention: The Voice of New York!* (Albany, NY: Albany Atlas, 1847), 14.

38 Edwin C. Rozwenc, ed., *Ideology and Power in the Age of Jackson* (Garden City, NY: Anchor Books, 1964), viii; Tocqueville, *Democracy in America*, 2:94; Lee Benson, *The Concept of Jacksonian Democracy: New York as a Test Case* (Princeton, NJ: Princeton University Press, 1961), 15.

39 Harold M. Hyman and William M. Wiecek, *Equal Justice Under Law: Constitutional Development, 1835–1875* (New York: Harper & Row, 1982), 79–81.

40 John C. Calhoun, *The Works of John C. Calhoun*, ed. Richard K. Cralle (New York: D. Appleton, 1851–57), 2:626–33, 4:511–12; John C. Calhoun, "Address," in *The Papers of John C. Calhoun*, ed. Clyde Wilson (Columbia: University of South Carolina Press, 1959–2003), 26: 239–41.

41 George Fitzhugh, *Cannibals All! Or, Slaves Without Masters* (Richmond, VA: A. Morris, 1857), xv; Jean Butenhoff Lee, ed., *Experiencing Mount Vernon: Eyewitness Accounts, 1784–1865* (Charlottesville: University of Virginia Press, 2006), 110.

42 Samuel F. B. Morse, *Imminent Dangers to the United States Through Foreign Immigration* (New York: E. B. Clayton, 1835), 13–19.

43 Michel Chevalier, *Society, Manners, and Politics in the United States*, ed. John W. Ward (Garden City, NY: Doubleday, 1961); William M. Gouge, *A Short History of Paper Money and Banking in the United States* (Philadelphia: T. W. Ustick, 1833), 91; Frances Trollope, *Domestic Manners of the Americans* (New York: Dodd, Mead, 1901), 99.

44 Ralph Waldo Emerson, *The Complete Works of Ralph Waldo Emerson*, ed. Edward Waldo Emerson (Boston: Houghton, Mifflin, 1904), 11:409; *The Journals of Ralph Waldo Emerson*, ed. Edward Waldo Emerson (Boston: Houghton, Mifflin, 1909–11), 6:361; Bell Gale Chevigny, ed., *The Woman and the Myth: Margaret Fuller's Life and Writings* (Boston: Northeastern University Press, 1994), 32, 239.

45 Sarah Grimké, *Letters on the Equality of the Sexes* (Boston: Isaac Knapp, 1838); Angelina Grimké, Sarah Grimké, and Theodore Weld, *American Slavery As It Is: Testimony of a Thousand Witnesses* (New York: American Anti-Slavery Society, 1839).

46 Elizabeth Cady Stanton, Susan B. Anthony, and Matilda Joslyn Gage, eds., *History of Woman Suffrage* (Rochester, NY: Charles Mann, 1881), 1:70–73.

47 Julius R. Ames, *The Legion of Liberty!*, 2nd ed. (New York: American Anti-Slavery Society, 1843), n.p.

48 Dorothy Sterling, ed., *We Are Your Sisters: Black Women in the Nineteenth Century* (New York: W. W. Norton, 1984), 162.

49 "Do the Various Races of Man Constitute a Single Species?," *United States Magazine and Democratic Review* 11 (August 1842): 113–39; "Natural History of Man," *United States Magazine and Democratic Review* 26 (April 1850): 328, 345.

50 John Van Evrie, *White Supremacy and Negro Subordination; or, Negroes a Subordinate Race, and (So-Called) Slavery Its Normal Condition* (New York:

Van Evrie, Horton, 1868), 52; *Congressional Globe*, 38th Congress, 1st sess., 709 (February 17, 1864).

51 John McKrum, "The True Functions of Government," *DeBow's Review* 4 (1847): 99–100.

52 Elizabeth Brown Pryor, *Reading the Man: A Portrait of Robert E. Lee Through His Private Letters* (New York: Viking, 2007), 260–61; Frederick Law Olmsted, *A Journey in the Back Country* (New York: Mason Brothers, 1863), 82.

53 George Fitzhugh, "The Message, the Constitution, and the Times," *DeBow's Review* 30 (February 1861): 162.

54 Mary Boykin Chestnut, *A Diary from Dixie*, ed. Ben Ames Williams (Cambridge, MA: Harvard University Press, 1962), 172, 534.

55 Frederick Douglass, "The Constitution of the United States: Is It Pro-Slavery or Anti-Slavery?," in *Frederick Douglass: Selected Speeches and Writings*, ed. Philip S. Foner (Chicago: Lawrence Hill Books, 1999), 381, 387.

CHAPTER 2:
THE SUPREME COURT CHOOSES INEQUALITY

1   Scott v. Sandford, 60 U.S. 19 How. 393 (1856); Passenger Cases, 7 How. 283, 482, 492 (U.S. 1849).

2   Don E. Fehrenbacher, *The Dred Scott Case: Its Significance in American Law and Politics* (New York: Oxford University Press, 1978), 3, 418.

3   John Codman Hurd, *The Law of Freedom and Bondage in the United States* (Boston: Little, Brown, 1858); Horace Gray and John Lowell, "The Case of Dred Scott," *Monthly Law Review* 20 (1857): 61–118; *Opinion of the Justices*, 44 (1857), Maine 505; Anderson v. Poindexter, 6 (1857) Ohio 623; *Washington Union*, November 17, 1857, quoted in *Congressional Globe*, 35th Cong., 1st sess., appendix ,199–200.

4   On *Dred Scott II*, the *Lemon* case in New York, see Paul Finkelman, *An Imperfect Union: Slavery, Federalism, and Comity* (Chapel Hill: University of North Carolina Press, 1981), 285–312; State of Vermont, *Report of the Select Committee on Slavery, the Dred Scott Decision, and the Action of the Federal Government Thereon* (Montpelier, VT: E. P. Walton, 1858), 7.

5   *Congressional Globe*, 35th Congress, 2nd sess., 985 (February 11, 1859).

6   Ibid., 36th Congress, 1st sess., 1840 (April 24, 1860).

7   *Political Debates Between Abraham Lincoln and Stephen A. Douglas in the Celebrated Campaign of 1858 in Illinois* (Cleveland: Arthur H. Clark, 1902), 237.

8   Ibid., 20, 71.

9   Ibid., 11, 124.

10 *Washington Union*, November 17, 1857, in James W. Sheahan, *The Life of Stephen A. Douglas* (New York: Harper & Brothers, 1860), 346; *Political Debates Between Lincoln and Douglas*, 98–100, 131–32.

11 *Political Debates Between Lincoln and Douglas*, 71, 132, 152–53, 162–63, 209–10, 261, 295–97, 308.

12 Ibid., 222.

13 Ibid., 110, 360–63.

14 Ibid., 36–37, 63, 93.

15 U.S. Congress, *Report of the Special Committee Appointed to Investigate the Troubles in Kansas* (Washington, DC: Cornelius Wendell, 1856), 357.

16 Abraham Lincoln, *The Collected Works of Abraham Lincoln*, ed. Roy P. Basler (New Brunswick, NJ: Rutgers University Press, 1953–55), 2:263.

17 Scott v. Sandford, 60 U.S. 19 How. 393 (1856).

18 Rice v. Foster, Delaware, 1847, 4 Harr. 479; Holmes v. Holmes, NY Supreme Court, 1848, 5 Barb. SC 295; White v. White, NY Supreme Court, 1849, 5 Barb. SC 474.

19 Carl Schurz, *Speeches, Correspondence and Political Papers of Carl Schurz*, ed. Frederic Bancroft (New York: G. P. Putnam's Sons, 1913), 1:57, 59–60.

20 James D. Richardson, ed., *A Compilation of the Messages and Papers of the Presidents, 1789–1902* (Washington, DC: Bureau of National Literature and Art, 1907), 3:298.

21 Phyllis F. Field, *The Politics of Race in New York: The Struggle for Black Suffrage in the Civil War Era* (Ithaca, NY: Cornell University Press, 2009), 117; William Russell Smith, ed., *The History and Debates of the Convention of the People of Alabama* (Montgomery: White, Pfister, 1861), 380; Michael P. Johnson, *Toward a Patriarchal Republic: The Secession of Georgia* (Baton Rouge: Louisiana State University Press, 1977), 47; Eric H. Walther, *William Lowndes Yancey and the Coming of the Civil War* (Chapel Hill: University of North Carolina Press, 2006), 260; Charles B. Dew, *Apostles of Disunion: Southern Secession Commissioners and the Causes of the Civil War* (Charlottesville: University Press of Virginia, 2001), 56.

22 Herbert Mitgang, ed., *Lincoln as They Saw Him* (New York: Rinehart, 1956), 205; Howard C. Perkins, "The Defense of Slavery in the Northern Press on the Eve of the Civil War," *Journal of Southern History* 9 (1943): 525.

23 L. Dummond, ed., *Southern Editorials on Secession* (New York: Century, 1931), 179, 202–3.

24 Douglas R. Egerton, *Year of Meteors: Stephen Douglas, Abraham Lincoln, and the Election That Brought on the Civil War* (New York: Bloomsbury, 2010), 282; Perkins, "The Defense of Slavery in the Northern Press," 506–7, 515, 522.

25 Egerton, *Year of Meteors*, 236; *The American Annual Cyclopaedia and Reg-
    ister of Important Events of the Year 1861* (New York: D. Appleton, 1864),
    189; *Congressional Globe*, 36th Cong., 2nd sess., 72–75 (December 12, 1860).

26 William E. Parrish, *David Rice Atchison of Missouri* (Columbia: University of
    Missouri Press, 1961), 127; William E. Dodd, *Jefferson Davis* (Philadelphia:
    George W. Jacobs, 1907), 107, 154.

27 *Richmond Whig*, November 6, 1860, 1.

28 *The Anti-Slavery History of the John-Brown Year* (New York: American Anti-
    Slavery Society, 1861), 167.

29 Michael Burlingame, *Abraham Lincoln: A Life* (Baltimore: Johns Hopkins
    University Press, 2013), 1:526; *Political Debates Between Lincoln and Doug-
    las*, 88.

30 Alexander H. Stephens, *Alexander H. Stephens in Public and Private: With
    Letters and Speeches*, ed. Henry Cleveland (Philadelphia: National Publishing,
    1866), 721; *Collected Works of Abraham Lincoln*, 4:160.

31 Egerton, *Year of Meteors*, 221, 274.

32   Stephens, *Alexander H. Stephens in Public and Private*, 721.

33 Richard E. Beringer, "A Profile of the Members of the Confederate Congress,"
    Journal of Southern History 32 (1967): 518–41; Henry Kidder White, ed., *Offi-
    cial Records of the Union and Confederate Navies in the War of the Rebellion*
    (Washington, DC: n.p., 1894–1922), series 2, 3:257.

34 *Constitution of the Confederate States of America* (Richmond: Wyatt M.
    Elliott, 1861), 8; U.S. Congress, *Journal of the Congress of the Confederate
    States of America, 1861–1865* (Washington, DC: Government Printing Office,
    1904–5), 1:851–96.

35 William Kauffman Scarborough, *Masters of the Big House: Elite Slaveholders
    of the Mid-Nineteenth-Century South* (Baton Rouge: Louisiana State University
    Press, 2003), 282.

36 David Blight, *Frederick Douglass' Civil War: Keeping Faith in Jubilee* (Baton
    Rouge: Louisiana State University Press, 1989), 60; Eric Foner, *Free Soil, Free
    Labor, Free Men: The Ideology of the Republican Party Before the Civil War* (New
    York: Oxford University Press, 1995), 223; *New York Herald*, October 30, 1860, 1.

37 Barron v. Baltimore, 32 U.S. (7 Pet.) 243 (1833).

38 Frederick Douglass, "What to the Slave Is the Fourth of July?" in *Narrative
    of the Life of Frederick Douglass, an American Slave, Written by Himself*, ed.
    David W. Blight, 2d ed. (Boston: Bedford/St. Martin's, 2003), 158.

39 "Letters of a Badger Boy in Blue: The Vicksburg Campaign," *Wisconsin Magazine
    of History* 4 (1920): 431–56; 5 (1921): 66–68.

40 L. Earnest Sellers, "Robert Smalls of South Carolina: Civil War Hero," *Negro
    Digest* 13 (April 1964): 24–27.

41 Elizabeth R. Varon, *Southern Lady, Yankee Spy: The True Story of Elizabeth Van Lew, a Union Agent in the Heart of the Confederacy* (New York: Oxford University Press, 2003), 166–68.

42 J. Matthew Gallman, *America's Joan of Arc: The Life of Anna Elizabeth Dickinson* (New York: Oxford University Press, 2006), 19–60.

CHAPTER 3:
LEARNING EQUALITY

1 Benjamin Quarles, *The Negro in the Civil War* (Boston: Little, Brown, 1953), 32–34.

2 Frederick May Holland, *Frederick Douglass: The Colored Orator* (New York: Funk & Wagnalls, 1891), 261.

3 Sara Agnes Pryor, *Reminiscences of Peace and War*, rev. ed. (New York: Macmillan, 1905), 109–12.

4 Herman V. Ames, *The Proposed Amendments to the Constitution of the United States During the First Century of Its History* (Washington, DC: Government Printing Office, 1897), 194; Michael Vorenberg, *Final Freedom: The Civil War, the Abolition of Slavery, and the Thirteenth Amendment* (Cambridge: Cambridge University Press, 2004), 9–18.

5 James D. Richardson, ed., *A Compilation of the Messages and Papers of the Presidents, 1789–1902* (Washington, DC: Bureau of National Literature and Art, 1907), 5:626, 638; Richard Bernstein with Jerome Agel, *Amending America: If We Love the Constitution So Much, Why Do We Keep Trying to Change It?* (New York: Random House, 1993), 84.

6 R. Alton Lee, "The Corwin Amendment in the Secession Crisis," *Ohio Historical Quarterly* 70 (1961): 1–26.

7 Abraham Lincoln, *The Collected Works of Abraham Lincoln*, ed. Roy P. Basler (New Brunswick, NJ: Rutgers University Press, 1953–55), 4:183.

8 Edward McPherson, ed., *The Political History of the United States of America, During the Great Rebellion*, 2nd ed. (Washington, DC: Philp & Solomons, 1865), 37.

9 Douglas R. Egerton, *Year of Meteors: Stephen Douglas, Abraham Lincoln, and the Election That Brought on the Civil War* (New York: Bloomsbury, 2010), 240, 265.

10 Bruce Levine, *The Fall of the House of Dixie: The Civil War and the Social Revolution That Transformed the South* (New York: Random House, 2013), 56; Richardson, ed., *Compilation of the Messages and Papers of the Presidents*, 6:276.

11 E. McPherson, ed., *Political History*, 103–4.

12 Charles Finney, *Memoirs of Rev. Charles G. Finney* (New York: A. S. Barnes, 1876), 352.

13 William H. Williams, *Slavery and Freedom in Delaware, 1639–1865* (Wilmington, DE: Scholarly Resources, 1999), 175; *Collected Works of Abraham Lincoln*, 5:29–30; Stephen D. Carpenter, *Logic of History: Five Hundred Political Texts: Being Concentrated Extracts of Abolitionism* (Madison, WI: S. D. Carpenter, 1864), 176.

14 Ames, *The Proposed Amendments to the Constitution of the United States During the First Century of Its History*, 365–66; Henry Winter Davis, *Speeches and Addresses Delivered in the Congress of the United States* (New York: Harper & Brothers, 1867), 392.

15 Vorenberg, *Final Freedom*, 23; Basil Thomasson, *North Carolina Yeoman: The Diary of Basil Armstrong Thomasson, 1853–1862*, ed. Paul D. Escott (Athens: University of Georgia Press, 1996), 351; Levine, *Fall of the House of Dixie*, 76.

16 Octavia E. Butler, *Parable of the Talents* (New York: Grand Central Publishing, 2000), 206; Albert V. House Jr., ed., "Deterioration of a Georgia Rice Plantation During Four Years of Civil War," *Journal of Southern History* 9 (1943): 102; Stephen V. Ash, *When the Yankees Came: Conflict and Chaos in the Occupied South, 1861–1865* (Chapel Hill: University of North Carolina Press, 1995), 223.

17 *The Diary of Edmund Ruffin*, ed. William K. Scarborough (Baton Rouge: Louisiana State University Press, 1989), 3:692.

18 George L. Wood, *The Seventh Regiment: A Record* (New York: James Miller, 1865), 77.

19 Frederick Douglass, *The Essential Douglass: Selected Writings and Speeches*, ed. Nicolas Buccola (Indianapolis: Hackett, 2016), 162; James M. McPherson, *The Struggle for Equality: Abolitionists and the Negro in the Civil War and Reconstruction* (Princeton, NJ: Princeton University Press, 1992), 62.

20 Benjamin F. Butler, *Private and Official Correspondence of Gen. Benjamin F. Butler During the Period of the Civil War* (Norwood, MA: Plimpton Press, 1917), 1:102–3, 116–17.

21 E. McPherson, ed., *Political History*, 195–96, 238, 244–45.

22 Leonard L. Richards, *Who Freed the Slaves? The Fight over the Thirteenth Amendment* (Chicago: University of Chicago Press, 2015), 25–27; Butler, *Private and Official Correspondence*, 1:185–88.

23 John Beatty, *The Citizen-Soldier: or, Memoirs of a Volunteer* (Cincinnati: Wilstach, Baldwin, 1879), 152–53.

24 Ira Berlin et al., eds., *Freedom: A Documentary History of Emancipation: 1861–1867*, series 1, vol. 1, *The Destruction of Slavery* (New York: Cambridge

University Press, 1985), 16–18, 28–29; E. McPherson, ed., *Political History*, 245–46; Dudley Taylor Cornish, *The Sable Arm: Negro Troops in the Union Army 1861–1865* (New York: W. W. Norton, 1966), 64–68.

25 E. McPherson, ed., *Political History*, 246; Vernon Volpe, "The Fremonts and Emancipation in Missouri," *Historian* 56 (1994): 339–54.

26 Berlin et al., eds., *The Destruction of Slavery*, 252–57.

27 E. McPherson, ed., *Political History*, 215.

28 Beatty, *The Citizen-Soldier*, 20, 119.

29 Theodore Parker, *The Collected Works of Theodore Parker*, ed. Francis Power Cobbe (London: Trubner, 1863), 5:328; Hinton Helper, *The Land of Gold: Reality Versus Fiction* (Baltimore: Henry Taylor, 1855); E. McPherson, ed., *Political History*, 239–40.

30 Howard C. Perkins, "The Defense of Slavery in the Northern Press on the Eve of the Civil War," *Journal of Southern History* 9 (1943): 523.

31 Quarles, *The Negro in the Civil War*, 25–28; Abraham Lincoln, *Abraham Lincoln: Complete Works*, eds. John G. Nicolay and John Hay (New York: Century, 1894), 2:235.

32 *Congressional Globe*, 37th Cong., 2nd sess. (1861–62), 3087, 3102, 3109, 3121–7; Richards, *Who Freed the Slaves?*, 41.

33 Peter H. Clark, *The Black Brigade of Cincinnati: Being a Report of Its Labors and a Muster-Roll of Its Members* (Cincinnati: J. B. Boyd, 1864), 4–5; Gerrit Smith, *Sermons and Speeches of Gerrit Smith* (New York: Ross & Tousey, 1861), 192.

34 Quarles, *The Negro in the Civil War*, 32; Steven J. Ramold, *Slaves, Sailors, Citizens: African Americans in the Union Navy* (DeKalb: Northern Illinois University Press, 2002).

35 Robert N. Scott et al., eds., *The War of the Rebellion: A Compilation of the Official Records of the Union and Confederate Armies* (4 series, 128 vols.; Washington, DC: Government Printing Office, 1880–1901) Series 1, vol. 15: 549, 557.

36 E. McPherson, ed., *Political History*, 196–97.

37 Lincoln, *Abraham Lincoln: Complete Works* 1:576; Gideon Welles, *Diary of Gideon Welles: Secretary of the Navy Under Lincoln and Johnson* (Boston: Houghton, Mifflin, 1911), 1:70–71.

38 Salmon P. Chase, *Inside Lincoln's Cabinet: The Civil War Diaries of Salmon P. Chase*, ed. David Donald (New York: Longmans, Green, 1954), 95–99.

39 E. McPherson, ed., *Political History*, 198–233.

40 "The Crisis of the American War," *Blackwood's Magazine* 92 (November 1862): 644; John Mercer Langston, *From the Virginia Plantation to the National Capitol* (Hartford, CT: American Publishing, 1894), 206; Samuel F. B. Morse

et al., *Papers from the Society for the Diffusion of Political Knowledge* (New York: The Society, 1863).

⁴¹ Jean H. Baker, *Affairs of Party: The Political Culture of Northern Democrats in the Mid-Nineteenth Century* (Ithaca, NY: Cornell University Press, 1983), 170–71; George Stillman Hillard, *Life and Campaigns of George B. McClellan, Major-General U.S. Army* (Philadelphia: J. B. Lippincott, 1864), 265.

⁴² Howard Hones, *Abraham Lincoln and a New Birth of Freedom: The Union and Slavery in the Diplomacy of the Civil Wars* (Lincoln: University of Nebraska Press, 1999), 152.

⁴³ Chauncey H. Cooke, "Letters of a Badger Boy in Blue: The Vicksburg Campaign," *Wisconsin Magazine of History* 4 (1920): 432–33.

⁴⁴ Ibid., 433; Scott et al., eds., *War of the Rebellion*, series 1, vol. 10: 162; Hannibal A. Johnson, *The Sword of Honor: A Story of the Civil War* (Worcester, MA: Blanchard Press, 1906), 30.

⁴⁵ Cooke, "Letters of a Badger Boy in Blue," 67.

⁴⁶ James M. McPherson, *The Negro's Civil War: How American Blacks Felt and Acted During the War for the Union* (New York: Ballantine Books, 1991), 102.

⁴⁷ Ibid., 104; Dorothy Sterling, ed., *We Are Your Sisters: Black Women in the Nineteenth Century* (New York: W. W. Norton, 1984), 162.

⁴⁸ William Wells Brown, *The Black Man: His Antecedents, His Genius, and His Achievements* (New York: Thomas Hamilton, 1863), 32, 35.

⁴⁹ Scott et al., eds., *War of the Rebellion*, series 1, vol. 14: 198; ibid., series 3, vol. 3: 177; Thomas Wentworth Higginson, *Army Life in a Black Regiment* (Boston: Fields, Osgood, 1870).

⁵⁰ Scott et al., eds., *War of the Rebellion*, series 3, vol. 3: 100, 1190; vol. 5: 121–24.

⁵¹ M. McPherson, *The Negro's Civil War*, 213.

⁵² Henry Steele Commager and Erik Bruun, eds., *The Civil War Archive: The History of the Civil War in Documents* (New York: Workman, 2000), 544; Robert Tomes and Benjamin G. Smith, *The War with the South: A History of the Late Rebellion* (New York: Virtue & Yorston, 1862–66), 3:18.

⁵³ William Wells Brown, *The Negro in the American Rebellion* (Boston: Lee & Shepard, 1867), 138–41.

⁵⁴ Charles Dana, *Recollections of the Civil War* (New York: D. Appleton, 1913), 86.

⁵⁵ Robert Cowden, *A Brief Sketch of the Organization and Services of the Fifty-Ninth Regiment of United States Colored Infantry* (Dayton, OH: United Brethren Publishing, 1883), 102; Cornish, *The Sable Arm*, 142–43.

⁵⁶ James Henry Gooding, *On the Altar of Freedom: A Black Soldier's Civil War Letters from the Front*, ed. Virginia M. Adams (Boston: University of Massachusetts Press, 1991), 38.

57 "Assassination of Lincoln," Report #104, *The Reports of the Committees of the House of Representatives Made During the First Session Thirty-Ninth Congress, 1865-66* (Washington, DC: Government Printing Office, 1866), 2; Joseph T. Glatthaar, *Forged in Battle: The Civil War Alliance of Black Soldiers and White Officers* (Baton Rouge: Louisiana State University Press, 1990), 155–57; Lonnie R. Speer, *Portals to Hell: Military Prisons of the Civil War* (Lincoln: University of Nebraska Press, 2005), 107–18.

58 Thomas J. Morgan, *Reminiscences of Service with Colored Troops in the Army of the Cumberland, 1863-1865* (Providence: Soldiers and Sailors Relief Society, 1885), 44–45, 48.

59 U.S. Congress, *Supplemental Report of the Joint Committee on the Conduct of the War* (Washington, DC: Government Printing Office, 1866), 1:427; Ulysses S. Grant to Abraham Lincoln, August 23, 1863, Abraham Lincoln Papers at the Library of Congress, online; Randall C. Jimerson, *The Private Civil War: Popular Thought During the Sectional Conflict* (Baton Rouge: Louisiana State University Press, 1988), 96.

60 William T. Sherman, *Memoirs of Gen. William T. Sherman* (New York: D. Appleton, 1891), 1:181.

61 M. McPherson, *The Negro's Civil War*, 214, 315; Edward M. Main, *The Story of the Marches, Battles and Incidents of the Third United States Colored Cavalry* (Louisville: Globe, 1908), 118–23.

62 *Douglass' Monthly* 5 (March 1863): 802.

63 Luis F. Emilio, *History of the Fifty-Fourth Regiment of Massachusetts Volunteer Infantry, 1863-1865* (Boston: Boston Book, 1894), 137, 220–28.

64 Charlotte Forten, "Life on the Sea Islands," *Atlantic Monthly* 13 (1864): 669.

65 Joseph T. Wilson, *The Black Phalanx: Negro Soldiers of the United States in the Wars of 1775-1812, 1861-'65* (Hartford, CT: American Publishing, 1890), 506.

66 Ash, *When the Yankees Came*, 150; Chandra Manning, "A 'Vexed Question': White Union Soldiers on Slavery and Race," in *The View from the Ground: Experiences of Civil War Soldiers*, ed. Aaron Sheehan-Dean (Lexington: University of Kentucky Press, 2007), 44.

67 James Hammond, *Secret and Sacred: The Diaries of James Henry Hammond, a Southern Slaveholder*, ed. Carol Blesser (New York: Oxford University Press, 1998), 297; Catherine Edmondston, *Journal of a Secesh Lady: The Diary of Catherine Ann Devereux Edmondston, 1860-1866*, eds. Beth G. Crabtree and James W. Patton (Raleigh: North Carolina Division of Archives and History, 1979), 529; Berlin et al., eds., *The Destruction of Slavery*, 705.

68 L. Earnest Sellers, "Robert Smalls of South Carolina: Civil War Hero," *Negro Digest* 13 (April 1964), 26.

69 J. G. Andrews to Richard Yates, Savannah, January 3, 1865, Abraham Lincoln Presidential Library and Museum, Springfield, IL, online; M. McPherson, *The Negro's Civil War*, 255–58.

70 M. McPherson, *The Negro's Civil War*, 292.

71 *Congressional Globe*, 38th Congress, 2nd sess., 155 (January 7, 1865).

72 Lincoln, *Collected Works of Abraham Lincoln*, 6:409.

73 Frederick Douglass, *The Life and Writings of Frederick Douglass*, ed. Philip S. Foner (New York: International Publishers, 1950–55), 3:354.

74 Vorenberg, *Final Freedom*, 37; M. McPherson, *The Negro's Civil War*, 195.

75 *Congressional Globe*, 38th Cong., 2nd sess., appendix, 65–68 (February 7, 1865).

76 Levine, *Fall of the House of Dixie*, 205–6.

77 John S. Wise, *The End of an Era* (Boston: Houghton, Mifflin, 1901), 366.

78 Howell Cobb to Secretary of War J. A. Seddon, January 8, 1865, *American Historical Review* 1 (1895–96): 97.

79 Walter L. Jenkins, *Seizing the Day: African Americans in Post–Civil War Charleston* (Bloomington: Indiana University Press, 2003), 30–31.

80 "A Typical Negro," *Harper's Weekly* 7 (July 4, 1863): 429.

81 Douglas R. Egerton, *Thunder at the Gates: The Black Civil War Regiments That Redeemed America* (New York: Basic Books, 2016), 336.

82 M. McPherson, *The Negro's Civil War*, 59–60, 191; Thomas Chester, *Thomas Morris Chester, Black Civil War Correspondent*, ed. R. J. M. Blackett (Baton Rouge: Louisiana State University Press, 1989), 220; Charlotte Forten, "Life on the Sea Islands," *Atlantic Monthly* 13 (1864): 668–70.

83 Barbara Gannon, *The Won Cause: Black and White Comradeship in the Grand Army of the Republic* (Chapel Hill: University of North Carolina Press, 2011), 104; Egerton, *Thunder at the Gates*, 336, 346; T. W. Higginson, "Regular and Volunteer Officers," *Atlantic Monthly* 14 (September 1864): 355–56.

84 W. Buck Yearns and John G. Barrett, eds., *North Carolina Civil War Documentary* (Chapel Hill: University of North Carolina Press, 1980), 98.

85 Walter D. Kamphoefner, Wolfgang Helbich, and Ulrike Sommer, eds., *News from the Land of Freedom: German Immigrants Write Home* (Ithaca, NY: Cornell University Press, 1991), 402.

86 Edward K. Spann, *Gotham at War: New York City, 1860–1865* (New York: SR Books, 2002), 74.

87 Elizabeth Kelly Kerstens, "Disguised Patriots: Women Who Served Incognito," *Ancestry* 18 (March/April 2000): 17.

88 Elizabeth Cady Stanton, Susan B. Anthony, and Matilda Joslyn Gage, eds., *History of Woman Suffrage* (Rochester, NY: Charles Mann, 1881), vol. 2, frontispiece, 47.

89 Ibid., 2:923; Wendy Hamand Venet, *Neither Ballots Nor Bullets: Women Abolitionists and the Civil War* (Charlottesville: University Press of Virginia, 1991), 46.

90 Edwin S. Redkey, ed., *A Grand Army of Black Men: Letters from African-American Soldiers in the Union Army, 1861–1865* (New York: Cambridge University Press, 1992), 175.

91 Chester, *Thomas Morris Chester*, 303–4.

92 Hallie Q. Brown, *Homespun Heroines and Other Women of Distinction* (New York: Oxford University Press, 1988), 157–58.

93 Virginia Writers' Project, *The Negro in Virginia* (New York: Hastings House, 1940), 201–2.

94 Thousands of these advertisements have been collected on the web page http://informationwanted.org; Kathryn L. Morgan, *Children of Strangers: The Stories of a Black Family* (Philadelphia: Temple University Press, 1980), 18.

95 C. C. Coffin, "Late Scenes in Richmond," *Atlantic Monthly* 15 (1865): 755.

96 John Wilkes Booth, *Right or Wrong, God Judge Me: The Writings of John Wilkes Booth*, eds. John Rhodehamel and Louise Taper (Urbana: University of Illinois Press, 1997), 15.

97 Holland, *Frederick Douglass*, 301.

CHAPTER 4:
FIXING THE CONSTITUTION

1 *Political Debates Between Abraham Lincoln and Stephen A. Douglas in the Celebrated Campaign of 1858 in Illinois* (Cleveland: Arthur H. Clark, 1902), 101.

2 J. David Hacker, "A Census-Based Count of the Civil War Dead," *Civil War History* 57 (2011): 306–47; Rice Bull, *Soldiering: The Civil War Diary of Rice C. Bull, 123rd New York Volunteer Infantry*, ed. K. Jack Bauer (Novato, CA: Presidio, 1995), 231–32.

3 Oliver Wendell Holmes Jr., *Dead, Yet Living: An Address* (Boston: Ginn, Heath, 1884), 6.

4 *Congressional Globe*, 39th Congress, 1st sess., 586 (February 1, 1866).

5 Joshua Lawrence Chamberlain, *The Passing of the Armies: An Account of the Final Campaign of the Army of the Potomac* (New York: G. P. Putnam's Sons, 1915), 242.

6 Alice Moore Dunbar, ed., *Masterpieces of Negro Eloquence* (New York: Bookery, 1914), 83.

7 Elaine Showalter, *A Jury of Her Peers: American Women Writers from Anne Bradstreet to Annie Proulx* (New York: Knopf, 2009), 131.

8 Louisa May Alcott, *Louisa May Alcott: Her Life, Letters, and Journals*, ed. Ednah D. Cheney (New York: Gramercy Books, 1995), 88; Louisa May Alcott, *Hospital Sketches* (Boston: James Redpath, 1863); Louisa May Alcott, *Work: A Story of Experience* (Boston: Roberts Brothers, 1873), 442; Louisa May Alcott, *A Long Fatal Love Chase* (New York: Random House, 1995), 3.

9 Bettina Friedl, ed., *On to Victory: Propaganda Plays of the Woman Suffrage Movement* (Boston: Northeastern University Press, 1986), 55–82.

10 Carol Farley Kessler, ed., *The Story of Avis* (New Brunswick, NJ: Rutgers University Press, 2001), 269–73.

11 Jeanne Boydston, Mary Kelly, and Anne Margolis, *The Limits of Sisterhood: The Beecher Sisters on Women's Rights and Woman's Sphere* (Chapel Hill: University of North Carolina Press, 1988), 267; Elaine Showalter, *The Civil Wars of Julia Ward Howe: A Biography* (New York: Simon & Schuster, 2016), 185.

12 Marietta Holley, *My Opinions and Betsy Bobbet's* (Hartford, CT: American Publishing, 1872); Lillie Devereux Blake, *Fettered for Life: or, Lord and Master* (New York: Sheldon, 1874).

13 Dawn Keetley and John Pettegrew, eds., *Public Women, Public Words: A Documentary History of American Feminism* (Madison, WI: Madison House, 1997), 1:246.

14 Abraham Lincoln, *The Collected Works of Abraham Lincoln*, ed. Roy P. Basler (New Brunswick, NJ: Rutgers University Press, 1953–55), 5:144–46, 152–53, 160–61; Leonard L. Richards, *Who Freed the Slaves? The Fight over the Thirteenth Amendment* (Chicago: University of Chicago Press, 2015), 58–59.

15 William E. Parrish, *Turbulent Partnership: Missouri and the Union, 1861–1865* (Columbia: University of Missouri Press, 1962), 185–95; Charles L. Wagandt, *The Mighty Revolution: Negro Emancipation in Maryland, 1862–1864* (Baltimore: Maryland Historical Society, 2004), 95–101, 217–30.

16 Alexander Tsesis, *For Liberty and Equality: The Life and Times of the Declaration of Independence* (New York: Oxford University Press, 2012), 182.

17 *Congressional Globe*, 38th Congress, 1st sess., 19–21 (December 14, 1863); ibid., 2nd sess., 531 (January 31, 1865).

18 Ibid., 521–22 (February 8, 1864), 1488–9 (April 8, 1864); ibid., 39th Congress, 1st sess., 322 (January 19, 1866), 503–4 (January 30, 1866), 702, 704 (February 7, 1866).

19 Ibid., 659–60, (February 15, 1864); *New York Times*, February 11, 1864, 4, and February 13, 1864, 6.

20 *Chicago Tribune*, March 4, 1864, 2; *New-York Tribune*, March 14 and 15, 1864, 4.

21 *New York Herald*, February 8, 1864, 4; Douglas Fermer, *James Gordon Bennett and the New York Herald: A Study of Editorial Opinion in the Civil War Era*

1854–1867 (New York: St. Martin's Press, 1986), 244–61; Michael Vorenberg, *Final Freedom: The Civil War, the Abolition of Slavery, and the Thirteenth Amendment* (Cambridge: Cambridge University Press, 2004), 73.

22 *Cincinnati Enquirer*, February 12, 1864, 2.

23 LaWanda Cox, "The Promise of Land for the Freedmen," *Mississippi Valley Historical Review* 45 (1958): 413–40; Brooks D. Simpson, "Land and the Ballot: Securing the Fruits of Emancipation?," *Pennsylvania History* 60 (1993): 176–88; M. McPherson, *The Negro's Civil War: How American Blacks Felt and Acted During the War for the Union* (New York: Ballantine Books, 1991), 280–85.

24 *Congressional Globe*, 38th Congress, 1st sess., appendix, 113 (April 4, 1864).

25 Ibid., 1364, appendix, 104 (March 30 and 31, 1864), 1419–24 (April 5, 1864).

26 Ibid., 1461 (April 7, 1864).

27 Ibid., 1484 (April 8, 1864).

28 Ibid., 1442, 1457, 1490 (April 6, 7, and 8, 1864), 2941 (June 14, 1864).

29 [David Croly and George Wakeman], *Miscegenation: The Theory of the Blending of the Races, Applied to the American White Man and Negro* (New York: H. Dexter, 1864); Samuel Cox, *Eight Years in Congress, from 1857–1865: Memoir and Speeches* (New York: D. Appleton, 1865), 264, 367–68; *Congressional Globe*, 37th Cong., 1st sess., 35–37; ibid., 38th Congress, 1st sess., 2941 (June 14, 1864).

30 *Congressional Globe*, 36th Congress, 2nd sess., 1488 (March 22, 1861); ibid., 38th Congress, 1st sess., 1490 (April 8, 1864).

31 Ibid., 38th Congress, 1st sess., 1489 (April 8, 1864).

32 Ibid., 2nd sess., 523 (January 31, 1865).

33 E. L. Godkin, "The Constitution, and Its Defects," *North American Review* 99 (1864): 119–20, 123, 131–32.

34 Gerrit Smith, *Speeches and Letters of Gerrit Smith (from January, 1864, to January, 1865 on the Rebellion)* (New York: American News, 1865), 2:55, 57, 60; Joseph Story, *Commentaries on the Constitution of the United States* (Boston: Little, Brown, 1858), 1:288.

35 *Congressional Globe*, 38th Congress, 1st sess., 1423, 1460, 1482 (April 5, 7, and 8, 1864).

36 Charles Sumner, *No Property in Man* (New York: Loyal Publication Society, 1864), 18.

37 *Congressional Globe*, 38th Congress, 1st sess., 1490 (April 8, 1864).

38 Ibid., 2949 (June 14, 1864).

39 See, for instance, ibid., 2943–5, 2983–91.

40 Ibid., 2951, 2962 (June 14–15, 1864).

41 Ibid., 2950–51, 2979 (June 15, 1864).

42 Ibid., 2980 (June 15, 1864).

43 Ibid., 2983–5, 2990 (June 15, 1864).

44 Ibid., 2995, 3357 (June 15 and 28, 1864).

45 Lincoln, *Collected Works of Abraham Lincoln*, 7:281–82.

46 Kirk H. Porter and Donald B. Johnson, eds., *National Party Platforms, 1840–1972* (Urbana: University of Illinois Press, 1973), 35–36.

47 Lincoln, *Collected Works of Abraham Lincoln*, 6:410, 7:380.

48 *Proceedings of the National Convention of Colored Men, Held in the City of Syracuse, N.Y., October 4, 5, 6, and 7, 1864* (Boston: Rock and Ruffin, 1864); Elizabeth Cady Stanton, Susan B. Anthony, and Matilda Joslyn Gage, eds., *History of Woman Suffrage* (Rochester, NY: Charles Mann, 1881), 2:78–94.

49 Sidney Kaplan, "The Miscegenation Issue in the Election of 1864," *Journal of Negro History* 34 (1949): 321n; *Abraham Africanus I: His Secret Life, as Revealed Under the Mesmeric Influence* (New York: J. F. Feeks, 1864).

50 Herald B. Hancock, *Delaware During the Civil War: A Political History* (Wilmington: Historical Society of Delaware, 1961), 129; "Miscegenation: Or the Millennium of Abolitionism," Library of Congress online.

51 *Congressional Globe*, 38th Congress, 1st sess., 2940 (June 14, 1864); ibid., 2nd sess., 151 (January 7, 1865).

52 Susan B. Anthony, *The Life and Works of Susan. B. Anthony*, ed. Ida Harper (Indianapolis: Bowen-Merrill, 1899), 1:227; Women's National Loyal League, "To the Women of the Republic," January 25, 1864, National Archives.

53 Stanton, Anthony, and Gage, eds., *History of Woman Suffrage* 1:747–48.

54 Benjamin W. Arnett, ed., *Orations and Speeches* (Philadelphia: A.M.E. Church, 1896), 300.

55 Lincoln, *Collected Works of Abraham Lincoln*, 8:149.

56 Frederick Douglass, *The Frederick Douglass Papers: Series One: Speeches, Debates, and Interviews*, eds. John W. Blassingame et al. (New Haven, CT: Yale University Press, 1979–92), 4:36; Vorenberg, *Final Freedom*, 178.

57 *Congressional Globe*, 38th Congress, 1st sess., 2940–2 (June 14, 1864); ibid., 2nd sess., 38 (December 14, 1864).

58 Ibid., 2nd sess., 260–61 (January 13, 1865).

59 Ariel and W. H. Drapier, *Brevier Legislative Reports: Embracing Short-Hand Sketches of the Journals and Debates of the General Assembly of the State of Indiana*, vol. 7 (South Bend: Forum Job Office, 1865), 190–91.

60 *Congressional Globe*, 38th Congress, 2nd sess., 141–42, 155–56, 189, 220–21, 242–44, 258 (January 6, 7, 10, 11, 12, and 13, 1865).

61 Ibid., 524–26 (January 31, 1865).

62 Ibid., 524 (January 31, 1865).

63 Ibid., 170–71 (January 9, 1865).

64 Ibid., 125 (January 5, 1865).

65 Vorenberg, *Final Freedom*, 203; *New-York Tribune*, January 3, 1865, 4.

66 Lincoln, *Collected Works of Abraham Lincoln*, 8:248.

67 *Congressional Globe*, 38th Congress, 2nd sess., 120–56, 174–75, 523–27 (January 31, 1865) (Herrick quote, 526).

68 Ibid., 530–31.

69 George W. Julian, *Political Recollections, 1840 to 1872* (Chicago: Jansen, McClurg, 1884), 251–52.

70 David Blight, *Frederick Douglass' Civil War: Keeping Faith in Jubilee* (Baton Rouge: Louisiana State University Press, 1989), 186.

71 Richards, *Who Freed the Slaves?*, 217; Ernest A. McKay, *The Civil War and New York City* (Syracuse, NY: Syracuse University Press, 1990), 295.

72 M. McPherson, *The Negro's Civil War*, 293–94.

73 Drapier and Drapier, *Brevier Legislative Reports*, 180, 222.

74 Ibid., 181–82.

75 *Journal of the House of Representatives of the State of Ohio*, vol. 61 (Columbus: Nevins, 1865), 155, 174.

76 Drapier and Drapier, *Brevier Legislative Reports*, 189–90.

77 *Journal of the Proceedings of the House of Delegates of the State of Maryland, January Session, 1865* (Annapolis: Richard P. Bayley, 1865), 125, 180–82; *The Anti-Slavery Reporter*, vol. 13 (London: British and Foreign Anti-Slavery Society, 1865): 229; Victor B. Howard, *Black Liberation in Kentucky: Emancipation and Freedom, 1862-1884* (Lexington: University Press of Kentucky, 1983), 72–78, 87–88.

78 *Congressional Globe*, 38th Congress, 2nd sess., 588 (February 4, 1865).

79 Lincoln, *Collected Works of Abraham Lincoln*, 8:402–5.

80 Drapier and Drapier, *Brevier Legislative Reports*, 191.

81 *The Liberator*, February 10, 1865, 2.

82 Binney to Lieber, March 14, 1864, Francis Lieber Manuscripts, Huntington Library, San Marino, CA; Edward Bates, *Opinion of Attorney General Bates on Citizenship* (Washington, DC: Government Printing Office, 1863).

83 "Anti-Slavery Measures in Congress," *The Nation*, December 6, 1865, 152–53.

84 Elizabeth Hyde Botume, *First Days Amongst the Contrabands* (Boston: Lee and Shepard, 1893), 169.

85 Douglass, *The Frederick Douglass Papers*, 4:83; C. Peter Ripley et al., eds., *The Black Abolitionist Papers, 1830-1865* (5 vols.; Chapel Hill: University of North Carolina Press, 1985-1992) 5:274, 300–301.

CHAPTER 5:
DEFINING AND DEFENDING CITIZENSHIP

1 James A. Garfield, *The Works of James Abram Garfield*, ed. Burke A. Hinsdale (Boston: J. R. Osgood, 1882–83), 1:86–87; Ira Rutkow, *James A. Garfield* (New York: Henry Holt, 2006), 27–29; Candice Millard, *Destiny of the Republic: A Tale of Madness, Medicine and the Murder of a President* (New York: Doubleday, 2011), 26–29.

2 *Congressional Globe*, 39th Congress, 1st sess., 586 (February 1, 1866).

3 Carl Schurz, *The Reminiscences of Carl Schurz* (3 vols.; New York: McClure, 1907–8), 3:150–59.

4 Ibid., 3:159–209.

5 Ibid., 3:209.

6 Carl Schurz, *Speeches, Correspondence and Political Papers of Carl Schurz*, ed. Frederic Bancroft (New York: G. P. Putnam's Sons, 1913), 1:305–6.

7 *Congressional Globe*, 39th Congress, 1st sess., 78–80 (December 19, 1865).

8 John R. Dennett, "The South As It Is," *The Nation*, April 12, 1866, 460.

9 Sidney Andrews, *The South Since the War: As Shown by Fourteen Weeks of Travel and Observation in Georgia and the Carolinas* (Boston: Ticknor and Fields, 1866), 218, 283, 319; Whitelaw Reid, *After the War: A Southern Tour* (New York: Moore, Wilstach & Baldwin, 1866), 404.

10 Reid, *After the War*, 71, 375; John R. Dennett, "The South As It Is," *The Nation*, February 1, 1866, 139; Andrews, *The South Since the War*, 290–99.

11 Andrews, *The South Since the War*, 22; Schurz, *Speeches*, 1:320.

12 Senate Executive Documents, 39th Congress, 1st sess., doc. 2, 93–94.

13 Schurz, *Speeches*, 1:348.

14 Andrews, *The South Since the War*, 371.

15 John Townsend Trowbridge, *The South: A Tour of Its Battlefields and Ruined Cities*, ed. J. H. Segars (Macon, GA: Mercer University Press, 2006), 435–36.

16 Schurz, *Speeches*, 1:372–73.

17 Samuel Q. Richardson to Governor A. J. Hamilton, September 1865, Records of Andrew Jackson Hamilton, Texas Office of the Governor, Archives and Information Services Division, Texas State Library and Archives Commission; Dennett, *The South As It Is*, 75.

18 Andrew Johnson, *The Papers of Andrew Johnson*, ed. Paul H. Bergeron et al. (Knoxville: University of Tennessee Press, 1967–2000), 9:469.

19 Julia Ward Howe, *Reminiscences: 1819–1899* (Boston: Houghton, Mifflin, 1900), 258.

20 Hans L. Trefousse, *Andrew Johnson: A Biography* (New York: W. W. Norton, 1997), 236; Andrew Johnson, *Speeches of Andrew Johnson, President of the United States*, ed. Frank Moore (Boston: Little, Brown, 1865), xl–xli, xlviii;

Edward McPherson, ed., *The Political History of the United States of America During the Period of Reconstruction*, 2nd ed. (Washington, DC: Philp & Solomons, 1871), 59–61.

[21] Eric McKitrick, *Andrew Johnson and Reconstruction* (New York: Oxford University Press, 1960), 153–85.

[22] Walt Whitman, *Walt Whitman: The Correspondence*, ed. Edwin H. Miller (New York: New York University Press, 1961), 1:266; Eric Foner, *Reconstruction: America's Unfinished Revolution, 1863-1877* (New York: HarperCollins, 1988), 180; Reid, *After the War*, 305.

[23] *Congressional Globe*, 39th Congress, 1st sess., 3–5 (December 4, 1865).

[24] McKitrick, *Andrew Johnson and Reconstruction*, 465–67; Edward L. Gambill, *Conservative Ordeal: Northern Democrats and Reconstruction, 1865-1868* (Ames: Iowa State University Press, 1981), 23, 102, 135.

[25] Charles H. Coleman, *The Election of 1868: The Democratic Effort to Regain Control* (New York: Octagon Books, 1971), 57–62, 68–72, 84–86, 106–26.

[26] Edward Steers Jr., ed., *The Trial: The Assassination of President Lincoln and the Trial of the Conspirators* (Lexington: University of Kentucky Press, 2003).

[27] *Congressional Globe*, 35th Congress, 2nd sess., 982–85 (February 11, 1859).

[28] Ibid., 37th Congress, 3rd sess., 266 (January 9, 1863).

[29] Ibid., 39th Congress, 1st sess., 14 (December 6, 1865), 1088 (February 28, 1866); Benjamin B. Kendrick, "The Journal of the Joint Committee of Fifteen on Reconstruction," PhD diss., Columbia University, 1914, 46–47; John A. Bingham, *One Country, One Constitution, and One People* (Washington, DC: Congressional Globe Office, 1866).

[30] *Congressional Globe*, 39th Congress, 1st sess., 1054–1095 (February 27–28, 1866).

[31] Ibid., 74 (December 18, 1865).

[32] Kendrick, "Journal of the Joint Committee of Fifteen," 53; *Congressional Globe*, 39th Congress, 1st sess., 357 (January 22, 1866).

[33] *Congressional Globe*, 39th Congress, 1st sess., 353–54, 356 (January 22, 1866).

[34] Ibid., 379–80 (January 23, 1866).

[35] Ibid., 490–91, 538, appendix, 57 (January 29 and 31, 1866).

[36] Ibid., 674, 685–86 (February 6, 1866).

[37] Ibid., 702, 704 (February 7, 1866).

[38] Ibid., 768–69 (February 9, 1866).

[39] Ibid., 880 (February 16, 1866).

[40] Ibid., 848–49 (February 15, 1866).

[41] Ibid., 1289 (March 9, 1866).

[42] William Blackstone, *Commentaries on the Laws of England*, 12th ed. (London: Strahan and Woodfall, 1793), 1:441.

43 *General Orders, 1866* (Washington, DC: Government Printing Office, 1867), nos. 3 and 44.

44 E. McPherson, ed., *Political History*, 72–74; U.S. Congress, *The Statutes at Large, Treaties, and Proclamations, of the United States of America*, vol. 14, ed. George P. Sanger (Boston: Little, Brown, 1868), 27.

45 *Congressional Globe*, 39th Congress, 1st sess., 317–18 (January 19, 1866).

46 Ibid., 323 (January 19, 1866).

47 Ibid., 365 (January 23, 1866).

48 George W. Curtis, "A Long Step Forward," *Harper's Weekly*, January 27, 1866, 50.

49 E. McPherson, ed., *Political History*, 74.

50 Ibid., 52–55.

51 Ibid., 70–71.

52 Thomas Nast, cartoon, *Harper's Weekly*, April 14, 1866, 232; *Congressional Globe*, 39th Congress, 1st sess., 926–43 (February 20, 1866); E. McPherson, ed., *Political History*, 74.

53 E. McPherson, ed., *Political History*, 56.

54 *Congressional Globe*, 39th Congress, 1st sess., 981–91 (February 23, 1866).

55 E. McPherson, ed., *Political History*, 78–80; *Congressional Globe*, 39th Congress, 1st sess., 606–7 (February 2, 1866).

56 *Congressional Globe*, 39th Congress, 1st sess., 528–29 (January 31, 1866), 1367 (March 13, 1866).

57 Ibid., 477 (January 29, 1866).

58 Ibid., 1117 (March 1, 1866); James Kent, *Commentaries on American Law* (2 vols.; New York: O. Halsted, 1832) 2:1.

59 E. McPherson, ed., *Political History*, 78–80; *Congressional Globe*, 39th Congress, 1st sess., 606–7 (February 2, 1866).

60 E. McPherson, ed., *Political History*, 70, 74–78.

61 *Congressional Globe*, 39th Congress, 1st sess., 1809 (April 6, 1866), 1861 (April 9, 1866).

62 Kendrick, "Journal of the Joint Committee of Fifteen," 82–85, 101, 115–20, 296–97.

63 Rembert W. Patrick, *The Reconstruction of the Nation* (New York: Oxford University Press, 1967), 45.

64 "The Moral of the Memphis Riots," *The Nation* 2 (May 15, 1866), 616–17.

65 McKitrick, *Andrew Johnson and Reconstruction*, 350–51.

66 *Congressional Globe*, 39th Congress, 1st sess., 2542 (May 10, 1866).

67 Ibid., 2459 (May 8, 1866).

68 James Brewer Stewart, *Wendell Phillips: Liberty's Hero* (Baton Rouge: Louisiana State University Press, 1986), 273; James M. McPherson, *The Struggle*

for Equality: Abolitionists and the Negro in the Civil War and Reconstruction
(Princeton, NJ: Princeton University Press, 1992), 355.

69 Elizabeth Cady Stanton, Susan B. Anthony, and Matilda Joslyn Gage, eds.,
History of Woman Suffrage (Rochester, NY: Charles Mann, 1881), 2:91–92.

70 Ibid., 2:93.

71 Ibid., 2:91, 153, 159, 171; Eleanor Flexner and Ellen Fitzpatrick, *Century of
Struggle: The Woman's Rights Movement in the United States* (Cambridge,
MA: Harvard University Press, 1996), 137.

72 *Congressional Globe*, 39th Congress, 1st sess., appendix, 133–34, 138 (February
26, 1866).

73 Ibid., 2538 (May 10, 1866).

74 Ibid., 2544–5 (May 10, 1866).

75 Report of the Committee on Reconstruction, 7, in *The Reports of the Committees of the Senate of the United States for the First Session Thirty-Ninth Congress,
1865-'66* (Washington, DC: Government Printing Office, 1866).

76 *Congressional Globe*, 39th Congress, 1st sess., 2766 (May 23, 1866).

77 Ibid., 2767 (May 23, 1866).

78 Ibid., 2891 (May 30, 1866).

79 Ibid., 2891–2 (May 30, 1866).

80 Ibid., 2939–40 (June 4, 1866).

81 Ibid., 2964, 2987 (June 5 and 6, 1866).

82 Ibid., 3148–9 (June 13, 1866).

83 E. McPherson, ed., *Political History*, 83.

84 James G. Hollandsworth Jr., *An Absolute Massacre: The New Orleans Race
Riot of July 30, 1866* (Baton Rouge: Louisiana State University Press, 2001).

85 Joseph B. James, *The Ratification of the Fourteenth Amendment* (Macon, GA:
Mercer University Press, 1984), 23.

86 Jean Edward Smith, *Grant* (New York: Simon & Schuster, 2001), 427.

87 Schurz, *Speeches*, 1:413.

88 U.S. State Department, *Documentary History of the Constitution of the
United States of America, 1787-1870* (Washington, DC: Department of State,
1894–1905), 5:534–38.

89 Alexander Hamilton, James Madison, and John Jay, *The Federalist, or The
New Constitution* (Norwalk, CT: Easton Press, 1979), 535.

CHAPTER 6:
EQUALITY FOR HALF

1   Elizabeth Cady Stanton, Susan B. Anthony, and Matilda Joslyn Gage, eds.,
History of Woman Suffrage (Rochester, NY: Charles Mann, 1881), 2:328–29.

2   Ann D. Gordon, ed., *The Selected Papers of Elizabeth Cady Stanton and Susan
B. Anthony* (New Brunswick, NJ: Rutgers University Press, 1997–2009),

2:127; Stanton, Anthony, and Gage, eds., *History of Woman Suffrage* 2:193–94.

3 Dawn Keetley and John Pettegrew, eds., *Public Women, Public Words: A Documentary History of American Feminism* (Madison, WI: Madison House, 1997), 1:238.

4 Edward McPherson, ed., *The Political History of the United States of America During the Period of Reconstruction*, 2nd ed. (Washington, DC: Philp & Solomons, 1871), 156.

5 Richard N. Current, *Old Thad Stevens: A Story of Ambition* (Madison: University of Wisconsin Press, 1942), 288.

6 William Gillette, *The Right to Vote: Politics and the Passage of the Fifteenth Amendment* (Baltimore: Johns Hopkins University Press, 1965), 27–28, 40.

7 *Charleston Mercury*, January 28 and February 20, 1868.

8 Allan Conway, *The Reconstruction of Georgia* (Minneapolis: University of Minnesota Press, 1966), 40–60, 162–81; Edmund L. Drago, *Black Politicians and Reconstruction in Georgia: A Splendid Failure* (Athens: University of Georgia Press, 1992), 35–65.

9 Jane Dailey, *Before Jim Crow: The Politics of Race in Postemancipation Virginia* (Chapel Hill: University of North Carolina Press, 2000), 15–47; John V. Orth, *The North Carolina State Constitution with History and Commentary* (Chapel Hill: University of North Carolina Press, 1995), 12–19; Richard Zuczek, *State of Rebellion: Reconstruction in South Carolina* (Columbia: University of South Carolina Press, 1996), 28–70; William Watson Davis, *The Civil War and Reconstruction in Florida* (New York: Columbia University Press, 1913), 491–516; James Wilford Garner, *Reconstruction in Mississippi* (New York: Macmillan, 1901), 186–204; Carl H. Moneyhon, *The Impact of the Civil War and Reconstruction on Arkansas: Persistence in the Midst of Ruin* (Fayetteville: University of Arkansas Press, 2002), 245–51; Lewis L. Laska, *The Tennessee State Constitution* (New York: Oxford University Press, 2011), 18–31; Carl H. Moneyhon, *Republicanism in Reconstruction Texas* (College Station: Texas A&M University Press, 2001), 82–103.

10 *The Nation*, November 16, 1868.

11 John M. Matthews, "Negro Republicans in the Reconstruction of Georgia," *Georgia Historical Quarterly* 60 (1976): 145–64.

12 Charles H. Coleman, *The Election of 1868: The Democratic Effort to Regain Control* (New York: Octagon Books, 1971), 362–84.

13 *Congressional Globe*, 40th Congress, 3rd sess., 904 (February 5, 1869).

14 William M. Stewart, *Reminiscences of Senator William M. Stewart of Nevada*, ed. George R. Brown (New York: Neale, 1908), 232–33.

15 *New York Times*, February 15, 1869; *Congressional Globe*, 40th Congress, 3rd sess., 673, 699, 707, 827.

16 *Congressional Globe*, 40th Congress, 3rd sess., 668 (January 28, 1869).

17 Ibid., appendix, 97–98 (January 29, 1869).

18 Ibid., 744–45 (January 30, 1869); E. McPherson, ed., *Political History*, 399–400.

19 *Congressional Globe*, 40th Congress, 3rd sess., 668 (January 28, 1869), 1010 (February 8, 1869).

20 Ibid., 985–86, 1012 (February 8, 1869).

21 Ibid., 863 (February 4, 1869).

22 Ibid., 862 (February 4, 1869), 1037, 1039 (February 9, 1869); Marion Mills Miller, ed., *Great Debates in American History* (New York: Current Literature Publishing, 1913), 8:99.

23 *Congressional Globe*, 40th Congress, 3rd sess., 1224–6, 1317–18, 1428 (February 15, 17, and 20, 1869); *National Anti-Slavery Standard* (New York), February 20, 1869; *New York Times*, February 24, 1869; *The Nation*, February 18, 1869.

24 *Congressional Globe*, 40th Congress, 3rd sess., 1623 (February 26, 1869).

25 Ibid., 1625, 1641 (February 26, 1869).

26 James D. Richardson, ed., *A Compilation of the Messages and Papers of the Presidents, 1789–1902* (Washington, DC: Bureau of National Literature and Art, 1907), 7:8.

27 Lydia Maria Child, *Lydia Maria Child: Selected Letters, 1817–1880*, ed. Milton Meltzer (Amherst: University of Massachusetts Press, 1982), 123, 279.

28 Ellen Carol DuBois, *Feminism and Suffrage: The Emergence of an Independent Women's Movement in America, 1848–1869* (Ithaca, NY: Cornell University Press, 1978), 59.

29 *Proceedings of the First Anniversary of the American Equal Rights Association* (New York: Robert J. Johnston, 1867), 7–8.

30 Dorothy Sterling, *Ahead of Her Time: Abby Kelley and the Politics of Antislavery* (New York: W. W. Norton, 1991), 347–48.

31 Child, *Lydia Maria Child*, 469; Rosalyn Terborg-Penn, *African American Women in the Struggle for the Vote, 1850–1920* (Bloomington: Indiana University Press, 1998), 32.

32 Stanton, Anthony, and Gage, eds., *History of Woman Suffrage*, 2:382–83.

33 Ibid., 2:320.

34 Dorothy Sterling, ed., *We Are Your Sisters: Black Women in the Nineteenth Century* (New York: W. W. Norton, 1984), 411; Stanton, Anthony, and Gage, eds., *History of Woman Suffrage*, 2:193.

35 Laura M. Towne, *Letters and Diary of Laura M. Towne: Written from the Sea Islands of South Carolina, 1862–1884*, ed. Rupert S. Holland (Cambridge, MA: Riverside Press, 1912), 183–84; Sterling, ed., *We Are Your Sisters*, 325–26.

36 Gillette, *The Right to Vote*, 82–83.

37 *National Anti-Slavery Standard* (New York), March 20, 1869; "The Constitutional Amendment," *The Nation*, February 18, 1869, 124–25; "Our Friends the Enemy," *Harper's Weekly* 13 (May 1, 1869): 274.

38 Gillette, *The Right to Vote*, 122, 135.

39 Ibid., 113.

40 San Antonio *Express*, February 24, 1870; *Daily Richmond Whig*, March 2, 1869.

41 Gillette, *The Right to Vote*, 131–39.

42 Ibid., 151–53.

43 Ibid., 140–45, 154–56.

44 C. Mildred Thompson, *Reconstruction in Georgia: Economic, Social, Political, 1865-1872* (New York: Columbia University Press, 1915), 259–70.

45 Richardson, ed., *Compilation of the Messages and Papers of the Presidents*, 7:55–56; *New York Times*, March 31, 1870.

46 "The Fifteenth Amendment," *Daily National Republican* (Washington, DC), March 31, 1870, 1; "At Last!," *Evening Telegraph* (Philadelphia), March 31, 1870, 1; "The Fifteenth Amendment," *New-York Tribune*, April 4, 1870, 1.

47 William A. Russ Jr., "The Negro and White Disfranchisement During Radical Reconstruction," *Journal of Negro History* 19 (1934): 181; Wendy Wolff, ed., *The Senate, 1789-1989: Addresses on the History of the United States Senate* (Washington, DC: U.S. Government Printing Office, 1991), 2:531.

48 Robert A. Warner, *New Haven Negroes: A Social History* (New Haven, CT: Yale University Press, 1940), 177–81, 287–91; Henry E. Cheaney, "Attitudes of the Indiana Pulpit and Press Toward the Negro, 1860–1880," PhD diss., Department of History, University of Chicago, 1961), 149–59.

49 Arthur M. Schlesinger Jr. and Fred L. Israel, eds., *My Fellow Citizens: The Inaugural Addresses of the Presidents of the United States, 1789-2009* (New York: Facts on File, 2010), 172.

CHAPTER 7:
THE SUPREME COURT STRIKES BACK

1 Walt Whitman, *Democratic Vistas, and Other Papers* (London: Walter Scott, 1888), 21, 35, 43, 61.

2 U.S. Congress, *Condition of Affairs in the Late Insurrectionary States*, 42nd Congress, 2nd session (Washington, DC: Government Printing Office, 1872.

3 William Peirce Randel, *The Ku Klux Klan: A Century of Infamy* (Philadelphia: Chilton Books, 1965), 18.

4 Richard Zuczek, *State of Rebellion: Reconstruction in South Carolina* (Columbia: University of South Carolina Press, 1996), 167, 172–78; Stephen Budiansky,

The Bloody Shirt: Terror After Appomattox (New York: Viking, 2008), 221–25; Green B. Raum, *The Existing Conflict Between Republican Government and Southern Oligarchy* (Washington, DC: Greene Printing, 1884), 231–87.

5 "A Terrible Indictment," *Daily Whig & Courier* (Bangor, ME), August 10, 1876.

6 Otis A. Singletary, *Negro Militia and Reconstruction* (New York: McGraw Hill, 1963), 135; Senate Report #527, 44th Congress, 1st sess., *Mississippi in 1875: Report of the Select Committee to Inquire into the Mississippi Election of 1875* (Washington, DC: Government Printing Office, 1876), 1:xiv, xx–xxii.

7 U.S. Congress, *Report and Testimony of the Select Committee of the U.S. Senate to Investigate the Causes of the Removal of the Negroes from the Southern States*, 46th Congress, 2nd sess., Senate Report #693 (Washington, DC: Government Printing Office, 1880), 110–11; Budiansky, *The Bloody Shirt*, 221; "Packard's Downfall," *Inter-Ocean* (Chicago), April 23, 1877.

8 Senate Report #855, 45th Congress, 3rd sess., *Report of the United States Senate Committee to Inquire into Alleged Frauds and Violence in the Elections of 1878* (Washington, DC: Government Printing Office, 1879), 1:xxviii.

9 Nell Irvin Painter, *Exodusters: Black Migration to Kansas After Reconstruction* (New York: Norton, 1992), 36–37.

10 Painter, *Exodusters*, 163; Senate Report #855, . . . *Alleged Frauds and Violence in the Elections of 1878*, 1:140–42.

11 "The Problem at the South," *The Nation*, March 23, 1871, 92–93; "An Illustration of Government at the South," *The Nation*, March 30, 1871, 212.

12 Alexander H. Stephens, *A Constitutional View of the Late War* (Philadelphia, 1868–70).

13 Henry Ward Beecher, "Reconstruction," New York *Independent*, July 6, 1865, 8.

14 Harriet Beecher Stowe, *Palmetto Leaves* (Gainesville: University Press of Florida, 1999), 269, 272; Harriet Beecher Stowe, "Life in Florida," *New-York Tribune*, February 17, 1877, 3; Harriet Beecher Stowe, "Our Florida Plantation," *Atlantic Monthly* 43 (1879): 648; Harriet Beecher Stowe, *Life and Letters of Harriet Beecher Stowe*, ed. Annie Fields (Boston: Houghton, Mifflin, 1897), 302–43.

15 "Our Augusta Letter," *Atlanta Constitution*, May 4, 1876; "A Revival Incident," *New York Times*, May 10, 1876, 2; Albert Taylor Bledsoe, "Moody and Sankey," *Southern Review* (Baltimore) 19 (1876): 186; "Mr. Douglass' Great Speech," New York *Freeman*, May 2, 1885.

16 Dorothy Sterling, ed., *We Are Your Sisters: Black Women in the Nineteenth Century* (New York: W. W. Norton, 1984), 374–75.

17 "Relief for the Refugees," *St. Louis Globe-Democrat*, March 18, 1879, 3; Painter, *Exodusters*.

18 Ari Hoogenboom, *The Presidency of Rutherford B. Hayes* (Lawrence: University Press of Kansas, 1988), 68; Painter, *Exodusters*, 249; "The Political South Hereafter," *The Nation*, April 5, 1877, 202.

19 "The Warning," *St. Louis Globe-Democrat*, March 31, 1877, 4.

20 *National Republican* (Washington, DC), March 27, 1877.

21 James Ford Rhodes, *History of the United States from the Compromise of 1850 to the Final Restoration of Home Rule at the South in 1877* (New York: Macmillan, 1920), 6:36–39.

22 Henry Adams, *The Education of Henry Adams* (New York: Vintage, 1954), 211–12.

23 "Universal Suffrage," *The Nation*, December 27, 1877, 391.

24 William James, "Great Men, Great Thoughts, and the Environment," *Atlantic Monthly* 46 (1880): 458; Charles Darwin, *The Descent of Man and Selection in Relation to Sex* (New York: D. Appleton, 1909), 100–136, 624–26.

25 W. G. Sumner, "Suggestions on Social Subjects," *Popular Science Monthly* 24 (1883–1884): 168; Barry Werth, *Banquet at Delmonico's: Great Minds, the Gilded Age, and the Triumph of Evolution in America* (New York: Random House, 2009), 185.

26 Rebecca Edwards, *New Spirits: Americans in the Gilded Age, 1865–1905* (New York: Oxford University Press, 2006), 120.

27 Francis Parkman, "The Failure of Universal Suffrage," *North American Review* 263 (July–August 1878): 7; E. L. Godkin, *The Gilded Age Letters of E. L. Godkin*, ed. William M. Armstrong (Albany: State University of New York Press, 1974), 55–56, 88, 283–84, 297, 312, 403–4, 455–56; Charles Francis Adams Jr., "The Protection of the Ballot in National Elections," *Journal of Social Science* 1 (June 1869): 108–9.

28 Elizabeth Cady Stanton, Susan B. Anthony, and Matilda Joslyn Gage, eds., *History of Woman Suffrage* (Rochester, NY: Charles Mann, 1881), 2:349.

29 Ibid., 2:408–10.

30 Linda K. Kerber, *No Constitutional Right to Be Ladies: Women and the Obligations of Citizenship* (New York: Hill and Wang, 1999), 88; Stanton, Anthony, and Gage, eds., *History of Woman Suffrage*, 2:418.

31 "The Week," *The Nation*, February 2, 1871, 65.

32 Stanton, Anthony, and Gage, eds., *History of Woman Suffrage*, 2:588, 598–99.

33 Minor v. Happersett, 88 U.S. 162 (1875).

34 Colorado Springs *Gazette*, February 17, March 10, July 7, 1877; *Daily Rocky Mountain News*, June 24, 1877.

35 Beverly Beeton, *Women Vote in the West: The Woman Suffrage Movement, 1869–1896* (New York: Garland, 1986), 106, 110; *Daily Rocky Mountain News*, November 16, 1877; Colorado Springs *Gazette*, September 8, 1877.

[36] *Daily Rocky Mountain News*, September 4, 9, 29, 30, October 3, 9, 14, 18, 1877.

[37] Eleanor Flexner and Ellen Fitzpatrick, *Century of Struggle: The Woman's Rights Movement in the United States* (Cambridge, MA: Harvard University Press, 1996), 165–70.

[38] Prigg v. Pennsylvania, 41 U.S. (16 Pet.) 539 (1842); *Congressional Globe*, 39th Congress, 1st sess., 1118 (March 1, 1866).

[39] Texas v. White, 74 U.S. 700 (1869); People v. Board of Education of Detroit, 18 Mich. 400 (1870).

[40] State v. Rash (Delaware), 345; Bowlin v. Kentucky, 2 Bush (1867): 15–29.

[41] U.S. v. Rhodes, 27 Fed. Cas. 151 (CCD KY, 1866): 788.

[42] Blyew v. U.S., US Reports 80 (1871): 644.

[43] *Slaughterhouse Cases*, 16 Wall. 36 (U.S. 1873); James H. Kettner, *The Development of American Citizenship, 1608–1870* (Chapel Hill: University Press of North Carolina, 1978), 348–49.

[44] *Slaughterhouse Cases*, 16 Wall 67 (1873); Harold M. Hyman and William M. Wiecek, *Equal Justice Under Law: Constitutional Development, 1835–1875* (New York: Harper & Row, 1982), 480.

[45] Stanton et al., eds., *History of Woman Suffrage*, 2:611.

[46] Ibid., 2:618.

[47] Bradwell v. State of Illinois, 83 U.S. 130 (1873); Rosalyn Terborg-Penn, *African American Women in the Struggle for the Vote, 1850–1920* (Bloomington: Indiana University Press, 1998), 38.

[48] Elizabeth Cady Stanton, *The Woman's Bible* (orig. 1895; Seattle: Coalition Task Force on Women and Religion, 1984).

[49] Francis Biddle, "Civil Rights and the Federal Law," in Robert Carr, ed., *Safeguarding Civil Liberties Today* (Ithaca, NY: Cornell University Press, 1945), 131.

[50] Texas v. Gaines, Fed. Cas. #13,837 (1874); U.S. v. Cruikshank, 92 U.S. 542 (1875).

[51] U.S. v. Reese, 92 U.S. 214 (1876).

[52] Virginia v. Rives, 100 U.S. 313 (1880); United States v. Harris, 106 U.S. 629.

[53] *Congressional Record*, 43rd Cong., 1st sess., 341 (December 19, 1873).

[54] *Civil Rights Cases*, 109 U.S. 26 (1883), 34.

[55] Santa Clara Co. v. Southern Pacific Railroad Co. et al., 118 US 394 (1886); C. Peter Magrath, *Morrison R. Waite: The Triumph of Character* (New York: Macmillan, 1963), 114–17.

[56] Plessy v. Ferguson, 163 U.S. 537 (1896).

[57] W. E. B. Du Bois, *Black Reconstruction in America, 1860–1880* (New York: Free Press, 1998), 188; Douglas A. Blackmon, *Slavery by Another Name: The*

Re-Enslavement of Black Americans from the Civil War to World War II (New York: Doubleday, 2008).

58 Hodges v. U.S., 203 U.S. (1906).

59 Prudential Insurance Co. v. Cheek, 259 U.S. 530, 543 (1922); Gitlow v. New York, 268 U.S. 652, 666 (1925).

60 Lochner v. New York, 198 U.S. 45 (1905).

61 Elaine Showalter, *The Civil Wars of Julia Ward Howe: A Biography* (New York: Simon & Schuster, 2016), 77, 173.

62 Elizabeth Cady Stanton, *Eighty Years and More: Reminiscences, 1815–1897* (Lebanon, NH: University Press of New England, 1993), 254–55.

63 Sterling, ed., *We Are Your Sisters*, 414, 434, 436–37. Majors found almost three hundred women to include; Monroe A. Majors, ed., *Noted Negro Women: Their Triumphs and Activities* (Chicago: Donohue & Henneberry, 1893).

64 Anna J. Cooper, *A Voice from the South* (Xenia, OH: Aldine, 1892), 144.

65 Beeton, *Women Vote in the West*, 148–56.

66 Philip S. Foner and Robert James Branham, eds., *Lift Every Voice: African American Oratory, 1787–1900* (Tuscaloosa: University of Alabama Press, 1998), 698.

67 Faith Berry, ed., *From Bondage to Liberation: Writings by and About Afro-Americans from 1700 to 1918* (New York: Continuum International Publishing, 2006), 447.

68 Carl Schurz, "The New South," in *Speeches, Correspondence and Political Papers of Carl Schurz*, ed. Frederic Bancroft (New York: G. P. Putnam's Sons, 1913), 4:368–400.

69 Ibid., 6:341.

70 Alexander Keyssar, *The Right to Vote: The Contested History of Democracy in the United States* (New York: Basic Books, 2000), 87.

EPILOGUE

1 James J. Creigh, *Address, Delivered at Paoli Massacre Ground, July 4, 1867* (West Chester, PA: N. T. Smith, 1867), 16–17.

2 Elizabeth Cady Stanton, Susan B. Anthony, and Matilda Joslyn Gage, eds., *History of Woman Suffrage* (Rochester, NY: Charles Mann, 1881), 2:193; Dorothy Sterling, ed., *We Are Your Sisters: Black Women in the Nineteenth Century* (New York: W. W. Norton, 1984), 254.

3 James G. Hollandsworth Jr., *Portrait of a Scientific Racist: Alfred Holt Stone of Mississippi* (Baton Rouge: Louisiana State University Press, 2008), 57.

4 William Faulkner, "On Fear: The South in Labor," *Harper's Magazine*, June 1956, 29–34, quote 31.

5   Carrie Chapman Catt and Nettie Rogers Shuler, *Woman Suffrage and Politics: The Inner Story of the Suffrage Movement* (New York: Charles Scribner's Sons, 1923), 107–110; Dawn Keetley and John Pettegrew, eds., *Public Women, Public Words: A Documentary History of American Feminism* (Madison, WI: Madison House, 1997), 1:234.

6   Josiah Strong, *Our Country: Its Possible Future and Its Present Crisis* (New York: American Home Missionary Society, 1885), 40–43.

7   Vincent J. Cannato, *American Passage: The History of Ellis Island* (New York: Harper, 2009), 95.

8   Brown v. Board of Education of Topeka, 347 U.S. 483 (1954).

9   Eisenstadt v. Baird, 405 U.S. 438 (1972); Wengler v. Druggists Mutual Insurance Co., 446 U.S. 142 (1980); Loving v. Virginia, 388 U.S. 1 (1967); Tennessee v. Lane, 541 U.S. 509 (2004); Emily Peck, "Girls Just Want to Wear Pants, Sometimes Leggings," *Huffington Post*, March 30, 2019.

10 Orr v. Orr, 440 U.S. 268 (1979).

11 Bowers v. Hardwick, 478 U.S. 186 (1986); Lawrence v. Texas, 539 U.S. 558 (2003); Obergefell v. Hodges, 576 U.S. __ (2015).

12 https://www.cruz.senate.gov, October 6, 2014; "Donald Trump: 14th Amendment Is Questionable," CNN, March 30, 2016.

13 http://www.truthrevolt.org, January 15, 2015.

14 David Brion Davis, "Free at Last: The Enduring Significance of the South's Civil War Victory," *New York Times*, August 26, 2001, "Week in Review" section, 1.

15 This imagery occurs in Micah 4:4, 1 Kings 4:25, and Zechariah 3:10. George Washington to the Hebrew Congregation in Newport, Rhode Island, August 18, 1790, National Archives.

Index